Rebecca Wetter
Meritocratic Beliefs and the Persistence of
Educational Inequality

Rebecca Wetter

Meritocratic Beliefs and the Persistence of Educational Inequality

A Study of Applicants to
Medical School in Germany

Budrich Academic Press
Opladen • Berlin • Toronto 2026

All rights reserved. No part of this publication may be reproduced, stored in or introduced into a retrieval system, or transmitted, in any form, or by any means (electronic, mechanical, photocopying, recording or otherwise) without the prior written permission of Verlag Barbara Budrich. Any person who does any unauthorized act in relation to this publication may be liable to criminal prosecution and civil claims for damages.

You must not circulate this book in any other binding or cover and you must impose this same condition on any acquirer.

A CIP catalogue record for this book is available from
Die Deutsche Nationalbibliothek (The German National Library):
https://portal.dnb.de.

The publication of this book was partly funded by the WZB Berlin Social Science Center.

© 2026 by Barbara Budrich Academic Press GmbH, Opladen, Berlin & Toronto

    ISBN   978-3-96665-106-6 (Paperback)
    eISBN 978-3-96665-889-8 (PDF)
    DOI   10.3224/96665106

Barbara Budrich Academic Press GmbH
Stauffenbergstr. 7. D-51379 Leverkusen Opladen, Germany| info@budrich.de
www.budrich-academic-press.de
86 Delma Drive. Toronto, ON M8W 4P6 Canada | info@budrich.de
www.budrich.eu

Cover design by Bettina Lehfeldt, Kleinmachnow, Germany –
   www.lehfeldtgraphic.de
Typesetting by Anja Borkam, Langenhagen – kontakt@lektorat-borkam.de
Printed in Europe on FSC®-certified paper by Libri Plureos, Hamburg

Acknowledgements

This book is based on a revised version of my dissertation, which I defended in October 2024 at the Free University of Berlin. Writing this dissertation has been an exciting, educational, inspiring, and certainly challenging journey. I am eternally grateful to the people who have accompanied and supported me intellectually and emotionally during this very special time.

First of all, I would like to thank my first supervisor, Heike Solga, for giving me the opportunity to work at the WZB in the research unit "Skill formation and labor markets (AAM)" and for supporting the start of my academic career in many ways, as well as for her extensive feedback and many important suggestions for improving this thesis. I would also like to thank Christian von Scheve for his support during my Master's studies and now as the second supervisor of this dissertation. A special thanks also goes to Claudia Finger for being my mentor throughout this whole process: I have learned so much from working on our project together, and I have always been able to count on you to support me, answer my questions, and provide valuable feedback. I would also like to thank Stefan Liebig, Jürgen Schupp, and Giuseppe Pietrantuono for being part of my thesis committee.

This dissertation largely resulted from my work in the project "Meritocratic beliefs, motivated reasoning, and goal (dis)engagement" and uses medical applicant data collected in this project and in the project "Social inequality in access to prestigious fields of study"—funded by the German Research Foundation (DFG) under grant number SO 430/13-1. Collecting the third wave of the data was a labor-intensive but exciting task and an opportunity from which this work has greatly benefited. In addition to Heike Solga and Claudia Finger, I would also like to thank Dorothea Kübler and Robert Stüber for collaborating on this project and the data collection, as well as all the student assistants who greatly supported the project and this dissertation: Robert Neuhaus, Birte Freer, Patrick Hölzgen, Victioria Hünewaldt, Julia Bersch, and Jonas Braun—thank you for your indispensable help.

Beyond the project, I have benefited greatly from the stimulating atmosphere in the AAM department. In particular, I would like to thank all the participants of the doctoral colloquium for their valuable constructive criticism of earlier versions of my thesis—for example, I would like to thank Jan Paul Heisig and Sascha dos Santos for their advice on any methodological issues. Beyond these formal contexts, I am also deeply grateful for all the lunches and coffee breaks shared with my colleagues, the many inspiring conversations, the mutual support, and encouragement. Thank you Misun Lim, Mona Joly, Agustina Marques Hill, Christian König, Carla Hornberg, Sophie Hofmeister, Martin Ehlert, Alessandra Rusconi, Matthias Flohr, Sönke Matthewes, and all the others who have accompanied and supported me over the past years at the WZB.

A special thanks also goes to Fiona Gogescu, with whom I had many inspiring conversations about meritocracy during her visit to the WZB and my visit to the LSE. The research stay at the LSE enriched my doctoral experience in a meaningful way, and—besides Fiona Gogescu—I would also like to thank Anne West for hosting me, Sam Friedman for insightful feedback on my work, and the other researcher at the Department of Social Policy and Sociology who made my visit such a pleasant experience.

Last but not least, I am especially grateful to my parents for their support and love throughout my life. I am also deeply grateful to my friends who have always been there to support and motivate me. Finally, I cannot thank Matúš enough for everything —for your love, support, and for always believing in me.

Berlin, November 2025

Rebecca Wetter

Table of content

List of tables	9
List of figures	12
1 Introduction	15
2 Institutional context	22
3 Theoretical framework for the formation of inequality beliefs and their consequences for educational inequality	27
3.1 Educational inequality	27
3.2 How parental education and educational experiences shape inequality beliefs	33
3.3 Consequences of inequality beliefs for perceptions of justice and distributive preferences	47
3.4 Inequality beliefs, persistence in goal pursuit, and educational inequality	58
3.5 Summary of hypotheses	66
4 Research design	71
4.1 Data collection	71
4.2 Variables	73
4.3 Samples	80
4.4 Weighting	81
4.5 Descriptive sample statistics	83
4.6 Representativeness of beliefs of medical applicants for adolescents in Germany	86
4.7 Overview of methods	91
5 Changes and persistence of inequality beliefs by educational experiences	94
5.1 Descriptive statistics: Patterns in inequality beliefs	94
5.2 Methodological approach	98
5.3 Social differences in inequality beliefs are shaped by educational experiences	99
5.4 Influence of experiences of success and failure on inequality beliefs	107
5.4.1 Causal effect of being admitted or rejected?	111
5.4.2 Effect of merit-based success or success in general?	114
5.5 The role of previous experiences as a frame for new experiences	116
5.6 Summary: Diverging paths in inequality beliefs	121

6 The complex relationship between parental education, inequality beliefs, perceptions of justice, and distributive preferences 126
   6.1 Descriptive statistics: Perceptions of justice and distributive preferences 126
   6.2 Methodological approach 128
   6.3 Distinct types of meritocratic and nonmeritocratic beliefs 129
   6.4 The complex relationship: Structural equation model results.... 133
      6.4.1 Associations between inequality beliefs and distributive preferences, and the role of perceptions of justice 135
      6.4.2 Social differences in inequality beliefs contribute to different distributive preferences 141
      6.4.3 The role of the admission outcome in the relationship between the concepts 143
   6.5 Summary: How inequality beliefs (de)legitimize educational inequality 149

7 The experience of rejection and the association between beliefs in meritocratic admission and persistence in goal pursuit 154
   7.1 Descriptive statistics: Persistence and beliefs in meritocratic admission 154
   7.2 Methodological approach 157
   7.3 Social differences in persistence and beliefs in meritocratic admission 158
   7.4 Influence of parental education and beliefs in meritocratic admission on persistence in goal pursuit 163
   7.5 Limitations due to sample selectivity and sample sizes 167
   7.6 Summary: Parental education does not affect persistence but beliefs do 168

8 Summary, discussion, and conclusion 172
   8.1 Theoretical arguments 172
   8.2 Key findings 175
   8.3 Discussion and contributions to theoretical debate and empirical research 178
   8.4 Limitations of study and avenues for future research 183
   8.5 Implications of findings 185

9 References 189

Appendix 199

Index 223

List of tables

Table 3.1:	Definitions of perceptions of justice and distributive preferences	48
Table 4.1:	Translated inequality beliefs scales in waves 1-3, and additional scale in wave 3	74
Table 4.2:	Descriptive statistics for different samples	84
Table 4.3:	Average inequality beliefs (W1 beliefs)	85
Table 4.4:	Average inequality beliefs in different samples of the NEPS data and the medical applicant data	88
Table 4.5:	Average GPA and distributions of parental education in different samples of the NEPS data and the medical applicant data	90
Table 4.6:	Overview of methods	92
Table 5.1:	Average beliefs in domain-specific belief cluster and societal belief cluster	96
Table 5.2:	Weighted admission rates and GPA by parental education	100
Table 5.3:	Average inequality beliefs by parental education (W1 beliefs)	102
Table 5.4:	Descriptive statistics of admitted and rejected applicants	108
Table 5.5:	Linear fixed-effects models with interaction term: Belief change*admission	110
Table 5.6:	Systematic illustration of results of hypotheses testing I	124
Table 6.1:	Average perceptions of justice and distributive preferences	127
Table 6.2:	Factor analysis results for domain-specific inequality beliefs	131
Table 6.3:	Factor analysis results for societal inequality beliefs	131
Table 6.4:	Average distinct types of inequality beliefs	132
Table 6.5:	Direct and total effects of parental education, inequality beliefs, and perceptions of justice on distributive preferences, and mediation mechanisms	133
Table 6.6:	Subgroup models: Direct and total effects of abilities beliefs on perceptions of justice and distributive preferences, separated by the belief that abilities are alterable vs. unalterable	140

Table 6.7:	Direct and total effects of parental education, admission outcome, inequality beliefs, and perceptions of justice on distributive preferences, and mediation mechanisms	144
Table 6.8:	Systematic illustration of results of hypotheses testing II	152
Table 7.1:	Description and distributions of persistence and inequality beliefs	156
Table 7.2:	Persistence in goal pursuit after a first rejection by parental education	158
Table 7.3:	Reapplication behavior and outcomes for each semester by parental education	160
Table 7.4:	Average domain-specific inequality beliefs by parental education	162
Table 7.5:	Effects of parental education and beliefs in meritocratic admission on persistence in goal pursuit	165
Table 7.6:	Systematic illustration of results of hypotheses testing III	170
Table A3.1:	List of hypotheses	199
Table A4.1:	Translated questionnaire items (from German) of main variables	200
Table A4.2:	Question wording and scales of inequality beliefs in NEPS data and medical applicant data	203
Table A5.1:	Correlation matrix of inequality beliefs (W1 beliefs)	204
Table A5.2:	Logistic regression model results: Effect of parental education on admission chances (marginal effects)	205
Table A5.3:	Robustness check with different weighting strategies: Admission rates by parental education	206
Table A5.4:	Robustness check with different weighting strategies: Average inequality beliefs by parental education (W1 beliefs)	207
Table A5.5:	Linear fixed-effects models with alternative weighting strategies	208
Table A5.6:	Fixed-effects ordered logit models (margins)	209
Table A5.7:	Fixed-effects fuzzy RDD models with interaction term: Belief change*admission	210
Table A5.8:	Heterogeneity in effect of admission on beliefs by admission quota: Linear fixed-effects models with interaction terms (belief change*admission quota)	211
Table A5.9:	Linear fixed-effects models with interaction terms: Belief change*parental education	212

Table A5.10: Linear fixed-effects models with interaction terms: Belief change*repeat applicant 213
Table A6.1: Weighted models: Direct and total effects of parental education and inequality beliefs on distributive preferences and mediation mechanisms 214
Table A7.1: Effect of parental education, beliefs in meritocratic admission, and self-predicted persistence on eventual success in admission 216
Table A7.2: Effects of beliefs in meritocratic admission on change in preferred field of study 217
Table A7.3: Robustness check including repeat and first-time applicants: Effects of parental education and beliefs in meritocratic admission on persistence in goal pursuit 218

List of figures

Figure 1.1:	Dissertation structure and main research questions	18
Figure 2.1:	Admission system to medical schools in Germany	25
Figure 3.1:	Stylized theoretical model of the effects of parental education and success or failure in admission on inequality beliefs	34
Figure 3.2:	Stylized theoretical model of the relationship between parental education, inequality beliefs, perceptions of justice, and distributive preferences	47
Figure 3.3:	Stylized theoretical model of social differences in beliefs in meritocratic admission and their consequences for persistence in goal pursui	58
Figure 3.4:	Hypotheses: The formation of inequality beliefs and their consequences for educational inequality	70
Figure 4.1:	Three survey waves of medical applicant data	72
Figure 4.2:	Samples of medical applicants used in analyses for three research objectives	81
Figure 5.1:	Dendrograms of belief patterns	95
Figure 5.2:	Effects of parental education on domain-specific inequality beliefs	104
Figure 5.3:	Effects of parental education on societal inequality beliefs	106
Figure 5.4:	Average inequality beliefs pre and post admission decision and belief changes	109
Figure 5.5:	Fuzzy cut-off point of drop in admission likelihood	112
Figure 5.6:	Average inequality beliefs pre and post admission decision and belief changes for applicants close to the fuzzy admission likelihood cut-off: GPA 1.3–1.4	113
Figure 5.7:	Average inequality beliefs pre and post admission and belief changes for admitted applicants through different quotas	115
Figure 5.8:	Average inequality beliefs pre and post admission decision and belief changes by parental education	117
Figure 5.9:	Average inequality beliefs pre and post admission decision and belief changes for first-time and repeat applicants	119
Figure 7.1:	Survival probabilities for reapplication behavior by parental education (discrete-time hazard models)	161

Figure A4.1: Distributions of societal effort and family background beliefs in NEPS and medical applicant data 220

Figure A5.1: Ordered logistic regression model results: Effects of parental education on domain-specific inequality beliefs 221

Figure A5.2: Ordered logistic regression model results: Effects of parental education on societal inequality beliefs 222

1 Introduction

In modern societies, educational attainment largely determines where one ends up on the social ladder. In Germany in particular, educational qualifications are strongly linked to labor market outcomes (Shavit et al., 2007):

> "It is mostly individuals' educational success or failure prior to labor market entry that determines […] social positioning in later life. As a consequence, the 'early winners' can safely enjoy lifelong returns and social status stability." (Solga, 2015, p. 205)

While individual effort and ability certainly contribute to educational success, there is clear empirical evidence that educational attainment remains strongly linked to social background (Autorengruppe Bildungsberichterstattung, 2022; Heisig et al., 2020). There is no level playing field for children from different backgrounds: Parental economic, social, and particularly cultural capital advantages children from privileged backgrounds in school (Bourdieu, 1977), making them more likely to attain a high level of education. Following the educational expansion, horizontal stratification also becomes increasingly important: Children from privileged backgrounds not only seek access to higher education, but specifically to selective fields of study with high returns in terms of income and prestige, and they are more successful in doing so than their less privileged peers (Lucas, 2001). Winning the educational game—and reaping the associated returns on the labor market—is possible for everyone, but the playing field is tilted in favor of those with better starting conditions. Highly educated parents are familiar with the norms and culture of the educational system and transfer this knowledge to their children (Bourdieu, 1984; Thaning, 2021). The interplay of educational gatekeeping processes and the ability of highly educated parents to understand and transmit the required cultural capital to their children results in educational inequality.

However, success against the odds occurs in individual cases. This may reinforce a widespread narrative that success primarily depends on individual merit, based on the notion that anyone can make it if they simply try hard enough. Regardless of the objective truth, beliefs have real-life consequences (Thomas & Thomas, 1928). Emphasizing differences in individual merit while disregarding that social background influences this merit may legitimize educational inequality as well as societal inequality in general (Mijs, 2016; Solga, 2015).

In his book 'The tyranny of merit,' Michael Sandel (2021), a professor in political philosophy at Harvard, criticizes meritocratic ideology and meritocratic university admission specifically:

> "Even a fair meritocracy, one without cheating or bribery or special privileges for the wealthy, induces a mistaken impression—that we have made it on our own.

The years of strenuous effort demanded of applicants to elite universities almost forces them to believe that their success is their own doing, and that if they fall short, they have no one to blame but themselves. This is a heavy burden for young people to bear. It is also corrosive of civic sensibilities. For the more we think of ourselves as self-made and self-sufficient, the harder it is to learn gratitude and humility. And without these sentiments, it is hard to care for the common good." (Sandel, 2021, p. 14)

This may explain why inequality is on the rise, but there seems to be no growing concern about this inequality among citizens (Mijs, 2021). Despite growing inequalities, a demand for an increasingly equal redistribution of resources fails to materialize, as inequality is seen as a problem of individuals rather than one of society. Those at the top may feel like they deserve their success, underestimating the privileges that they have enjoyed, while those at the bottom may blame themselves for their failure, underestimating the structural barriers they have had to face (Destin, 2020).

Marxist theory suggests that elites create structures and ideologies to maintain their privileges and prevent disadvantaged groups from working together to change the social order (Marx & Engels, 2004 [1845/46]). Meritocratic ideology can be seen as a modern way of the elites to legitimately transmit their status to their children by preparing them to achieve the required educational merit. Given unequal educational opportunities, attributing success solely to merit leads to a misconception of inequality, legitimizes intergenerational transmission of status, and contributes to the persistence of (educational) inequality (Bills, 2019; Mijs, 2016; Solga, 2015).

Meritocratic beliefs—beliefs that success primarily depends on individual effort and abilities—do not arise in a vacuum but rather are gradually formed through socialization and experiences, particularly through educational experiences in early adulthood (Mijs, 2017). Educational experiences of success and failure vary by social background. As parental education has been found to be the strongest predictor of educational success among social background characteristics (Thaning, 2021), in this dissertation, I focus on parental education as a resource that advantages or disadvantages applicants to medical school in achieving a very good grade-point-average (GPA) and thus influences their admission chances.

I propose that inequality beliefs (i.e., meritocratic and nonmeritocratic beliefs) are shaped by these educational experiences of success and failure and that interpersonal differences in beliefs may amplify their consequences for educational inequality: People from privileged backgrounds and the winners of the educational game are more likely to end up in positions of power. If those people hold stronger meritocratic and weaker nonmeritocratic beliefs than their less privileged peers and those who experience failure in education, they are more likely to perceive inequality as legitimate and less likely to support inequality-reducing policies. Furthermore, even when experiencing failure, stronger meritocratic beliefs among those from privileged backgrounds may advantage them by increasing their persistence in goal pursuit. Understanding how inequality beliefs are formed and their consequences for educational inequality could inform policies to promote a balanced understanding of success and structural barriers among adolescents, thereby increasing support for inequality-reducing policies and paving the way for a more equal and just society.

The broader research objective of this dissertation is to explore how parental education and educational experiences shape inequality beliefs, and what consequences these beliefs have for the legitimation and reproduction of educational inequality.

I propose a theoretical framework and test it using longitudinal data on applicants to the most selective study programs in Germany: public medical schools. The medical applicant data (Finger et al., 2023) includes a total of three waves that were collected via online surveys in August and November 2018, and February 2021. Between wave 1 and wave 2, all applicants received an admission decision (i.e., they were either admitted or rejected), and wave 2 and wave 3 followed up on admitted as well as rejected applicants.

Examining changes in inequality beliefs through the real-life experience of admission to medical school enables gaining an in-depth understanding of how educational experiences—experiences that differ by parental education—shape inequality beliefs during a life stage where these beliefs are likely not yet consolidated. As admission is a crucial event for applicants' future social positioning, experiencing success or failure in it may influence their inequality beliefs not only regarding the admission procedure but also regarding societal inequalities in general.

Admission to medical school in Germany is a highly selective procedure where the narrative of selection based on merit is predominant. Studying applicants' evaluation of this procedure is a good example to examine how (non)meritocratic beliefs may (de)legitimize such selection procedures, despite the tilted playing field to achieve the required merit of excellent school grades. Furthermore, applicants to medical schools are a positively selective group in terms of previous educational experiences, and for many of them, a rejection may be their first experience of failure. This dissertation examines how applicants from different social backgrounds deal with this experience of failure, and explores the role of inequality beliefs for differences in the persistence in pursuing admission to the most selective field of study—and thus for reproducing educational inequality.

Research gaps, contributions, and research questions

This dissertation makes a contribution to previous research by developing a theoretical framework for the formation of (non)meritocratic inequality beliefs and their consequences for educational inequality by combining sociological theories of intergenerational status transmission in education (e.g., Boudon, 1974; Bourdieu, 1977; Breen & Goldthorpe, 1997) and cumulative disadvantage (DiPrete & Eirich, 2006), sociological and social psychological theories on the formation of inequality beliefs (e.g., Bénabou & Tirole, 2016; Jost & Banaji, 1994; Mijs, 2017), sociological theories of meritocracy as an inequality-legitimizing ideology (e.g., Bills, 2019; Mijs, 2016; Solga, 2015), and social psychological attributional (Weiner, 1985) and motivational theory (Heckhausen & Schulz, 1995; Heckhausen et al., 2010).

Figure 1.1: Dissertation structure and main research questions

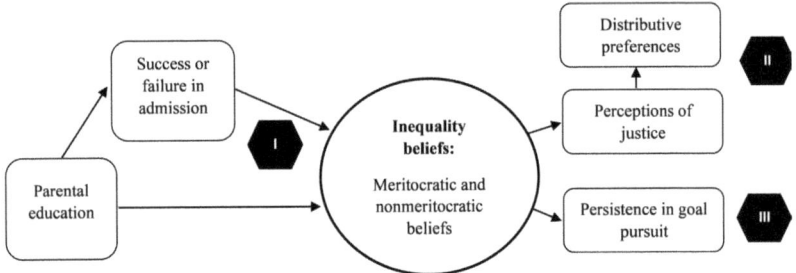

Note. Author's illustration.

Figure 1.1 illustrates the three main research objectives that structure the theoretical and empirical parts of this dissertation. The Roman numerals displayed in this figure will be used to number the hypotheses regarding these different research objectives.

To test this framework empirically, I use unique medical applicant data containing information on applicants' parental education, their (re)application behavior, and application outcomes. Furthermore, it entails their inequality beliefs (i.e., meritocratic and nonmeritocratic beliefs), their perceptions of justice, and distributive preferences. All three concepts pertain to two dimensions: a domain-specific one, referring to their own admissions; and a societal one, referring to societal success and inequalities in general. Inequality beliefs are defined as beliefs about sources of inequality (i.e., beliefs that success depends on meritocratic or nonmeritocratic factors), while perceptions of justice are defined as perceptions of the admission procedure or inequality in society in general as just. Distributive preferences are preferences for the distribution of places in the program or income based on different justice principles such as equality and educational meritocracy.

The first empirical contribution of this dissertation is to gain an in-depth understanding of how parental education and educational experiences of success and failure shape inequality beliefs. Existing research on how inequality beliefs are formed has primarily focused on the relationship between individuals' social position and inequality beliefs (e.g., Kluegel & Smith, 1986; Kreidl, 2000), or described changes in inequality beliefs among the successful group (Warikoo, 2016). This prompts the question concerning what role social origin plays for the formation of inequality beliefs, and how failure influences such beliefs. Experimental game studies could identify changes in winners' and losers' inequality beliefs and show that winners are more likely to attribute their success to talent and effort, while losers are more likely to attribute their losses to external factors—regardless of their initial condition in the game (Fehr & Vollmann, 2020; Molina et al., 2019). However, these game studies have been conducted in an artificial setting and are lacking the relevance of a real-life experience—their external validity remains unclear. Taking the real-life experience of success or failure in admission to medical school, I am able to longitudinally examine how such an experience changes their domain-specific inequality beliefs about their own admission and their societal inequality beliefs. The data further allows me to assess the effects of parental education on inequality beliefs and the role of parental education in the effects of experiences of success and failure on inequality beliefs: Parental education is often missing in previous studies on inequality beliefs (e.g., Bénabou & Tirole, 2016; Kluegel & Smith, 1986; Kreidl, 2000).

Hence, with research objective I (see Figure 1.1) I will address the following research questions: Do success in admission and inequality beliefs differ by parental education? How do experiences of success and failure shape inequality beliefs, and do differences in experiences explain social differences in beliefs? I will further explore whether the effects of success and failure differ depending on applicants' previous experiences.

The second contribution is to explore the complex mechanisms concerning how inequality beliefs legitimize or delegitimize inequality by influencing distributive preferences. Empirical research has explored the effects of inequality beliefs on perceptions of justice (e.g., Batruch et al., 2022; Mijs, 2021; Sachweh & Sthamer, 2019) and the preference for equal distribution (e.g., Alesina & Giuliano, 2011; García-Sánchez et al., 2020; Marquis & Rosset, 2021), but the inequality-legitimizing effect of the belief in the importance of abilities for success as well as the effect of inequality beliefs on the preference for distribution based on educational meritocracy have been understudied.

Furthermore, while existing studies assume that inequality beliefs affect distributive preferences through the perception of inequality as just (e.g., Alesina & Giuliano, 2011; Marquis & Rosset, 2021), empirically this theoretical assumption has yet to be tested, as most studies have focused on only one of these outcomes rather than combining them and investigating their relationship. Additionally, previous research suggests that people from similar backgrounds tend to have similar distributive preferences (Liebig & Sauer, 2016). I propose that social differences in distributive preferences could partly be explained by differences in inequality beliefs, resulting from differences in experiences.

With research objective II, I address the legitimizing function of inequality beliefs, and ask: How do inequality beliefs influence distributive preferences through perceptions of justice? Do social differences in inequality beliefs, and the resulting perception of justice, partly explain the association between parental education and distributive preferences?

Third, this dissertation contributes to research on the secondary effects of parental education on educational attainment. Previous research has explored the association between inequality beliefs and persistence in goal pursuit (e.g., Hu et al., 2020; Shane & Heckhausen, 2013, 2017), but has not considered how it may contribute to educational inequality. I propose that social differences in inequality beliefs may partly explain social differences in educational choices, namely differences in persistence. As the data on medical school applicants includes information on applicants' persistence in goal pursuit after failure, I am able to test this newly developed argument empirically, exploring the effects on different concepts of persistence (self-predicted persistence and actual reapplication behavior).

Thus, with research objective III I explore how (social differences in) inequality beliefs affect the persistence in goal pursuit: Are there social differences in the persistence in goal pursuit after a first rejection? Do beliefs in meritocratic admission increase applicants' persistence? Do social differences in their beliefs in meritocratic admission explain part of the effect of parental education on persistence? Furthermore, I will explore whether the effect of the belief in meritocratic admission differs by parental education.

Finally, this dissertation makes an overarching contribution by considering conceptionally different meritocratic and nonmeritocratic beliefs (e.g., hard work vs. ability belief, luck vs. social background belief) throughout its different parts. Previous studies often either include only a small selection of inequality beliefs or aggregate them into indices (e.g., Mijs, 2021; Shane & Heckhausen, 2013), even though attributional theory and previous empirical studies suggest that there may be different consequences of distinct types of inequality beliefs for the legitimation of inequality and persistence (e.g., Friedman et al., 2023; Marquis & Rosset, 2021; Smith & Skrbiš, 2017). In addition, research suggests that experiences of success or failure may affect domain-specific inequality beliefs differently than societal inequality beliefs (Shane & Heckhausen, 2017) and that people may use different criteria to assess justice and form distributive preferences depending on the situation to be evaluated (van Hootegem et al., 2020)—a distinction that is also considered throughout this dissertation.

Structure of dissertation

After this first introductory chapter, this dissertation will continue with a chapter on the institutional context of Germany's stratified educational system and admission to medical schools, as this is crucial for understanding the specific case and sample observed here (Chapter 2).

In Chapter 3, I will discuss theories and empirical research on the formation of inequality beliefs and their consequences for educational inequality, and present a theoretical framework. In Chapter 3.1, I will introduce mechanisms behind educational inequality, discuss and hypothesize my basic assumption that chances of admission to medical school vary by parental education, and argue that meritocratic ideology may play a crucial role in legitimizing this educational inequality. Subsequently, in Chapters 3.2, 3.3, and 3.4, I will discuss theories and empirical evidence on the formation of inequality beliefs and their consequences for educational inequality. I will draw hypotheses regarding research objective I in Chapters 3.1 and 3.2, regarding research objective II in Chapter 3.3, and regarding research objective III in Chapter 3.4 (see research objectives in Figure 1.1). Finally, in Chapter 3.5, I will integrate these hypotheses into one theoretical framework.

In Chapter 4, I will present the research design of this study by describing the data collection and variables. Furthermore, I will describe the different (sub)samples used to examine the different research objectives, discuss the applied weighting strategies, and provide sample statistics on the characteristics of the different subsamples and applicants' inequality beliefs. Furthermore, I will use data from the German National Educational Panel Study (NEPS) to provide an idea of the representativeness of inequality beliefs of medical school applicants compared to the inequality beliefs of other groups of adolescents in Germany. Finally, I will present an overview of the methods applied.

In Chapters 5, 6, and 7, I will present the analyses and findings to answer the research questions empirically. In each chapter, I will include descriptive statistics on the sample observed in the specific empirical part as well as more in-depth information on the applied methodological approach. Subsequently, the findings will be presented, and each chapter will conclude with a brief summary of the main findings.

Finally, in Chapter 8, I will summarize the main theoretical arguments and key findings before discussing the contributions of this study to the theoretical debate and previous empirical research. Subsequently, I will state the limitations of this research and suggest avenues for future research. I will conclude this dissertation by discussing how this research contributes to understanding the role of inequality beliefs in legitimizing, reproducing, and perpetuating inequality, as well as how the findings could help to pave the way for a more equal society in terms of outcomes and opportunities.

2 Institutional context

In this dissertation, I use a sample of applicants to public medical schools in Germany to answer my research questions. The focus on this specific group allows me to study how 1) experiences of success and failure in highly selective university admission shape inequality beliefs, 2) inequality beliefs about admission may shape justice perceptions and distributive preferences in a setting where the narrative and ideology of meritocracy is predominant, and 3) these beliefs may contribute to educational inequality in access to the most selective field of study that come with high returns in terms of prestige and income. In this chapter, I will provide a brief overview of the German educational system generally as well as admission to medical school specifically, while describing social selectivity at the different steps on the way to higher education (HE) and medical school specifically.

Germany's stratified educational system

Entry to HE in Germany is highly stratified and socially selective, despite the low tuition costs of HE. The main reasons for this are the dual system of HE and vocational education and training (VET), as well as a strongly segregated educational system (Finger, 2022; Powell & Solga, 2011).

After primary school (after grade 4 or 6, when children are about age 10 or 12 years old, depending on the federal state), children are sorted into different educational tracks, which prepare children for either HE or VET. The sorting is based on teachers' track recommendations considering children's abilities and performance in primary school. In some federal states, recommendations are binding, while in most federal states, parents can choose freely on which track to enroll their children based on this recommendation. This early sorting is legitimized by the idea that children have either practical talents or theoretical abilities (Gogescu, 2024; Powell & Solga, 2011). Changes between these tracks are possible but rare, and thus this early selection largely predetermines children's future educational pathways and opportunities in the labor market (Powell & Solga, 2011).

Traditionally, children are sorted into the three school types lower-secondary schools ('Hauptschule'), intermediate-secondary schools ('Realschule'), or upper-secondary schools ('Gymnasium'). However, children can also attend comprehensive schools with options to obtain different school-leaving certificates, reflecting an increasingly important school type.[1] Only the school-leaving certificate obtained on the academic track at upper-secondary schools (or on the upper-secondary track at comprehensive schools)—the so-called 'Abitur'—qualifies adolescents to enter HE.[2] In 2018, only 51 % of all secondary school students obtained their Abitur. Furthermore, only around 75 % of these eligible students ultimately entered HE (Autorengruppe Bildungsberichterstattung, 2020, p. 184).

Different steps on the way to entering HE are highly socially selective, with reports on education in Germany (Autorengruppe Bildungsberichterstattung, 2020, 2022) showing social differences at the initial sorting on an educational track and at entering HE. The mentioned reports draw from data from the National Educational Panel, following children from the fifth grade in 2010 to 2019/20 (Autorengruppe Bildungsberichterstattung, 2022, pp. 159–161). Among children from high socio-economic backgrounds—measured as highest parental occupation (hereafter called high SES)—79 % attended upper-secondary schools, compared to only 50 % among those with medium and only 27 % among those with low SES. Among high and medium SES children, 8 % attended comprehensive schools with the option to obtain the Abitur, and among low SES children, 10 % attended such schools. When looking at who obtained the Abitur, social differences do not go beyond initial sorting: Among adolescents from high SES, 79 % obtained the Abitur, compared to 57 % from medium SES and 31 % from low SES.

However, based on analyses of adolescents eligible to enter HE in 2015 (DZHW), the report shows social differences in the decision to enter HE (Autorengruppe Bildungsberichterstattung, 2020, pp. 185–186). Among those with at least one college-educated parent, 86 % decided to enter HE compared with only 76 % among those without college-educated parents. Even among those who have successfully gone through the different steps on the way to be eligible to enter HE, and despite low tuition costs and the possibility of means-tested subsidiaries for children from low-income families, for many adolescents from low SES backgrounds, the VET system may be more attractive (Powell & Solga, 2011). Even though HE leads to more opportunities in the labor market and higher salaries in the long run, VET also leads to relatively well-paid occupations and allows a faster entry into the labor market.

---

1 In 2006, among those who obtained the Abitur, 6 % attended comprehensive school, while the share increased to 9 % in 2018 (Autorengruppe Bildungsberichterstattung, 2020, p. 147).
2 Besides obtaining the Abitur, there are also possibilities to enter HE later in life by obtaining the entry certificate by visiting so-called evening colleges (Abendgymnasium) or through prior working experiences. However, these paths are relatively rare: In 2014, only 6 % of students entered HE through these paths (Autorengruppe Bildungsberichterstattung (2016, p. 299).

Furthermore, social differences in the decision to enter HE can be explained by social differences in school grades (Autorengruppe Bildungsberichterstattung, 2020, p. 186). Lower school grades may prevent adolescents from less privileged backgrounds from entering HE, as access to some fields of study is limited, and admission is often based on performance in school (Mayer et al., 2007). More precisely it is often based on their GPA, ranging from 1.0 (the best score) to 4.0 (the worst score), an average that is calculated based on students' grades in their last two years at upper-secondary schools and their grades in the final exams. An insufficient score may prevent students from applying to selective fields of study, as it crucially determines their admission chances.

Admission to medical schools in Germany

Unlike educational systems with strong differences in prestige between universities such as the United States or the United Kingdom, German universities are rather alike in their institutional prestige and quality (Finger, 2022; Mayer et al., 2007). However, differences between fields of study are pronounced, with medical programs offering exceptionally high returns in terms of income and occupational prestige (Finger, 2022). Medical programs are also the most selective, with rates of admission averaging around 25 %.

Aspiring applicants to medical programs at one of the 39 public universities must apply through a central clearinghouse, the Stiftung für Hochschulzulassung (SfH).[3] Until 2019, places were allocated via three quotas: (a) 20 % exclusively based on their GPA, (b) 20 % based on their waiting-period, and (c) 60 % based on university-specific criteria.[4] To be admitted via the first quota, applicants need an excellent GPA, usually the best grade of 1.0. To be admitted via the second quota, applicants must wait for approximately six to seven years, during which they cannot study at universities in Germany. For the third quota, applicants' GPA is the most important selection criterion, although universities typically use additional criteria (e.g., test scores or work experience) to select applicants.

Applicants may rank up to six universities in each admission quota, and they can only be admitted to one university (Finger & Solga, 2023; Finger et al., 2024). Step-wise admission takes place where the allocation of places in

---

3   There are only very few private universities with limited places in the program that offer to study medicine in Germany. Furthermore, some aspiring applicants from Germany decide to (additionally) apply to study medicine abroad where admission is less selective. In this dissertation, I will only focus on applicants to public medical schools in Germany.
4   There is also a very small share of applicants who may be admitted via other routes; for instance, in case of social hardship or through a lottery as a final step for wait-listed candidates.

the program starts with the first university listed in the GPA quota and ends with the last university listed in the university-specific quota. Figure 2.1, an illustration by Finger and Solga (2023), shows the admission system that was in place until 2019.

Figure 2.1: Admission system to medical schools in Germany

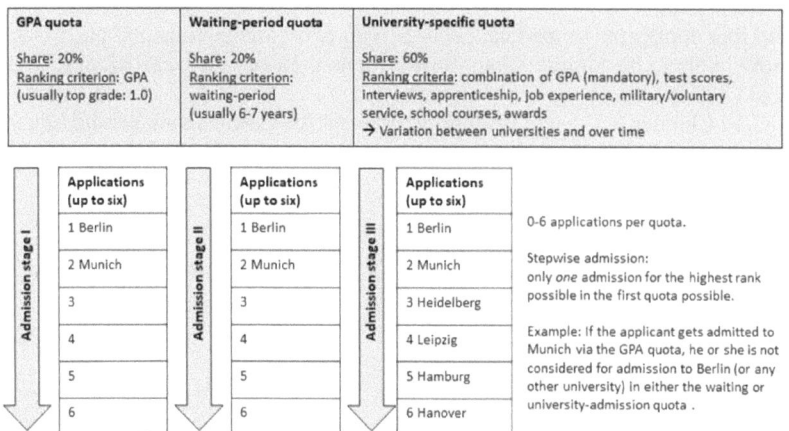

Note. Source: Illustration from Finger and Solga (2023). Slightly adapted by the author.

The GPA and the university-specific quotas can be regarded as merit-based, whereas admission through the waiting-period quota relies on a nonmeritocratic factor. A debate has recently emerged on the meritocratic foundation of admission to public medical schools in Germany, mainly criticizing admission through the waiting-period quota and the (lack of) comparability of GPAs across German federal states. A 2017 ruling by the Federal Constitutional Court required changes in the usage and weighting of the criteria for admission.

Since 2020, 30 % of the successful applicants are admitted by the GPA quota, a further 10 % are admitted by an eligibility quota based on criteria besides the GPA, and 60 % are admitted by university-specific criteria. In the last quota, more emphasis has been placed on test scores compared to the previous system, such as scores from the test for medical programs (TMS). Nevertheless, applicants' GPA remains the most important admission criterion. When examining changes in inequality beliefs through success or failure in admission (Chapter 5), I observe admission in 2018 following the old system, although the preceding public debate about the admission procedure might have influenced applicants' beliefs. When examining reapplication behavior (Chapter 7), some applicants might have applied through the old as well as the new admission system. However, the changes in the admission procedure are not in the focus of this dissertation, but rather how educational experiences shape inequality beliefs, and how these beliefs contribute to educational inequality.

There are strong social differences in being eligible to and choosing to enter HE, as well as social differences in school grades—the most important selection criteria for admission to medical school. Hence, unsurprisingly, research shows that adolescents from privileged backgrounds are highly overrepresented among medical students (R. Becker et al., 2010; Lörz, 2012) and that applicants to medical schools with two college-educated parents are more likely to be admitted than those with no college-educated parent (Finger et al., 2024).

In Chapter 3.1, I will discuss theories on the mechanisms behind educational inequality generally and in application and access to medical school specifically.

3 Theoretical framework for the formation of inequality beliefs and their consequences for educational inequality

The overall purpose of Chapter 3 is to discuss and combine theories and empirical evidence to propose a theoretical framework for the formation of inequality beliefs and their consequences for educational inequality.

In Chapter 3.1, I will first provide a broader framework on the mechanisms behind educational inequality and introduce theories on how this inequality may be legitimized by meritocratic ideology. I will then discuss theories and empirical evidence for my narrower research objectives: In Chapter 3.2, I will argue how parental education and educational experiences may shape inequality beliefs. In Chapter 3.3, I will discuss the consequences of inequality beliefs for perceptions of justice and distributive preferences. In Chapter 3.4, I will address how inequality beliefs may affect persistence in goal pursuit and contribute to reproducing educational inequality. In Chapter 3.5, I will summarize my hypotheses and integrate them into one theoretical framework.

3.1 Educational inequality

A central concern of educational sociology is to understand why social background remains strongly linked with children's educational attainment. In this chapter, I will argue why I expect social inequality in admissions to prestigious and selective fields of study. For this purpose, I will present prominent theoretical explanations of educational inequality, and discuss how they relate to inequality in access to selective fields among applicants. This brief introduction to educational inequality leads to the central question concerning what legitimizes this persistent inequality, whereby I argue that meritocratic ideology plays a crucial role in this legitimation.

Primary and secondary effects as mechanisms behind educational inequality

A widely used concept in educational sociology is the distinction between two main mechanisms behind educational inequality, namely performance and educational decisions that vary by social background (Boudon, 1974; Jackson, 2013). Boudon (1974) calls these mechanisms primary and secondary effects. Together, both primary and secondary effects can explain social differences in educational attainment. This distinction enables identifying the determinants of and processes behind educational inequality more precisely. As an introduction to educational inequality, I will now present prominent theories on mechanisms behind primary and secondary effects, which I will consider in this dissertation when discussing the role of inequality beliefs in educational inequality.

Performance differences that lead to unequal attainment (i.e., primary effects) arise from differences in capital that advantage children from privileged backgrounds (Boudon, 1974; Bourdieu, 1977; Bourdieu & Passeron, 1990; Schindler & Lörz, 2012). Bourdieu (1986) distinguishes between three types of capital that can be transmitted from parents to their children: economic, social, and cultural capital. Economic capital refers to resources such as money, assets, and property, and social capital refers to current or potential resources associated with one's network or institutionalized relationships (Bourdieu, 1986). When explaining educational inequality and performance differences between children from different social backgrounds, Bourdieu focuses on a third type of capital that can be transmitted: cultural capital (Bourdieu, 1977; Bourdieu & Passeron, 1990). Cultural capital includes objectified cultural capital (e.g., artwork, instruments), institutionalized cultural capital (e.g., educational certificates, professional qualifications), and embodied cultural capital—the most important type of cultural capital to explain intergenerational status transmission and social reproduction.

Embodied cultural capital refers to a person's characteristics such as class-specific cultural and linguistic competencies, and behaviors.[5] Subconsciously learned and internalized values, preferences, and behavior translate into a class-specific habitus (Bourdieu, 1977; Bourdieu & Passeron, 1990). This embodied cultural capital—and the resulting habitus—is primarily shaped in early childhood through socialization within the family. While different dimensions of social class and capital can influence children's success in school, Bourdieu (1984) argues that social reproduction often occurs with a focus on one type of capital: Highly educated parents are more likely to invest in their children's (educational) cultural capital, while wealthy parents are more likely to invest in their economic capital (Bourdieu, 1984; Thaning, 2021). Following this theoretical argument, parental education should be the social background charac-

---

5 While Bourdieu's definition of cultural capital is rather vague, subsequent research has theoretically and empirically explored different interpretations of cultural capital. In contrast to the classical interpretation of Bourdieu's work, Graaf et al. (2000) found that reading to children—rather than participating in high-brow activities such as attendance at theatres, concerts, and museums—increased children's educational attainment. Further research has also stressed the role of class-specific parenting style and parental expectations as strong predictors of children's success that partially explain educational inequality (Barone, 2006; Graaf et al., 2000; Lareau, 2003; Roksa and Potter, 2011).

teristic that is most strongly associated with children's educational attainment and educational inequality—an assumption that has been supported by recent empirical studies in Sweden (e.g., Hällsten & Thaning, 2018; Thaning, 2021).

Educational institutions act as gatekeepers and define which cultural competencies are rewarded in the school context (Karabel, 1984, 2005). Highly educated parents are familiar with the norms and culture of the educational system and transfer this knowledge, but also subconsciously a certain habitus, to their children (Bourdieu, 1984; Thaning, 2021). The interplay of educational gatekeeping processes and the ability of (highly educated) parents to understand and transmit the required cultural capital to their children results in educational inequality. Accordingly, children with highly educated parents are better equipped to adapt to the academic culture at school, which is more familiar to them than to their less privileged peers. As a result, they are more likely to thrive in educational settings and perform better (Bourdieu, 1977; Bourdieu & Passeron, 1990).

In addition to primary effects, secondary effects constitute differences in educational choices and transition decisions that depend on someone's background and associated beliefs and opportunities (Boudon, 1974; Schindler & Lörz, 2012). Empirical research confirms that these social differences in educational choices persist even after accounting for primary effects (Heiskala et al., 2023; Jackson, 2013).

According to Breen and Goldthorpe's (1997) rational choice model for educational decisions, adolescents act rationally in choosing among different educational options. Based on their perceived likelihood of success in achieving educational outcomes, they chose certain educational goals, considering the costs and benefits. Social differences in educational decisions are explained as the consequence of differences in resources and constraints. Furthermore, the theory suggests that adolescents are motivated to avoid the risk of downward mobility relative to their parents' status, and at least replicate the social status and educational level of their parents—also known as status maintenance (Breen & Goldthorpe, 1997).

Thus, on average, adolescents with college-educated parents are more likely to set themselves high educational goals, such as obtaining a college degree. However, there are also young people with high educational aspirations among adolescents without college-educated parents, especially if they show a high academic potential at an early age and receive (sufficient) support from their parents (Bourdieu & Passeron, 1971; Finger, 2022).

Bourdieu's (1977) theory of social reproduction may not only explain primary effects but also secondary effects. Class-specific habitus advantages children from privileged backgrounds to perform well in school but embodied cultural capital and habitus may also entail values of strong commitment to high educational goals and persistence in pursuing them—aspects of educational decisions that I will discuss in Chapter 3.4. In Chapter 3.2, I will further argue that motivating meritocratic beliefs may be a form of cultural capital that is transmitted by highly educated parents to their children.

Inequality in application and admission to selective fields of study

Educational inequality entails not only vertical stratification between educational levels but also horizontal stratification between the fields of study. The expansion of the education system has increased this horizontal stratification, as university certificates lose value and those from privileged backgrounds switch to more profitable forms of education to ensure status reproduction. Lucas' (2001) effectively maintained inequality hypothesis suggests that those from a privileged social background are not only more likely to pursue HE but will also make more beneficial educational choices within HE. In the German context, empirical research has confirmed that adolescents from privileged backgrounds are more likely to apply and enter selective fields of study (e.g., R. Becker et al., 2010; Lörz, 2012; Schindler & Lörz, 2012).

Both primary and secondary effects contribute to inequality in selective fields of study. Selection is commonly primarily based on performance in school, increasing the admission likelihood of applicants from privileged backgrounds due to their advantaged position in school (Bourdieu, 1977; Bourdieu & Passeron, 1990). In addition, R. Becker et al. (2010) argue that the choice of study field follows similar mechanisms of rational decision-making as the choice to enter HE in general. Based on their perceived likelihood of success—which in turn depends on their performance—adolescents decide whether or not to apply to these selective fields of study. Furthermore, according to the mechanism of status maintenance, adolescents are motivated not only to replicate their parents' educational level but also their social status (Breen & Goldthorpe, 1997). From a Bordieuan perspective, class-specific cultural capital and habitus make it easier for adolescents from privileged backgrounds to identify educational options that come with high returns in terms of income or prestige (Bourdieu, 1994). For those from less privileged backgrounds, these options may be perceived as a poor fit due to the high value that cultural capital may have in these selective fields of study (Bourdieu & Passeron, 2007).

In this dissertation, I observe applicants to medicine—the most selective field of study in Germany. Medical schools act as gatekeepers by choosing selection criteria such as GPA (Karabel, 1984, 2005), a choice that shapes the composition of the student body and excludes certain groups from entering this selective field of study. Primary and secondary effects and the interplay with institutional gatekeeping are likely to lead to an overrepresentation of students with two college-educated parents among medical students.

My sample consists only of applicants: adolescents who have already decided to apply. Hence, I only observe social differences in access to medical school among a positively selective group and not secondary effects in terms of initial educational choices. However, as GPA is the most important selection criterion for medical schools, primary effects are likely to contribute to unequal admission between applicants from different social backgrounds. Furthermore, applicants from privileged backgrounds may be more strategic and flexible in choosing universities for their ranking (secondary effects).

Empirical research confirms social differences in the realization of study aspirations in Germany. Spangenberg et al. (2011, p. 83) showed that among adolescents who aspired to study medicine, those with two college-educated parents were 33 percentage points more likely to realize these aspirations and enter medical school than those with no college-educated parent. This social difference in the realization of study field aspirations was the most pronounced for medicine and much less pronounced for less selective fields of study (e.g., economics or social sciences).

Finally, a recent study observed the admission likelihood among those who decided to apply to medical school (Finger et al., 2024), using the same data as this dissertation—namely the medical applicant data (Finger et al., 2023). The authors found that applicants with two college-educated parents were 6 percentage points more likely to be admitted than applicants with no college-educated parent (Finger et al., 2024). They further showed that social differences in admission likelihood were driven entirely by social differences in applicants' performance (in GPA and test scores), and not by differences in application strategies (Finger et al., 2024), contradicting the argument of secondary effects on admission likelihood.

Even though this study has already shown differences in admission likelihood for medical applicants by parental education, for reasons of comprehensiveness, I will replicate Finger et al.'s (2024) findings of social differences in admission likelihood with my specific sample. Accordingly, I expect that:

HI.1: Applicants from privileged backgrounds are more likely to be admitted to medical school than their less privileged peers.

While this base hypothesis addresses differences in admission among those who decided to apply, in Chapter 3.4, I will further argue that differences in educational decisions (secondary effects)—specifically persistence after a first rejection—also contribute to unequal admission between applicants from different social backgrounds.

Following arguments on within-capital transmission (Bourdieu, 1984; Thaning, 2021), when discussing the role of social background in this dissertation, I focus on applicants' parental education because this capital, even though it is of course linked to other types of capital, is the strongest predictor of educational success (Bourdieu, 1984; Hällsten & Thaning, 2018; Thaning, 2021). Hence, throughout this dissertation, the term 'applicants from privileged backgrounds' refers to applicants with two college-educated parents, and the term 'applicants from less privileged backgrounds' to applicants with no college-educated parent, while applicants with one college-educated parent fall in the middle of these poles. I purposely use the term less privileged instead of disadvantaged, as even applicants to medical school with no college-educated parent may have had a certain level of support that allowed them to pursue their application to medical school that more disadvantaged groups of adolescents may not have had.

Legitimation of educational inequality

Educational inequality is particularly problematic because educational attainment may be perceived as a result of individual merit, which contributes to its persistence. Emphasizing differences in individual performance while neglecting that social background influences performance may legitimize unequal educational attainment and the intergenerational transmission of status (Bills, 2019; Solga, 2015).

In his famous satire, Michael Young—who introduced the term 'meritocracy'—defined merit as "I.Q. + effort = merit" (Young, 1994 [1958], p. xiii). According to the principle of meritocracy, social positions and privileges should be distributed solely based on people's individual merit (Mijs, 2016; Young, 1994 [1958]). Although Young (1994 [1958]) portrayed the meritocratic society as a dystopian society of the future United Kingdom in his book, nowadays the meritocratic ideology has found strong support in society, particularly as a guiding principle in education (Bills, 2019; Solga, 2015). Students' merit should be rewarded with good grades, which in return will grant them access to highly selective study programs and eventually to high positions in the social hierarchy (Bills, 2019; Mijs, 2016). Mijs (2016) has problematized this "pervasiveness of meritocracy in educational policy, which threatens to crowd out need and equality as principles of justice, to the detriment of equality of opportunity" (Mijs, 2016, p. 16).

Meritocracy is a system-justifying ideology (Jost et al., 2003). It strives for equality of opportunities while embracing and legitimizing equality of outcomes (Bills, 2019). Solga (2015) has argued that meritocratic ideology comes with five key features that lead to a misinterpretation of the nature of educational inequality and contribute to its legitimization: First, it deems a certain level of inequality of outcomes as necessary for the division of labor and to motivate people to reach their full potential and work in demanding occupations (Davis & Moore, 1945). Second, in meritocratic societies, educational and social inequalities are portrayed as a natural result of differences in individual's efforts and, particularly, in talents: The belief that people are born with these differences in innate talents makes inequality seem natural, unchangeable, and unescapable (Friedman et al., 2023; Solga, 2015). Third, educational processes are organized in such a way that educational institutions can signal qualifications and skills to employers. Thus, what is important for a person's social position are rather educational certificates than the actual skills, and according to Bourdieu (1986), the intergenerational transmission of 'institutionalized capital' contributes to social reproduction. Fourth, Solga (2015) argues that in the meritocratic ideal, inequality is framed as the result of individual achievement, replacing differences based on social categories such as social background or gender. The meritocratic narrative neglects previously described mechanisms of status reproduction, leading to social differences in performance and educational choices. Fifth, meritocratic ideology ignores that merit is not a fixed construct, but rather socially constructed: Elites in society define what merit means in a particular historical and social context (Mijs, 2016; Solga, 2015).

In the educational context, selection criteria and the definition of merit have changed over time. The choice of selection criteria (e.g., selection based on school grades or admission tests) always favors certain groups over others. Karabel (2005) suggests that "those who are able to define ''merit'' will almost invariably possess more of it, and those with greater resources—cultural, economic, and social—will generally be able to ensure that the educational system will deem their children more meritorious" (Karabel, 2005, p. 550). This assumption follows Marxist theory, namely the notion that elites create structures and ideologies to maintain their privileges and prevent disadvantaged groups from working together to change the social order (Marx & Engels, 2004 [1845/46]). According to this conflict theory, meritocratic ideology allows higher social classes to legitimize their position and transmit their status to their children by preparing them to achieve the required merit. Weber (1991 [1921]) stated that "today, the 'examination' is the universal means for monopolization" (Weber, 1991 [1921], p. 242).

The Thomas Theorem claims that beliefs—regardless of the objective truth—have real-life consequences (Thomas & Thomas, 1928). Whether people believe that they live in a meritocratic society and which factors they believe influence whether someone is successful—in admission to medical school or more broadly in society—matters for the legitimation of (educational) inequality.

3.2 How parental education and educational experiences shape inequality beliefs[6]

Beliefs about inequality do not arise in a vacuum nor are they something that people are born with, but I suggest that they are rather something that is grad-

---

6   Parts of this chapter, particularly adapted versions of the sections on theories of biased inequality beliefs and previous experiences as a frame for new experiences

ually formed through socialization and through educational experiences: experiences such as being admitted or rejected when applying to medical school. After discussing a) how the likelihood of success and failure in admission may vary by parental education, in this chapter, I will discuss b) whether and how parental education influences inequality beliefs, c) whether and how experiences of success and failure influence inequality beliefs, and d) whether and how the effects of these experiences vary by previous experiences.

First, I will first provide a definition of inequality beliefs, and explain how these beliefs crystallize primarily in early adulthood. I will then discuss the relationship between parental education and inequality beliefs, and present theories of biased inequality beliefs, as well as my expectations of how success and failure in admission to medical school shape inequality beliefs in a self-serving way. Finally, I will present arguments that prior experiences provide a frame for new experiences of success and failure, and thus influence the effect of success or failure in admission on inequality beliefs. Figure 3.1 displays the proposed effects of parental education and success or failure in admission on inequality beliefs, including the moderation of the later effects by previous experiences.

Figure 3.1: Stylized theoretical model of the effects of parental education and success or failure in admission on inequality beliefs

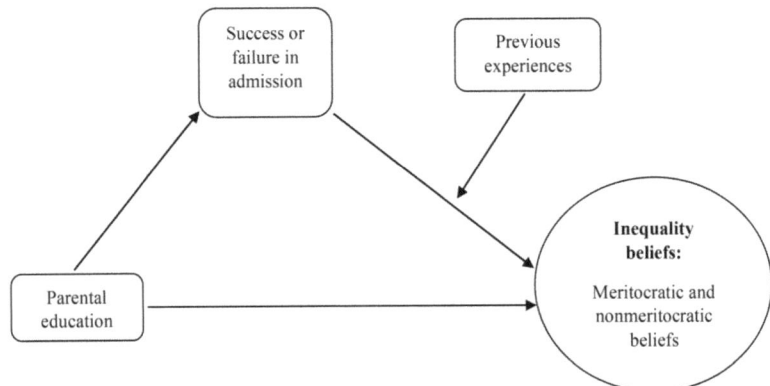

Note. Author's illustration.

have been published in a co-authored article with Claudia Finger (Wetter & Finger, 2023).

What are inequality beliefs?

People differ in their inequality beliefs—their beliefs about the extent to which success depends on different factors. The main distinction made in this dissertation is the distinction between meritocratic and nonmeritocratic beliefs.

Meritocratic and nonmeritocratic beliefs are not mutually exclusive. Indeed, most people believe that an interplay of meritocratic and nonmeritocratic factors determines success and inequality of outcomes (Kreidl, 2000). However, there are individual differences in beliefs about the extent to which unequal outcomes are based on meritocratic or nonmeritocratic factors—differences that may be shaped by people's experiences and have consequences for educational inequality.

Meritocratic beliefs are all beliefs that attribute success or failure to individual differences in merit. Typically, both hard work (e.g., effort, perseverance, and drive) and abilities (e.g., talent, intelligence, and skills) constitute merit (Mijs, 2016; Young, 1994 [1958]). Beliefs about the importance of hard work and abilities for success are sometimes combined into a single 'meritocratic belief' index (Shane & Heckhausen, 2013, 2017).

However, according to Weiner's (1985) attributional theory, there is a structure behind beliefs about reasons for success and failure, comprising three dimensions such as locus (internal versus external), stability (stable or unstable), and control (alterable or unalterable). Following Weiner's (1985) argument, the beliefs about the importance of hard work and abilities may be two distinct types of beliefs, as these factors differ in their perceived controllability and stability. People might perceive abilities as unalterable and stable, while they see hard work as unstable, alterable, and controllable by the individual (Skinner et al., 1998; Weiner, 1985).[7] Hence, these two meritocratic beliefs may be affected differently by experiences of success and failure, have different inequality-legitimizing consequences, and have different implications for persistence in goal pursuit.

Ideally, school grades should be distributed based on a combination of hard work and abilities, reflecting merit in school. Hence, the belief in the importance of school grades for success constitutes another distinct meritocratic belief. Unlike hard work and abilities, school grades are easily observable, and—according to the principle of educational meritocracy—a distribution of desired social positions based on grades and educational certificates is often considered legitimate (Bills, 2019; Solga, 2015).

Nonmeritocratic beliefs include fatalistic and structural beliefs—in this dissertation also referred to as luck and social background beliefs. Fatalistic

---

7   However, Dweck (2006) suggests that not everyone views abilities as unalterable but that some people view abilities as stable (i.e., 'fixed mindset'), while others may view them as alterable (i.e., 'growth mindset')—an argument that will be considered in the theoretical arguments and analyses.

beliefs refer to the perception that success is simply due to differences in luck between individuals (Shane & Heckhausen, 2013). Structural beliefs recognize that deeply ingrained structural inequality in our society results in unequal distribution of opportunities across social groups. Ascriptive characteristics such as gender and ethnicity, or differences in economic, social, and cultural capital due to parents' socio-economic status, influence an individual's likelihood of success (Mijs, 2016). While both luck and structural factors have an external locus of control, attributional theory suggests that they are distinct nonmeritocratic beliefs: Luck is an unstable factor that typically fluctuates throughout a person's life and affects everyone equally, while structural factors influence an individual throughout their life (Weiner, 1985). In this dissertation, I will explore these distinct inequality beliefs and examine changes in those beliefs and their consequences separately.

Furthermore, inequality beliefs may refer to different reference points and thus be more or less strongly linked to individual experiences. Shane and Heckhausen (2017) distinguish between beliefs about one's own success in society, and beliefs about the success of others. Beyond this distinction, inequality beliefs may also differ in whether they refer to the allocation of outcomes in a specific domain, such as admission to medical school, or social inequality in general. Research suggests that people may use different criteria to evaluate inequality contingent on the circumstances (van Hootegem et al., 2020). Thus, inequality beliefs may be more or less affected by educational experiences and have different consequences for educational inequality depending on the reference point.

Some studies have examined inequality beliefs about specific outcomes, such as students' attribution of academic success to meritocratic or nonmeritocratic factors (Lohbeck et al., 2017) and students' beliefs in meritocratic admission (Warikoo, 2016). Other studies have examined beliefs about societal inequality more generally (Kluegel & Smith, 1986; Kreidl, 2000; Mijs, 2021), although few have combined the two concepts of domain-specific and general societal inequality beliefs (Wiederkehr et al., 2015).[8] In this dissertation, I address this research gap by observing meritocratic and nonmeritocratic beliefs about one's own admission to medical school (domain-specific beliefs) and about success in society in general (societal beliefs).

---

8   Wiederkehr et al. (2015) studied how students' belief that success in school depends on effort is associated with their belief that they live in a just and meritocratic society. However, their study does not address how these beliefs are shaped by educational experiences and what consequences they have for educational inequality.

Crystallization of inequality beliefs in early adulthood

In early adulthood, a period of change and transitions from school to HE or the labor market, inequality beliefs are likely not yet consolidated. The impressionable years hypothesis (Alwin & Krosnick, 1991) proposes that sociopolitical attitudes and beliefs remain subject to considerable change in early adulthood, while they tend to become more stable over a person's life course—a consistent finding in political psychology (Alwin & Krosnick, 1991; Sears & Funk, 1999). It can be assumed that this is also true for inequality beliefs. Indeed, findings from a study on intergenerational differences in meritocratic beliefs in Poland suggest that historical experiences during adolescence have shaped people's meritocratic beliefs held throughout their life course (Wysmułek & Wysmułek, 2024).

In the life stage of early adulthood, the direct influence of the parents may become less important, while educational institutions may play a crucial role in the crystallization of inequality beliefs. Mijs (2017) has developed a framework of educational institutions as 'inferential spaces.' He explains that educational institutions such as schools or universities are places of socialization that "young adults draw from in developing an understanding of the society they live in" (Mijs, 2017, p. 64). Beyond the family, educational institutions play an important role in shaping adolescents' values and beliefs, and their social network. Mijs' (2017) study showed that inequality beliefs still change substantially in early adulthood, and are shaped by educational institutions and the (racial) composition of the peer group associated with them.

Selection into these institutions matters for the composition and diversity of the student body—the peer group that influences adolescents' inequality beliefs. As discussed in Chapter 3.1, a selection based on school grades reproduces educational inequality (Boudon, 1974; Bourdieu & Passeron, 1971; Finger, 2022). Beyond these consequences of the selection procedure for inequality beliefs due to the composition of the student body and peer socialization, the admission procedure itself may shape young adults' meaning-making and their beliefs about merit and justice. Qualitative interviews with undergraduates attending elite universities in the United States and the United Kingdom revealed that admitted students appear to adapt—rather than challenge—the university's values of what constitutes merit and the criteria on which admission should be based (Warikoo, 2018). To make sense of and legitimize their own success, they seem to develop a strong belief that they were selected based on their merit and underestimate the privileges that they might have had. Furthermore, Warikoo (2018) suggests that these meritocratic beliefs likely transcend beliefs about the admission procedure of elite universities and that the admission procedure may shape young adults' inequality beliefs in other domains and influence their future decision-making.

In this dissertation, I observe the change in young adults' inequality beliefs at a particular life stage and in a highly selective educational setting: at the stage when they are trying to enter medical school. For most applicants, their application is their first step in attempting to achieve their desired career goal, which is associated with high prestige and returns: becoming a doctor. The experience of success or failure in admission is a pivotal event for adolescents with this particular goal. It is likely to have long-term consequences for their social positioning, but also for their worldview and inequality beliefs throughout their lifetime. Studying young adults' inequality beliefs, and the formation of these beliefs and interpersonal differences in them, is particularly important because these young adults may influence social change in the future.

Parental education and inequality beliefs

System-justification theory (Jost & Banaji, 1994) claims that in certain situations, people tend to uphold beliefs that justify and legitimize the existing system and differences in status, even if they are in a disadvantaged position themselves. Trying to justify the social order, people may develop negative stereotypes about disadvantaged groups to explain their lower likelihood of success in society, notions that persist among majority-group members, but even among the discriminated groups themselves (Hoyt et al., 2021; Jost & Banaji, 1994). As education is their main pathway for upward mobility, they are motivated to believe that they can make it if they simply work hard enough (Wiederkehr et al., 2015)—and may downplay structural barriers by blaming their peers' failure on their lack of effort.

However, I argue that in most cases, socialization and reoccurring experiences of failure for the disadvantaged will partly outweigh this system-justification motivation, and lead to differences in inequality beliefs between applicants from different social backgrounds. In the following, I will present three arguments as to why I expect inequality beliefs to differ by parental education.

First, parental beliefs may be transmitted to their children. According to reproduction theory (Bourdieu, 1977; Bourdieu & Passeron, 1990), children adopt a certain class-specific habitus and cultural norms, values, and beliefs from their parents. Meritocratic ideology is a guiding principle in education (Bills, 2019; Solga, 2015), and the idea that success in education primarily depends on individual merit may be a belief more strongly held by those who have been successful in their educational pursuits. As previously suggested, HE institutions may have shaped their values and beliefs—beliefs that they may transmit to their children.

Second, parental education may shape inequality beliefs by influencing the environment in which children grow up. Individuals form 'cognitive landscapes' based on their experiences and observations (Sampson & Bartusch,

1998). Children from privileged backgrounds tend to grow up surrounded by people with similar life circumstances. Drawing from contact theory (Allport, 1954), Mijs (2017) argues that a more heterogeneous environment (e.g., in school) leads to more intergroup contact between young adults from different backgrounds, which strengthens the understanding of these groups and an awareness of the structural barriers that they face. Mijs (2017) tested this theoretical framework of educational institutions as 'inferential spaces' for racial diversity in college. He found that greater racial heterogeneity of the student body, the frequency of outgroup interactions, and having a roommate of a different ethnicity were associated with an increase in structural beliefs during the college years.

Mijs' theoretical framework can also be applied to diversity in social backgrounds and the German context. The educational system in Germany is highly stratified with early tracking procedures (see Chapter 2). In schools for the academic track (i.e., 'Gymnasium'), children from privileged backgrounds are strongly overrepresented (Autorengruppe Bildungsberichterstattung, 2022; Heisig et al., 2020) due to mechanisms of social reproduction and intergenerational status transmission (Boudon, 1974; Bourdieu, 1977; Bourdieu & Passeron, 1990). Thus, children from privileged backgrounds who end up on this educational track may mostly have friends from a similar social background and little contact with children from less privileged backgrounds. Moreover, according to Bourdieu's perspective, it may be advantageous for children from less privileged backgrounds to adopt a 'high-class' habitus. Especially children without college-educated parents who end up on the academic track, perform well, and pursue a selective field of study may try to conform to the dominant culture at school. To fit in with their peers, they may avoid talking about the structural challenges that they had to face or even avoid talking about their social upbringing altogether. Previous research supports this assumption, finding that in the context of HE in the United Kingdom, students from working-class backgrounds tend to try to hide their social background and avoid signaling it through their accents, for example (Loveday, 2016).

Third, young adults' inequality beliefs are shaped not only by parental beliefs and their social environment, but their own educational experiences may also shape them. Due to previously discussed mechanisms of social reproduction (Boudon, 1974; Bourdieu & Passeron, 1990), children from advantaged backgrounds are more likely to experience success in education and in other related life domains. These social differences in experiences of success and failure may further contribute to stronger meritocratic and weaker nonmeritocratic beliefs among adolescents from privileged backgrounds. How I expect experiences of success and failure to shape inequality beliefs in a self-serving way will be discussed in the following chapter.

Overall, I argue that parental education influences young adults' inequality beliefs through the transmission of parental beliefs, differences in the heterogeneity of the social environment in which they grow up, and differences in experiences of success and failure in education. Therefore, I expect, also for applicants to medical school, that:

HI.2: Applicants from privileged backgrounds hold stronger meritocratic and weaker nonmeritocratic beliefs than those from less privileged backgrounds.

Theories of biased inequality beliefs

Our experiences shape how we see the world. In this chapter, I will discuss theories of biased inequality beliefs, and draw conclusions for the specific case of how success or failure in admission to medical school may change applicants' inequality beliefs. Self-serving beliefs theory (Bénabou & Tirole, 2016) suggests that experiences of success and failure bias inequality beliefs in a way that serves one's self-image, whereas system-justification theory (Jost & Banaji, 1994) proposes that in certain situations, anyone—including those who fail or are in a disadvantaged position—might endorse meritocratic beliefs to justify the system in which they live.

According to the theory of self-serving beliefs (Bénabou & Tirole, 2016), people are motivated to defend their own and their group's self-image by attributing success to meritocratic factors such as hard work, and failure to external factors such as luck. Success is perceived as legitimate and deserved, and failure is not attributed to a lack of one's own efforts and capability. The attribution bias justifies success and the rewards connected to high social positions (Mijs 2016; Warikoo 2016), and it reduces the negative effects of failure, such as a decline in self-esteem (Jost & Hunyady, 2003).

According to this perspective—from which economic position and self-interest are important factors in opinion formation (Newman et al., 2014)—inequality beliefs differ by how successful people are. Research indeed shows that high-income earners believe more strongly in meritocratic explanations of inequality compared to low-income earners, who believe more strongly in structural and fatalistic explanations of unequal outcomes (Kluegel & Smith, 1986; Kreidl, 2000). However, this observation does not sufficiently prove that high-income earners' success increased their meritocratic beliefs. Meritocratic beliefs have a motivational function, which helps people achieve their goals (Heckhausen et al., 2010; Shane & Heckhausen, 2013), suggesting the possibility of reverse causality. Furthermore, a higher educational level may also be positively associated with more awareness of structural inequality, as shown regarding beliefs about racial inequality (Wodtke, 2012, 2018).

However, educational research has shown that elementary school children (Lohbeck et al., 2017) and university students (Mkumbo & Amani, 2012) tend to ascribe their success to effort and ability and their failure to external factors such as task difficulty or poor learning conditions. Moreover, high academic performance in school seems to bolster parental beliefs that good grades depend on skills and hard work, showing the legitimizing role of self-serving inequality beliefs (Olivos, 2021). While a higher level of education may increase nonmeritocratic beliefs, within educational groups, success may indeed be positively associated with meritocratic beliefs and negatively with nonmeritocratic beliefs.

The discussed studies do not consider the role of social background. However, as discussed in the previous chapter, children from advantaged groups may tend to have stronger meritocratic and weaker structural beliefs than those from disadvantaged backgrounds. As advantaged groups have greater chances of succeeding in the educational and work setting, perhaps the association between success and meritocratic beliefs is due merely to different social upbringings. To some extent, experimental studies could resolve issues of unclear causality and confounding variables. Participants in those game studies had unequal and more or less merit-based chances to win. In all conditions, winners were more likely than losers to attribute their success to talent and effort, and losers were more likely to attribute their losses to external factors, regardless of their initial condition in the game (Fehr & Vollmann, 2020; Molina et al., 2019). "It's not just how the game is played, it's whether you win or lose" (Molina et al., 2019, p. 1). In other words, experimental studies suggest a direct effect of experiencing success or failure on inequality beliefs: a self-serving bias in explanations of social outcomes, which transcends the individual's initial advantages or disadvantages.

Contrary to self-serving beliefs theory, in certain situations, people may uphold beliefs that justify and legitimize the existing system and differences in status, even if these beliefs contradict their interests. People are motivated to believe in a legitimate system. While beliefs in a just-world theory (Lerner, 1980) argues this motivation stems from a universal human need to believe in a just world where people can control their own destiny, system-justification theory rather argues for a justification process which "lead[s] people to rationalise the way things are" (Jost & Hunyady, 2003, p. 116); for example, through meritocratic ideology (Jost et al., 2003). Reasons for this mechanism are diverse and include socialization, the need to reduce ideological dissonance, and the palliative function of these beliefs, which helps accept their own position in the social hierarchy (Jost et al., 2003).

However, losers of the system do not always support the existing order. Instead, system-justification motivation competes with—for instance—self-serving motivations. System-justification is more likely to occur in a context where meritocratic explanations of outcomes are pervasive (Jost et al., 2003). It might furthermore be the dominant pattern in situations in which it is hardly possible to 'escape' the system.

In the specific case of admissions to highly selective medical schools, I expect self-serving bias to outweigh system-justification in explaining the admission outcome. First, recurring public debates about the legitimacy of admission procedures to medical schools in Germany expressed serious doubts about their fairness and legitimacy. Recently, a debate emerged on the meritocratic foundation of admission to public medical schools in Germany, which led to the implementation of changes in the admission procedure (see Chapter 2). The data used in this study to explore the change in inequality beliefs through success or failure in admission relate to applicants from 2018, who are unaffected by these formal changes but might have followed the preceding debate. Thus, meritocratic explanations of admission outcomes—while still widespread—are not unchallenged.

Second, applicants to medical schools should not have a very pronounced motivation to justify the admission system since they are not locked in the system. Given that they belong to a rather positively selective group of high school graduates—who, on average, have very good school grades—similarly prestigious, alternative career paths are available to them.

With these considerations in mind, I expect self-serving bias to outweigh system-justifying mechanisms in domain-specific beliefs about admission to medical school. Can the same pattern be expected regarding general societal inequality beliefs? Based on the impressionable years hypothesis (Alwin & Krosnick, 1991), I have argued that in early adulthood worldviews, values, and beliefs, such as inequality beliefs, are not yet consolidated. In this life stage, educational institutions and their admission procedure play a crucial role in shaping young adults' worldviews (Mijs, 2017; Warikoo, 2018). Thus, success or failure in admission to medical school—a crucial event for adolescents with this career goal—is likely to shape inequality beliefs beyond the specific case of admission. For most applicants, it is one of their first attempts to pursue their career goal and reach a high social position. In particular, being rejected may cause these applicants to question their former beliefs, as for many of them it might be their first experience of failure in the educational context. Overall, I expect that:

H1.3: Success strengthens meritocratic beliefs and weakens nonmeritocratic beliefs, whereas failure weakens meritocratic beliefs and strengthens nonmeritocratic beliefs.

The self-serving bias might be weaker for societal beliefs than for domain-specific beliefs. This might, first, stem from the fact that certain life experiences are linked more strongly to beliefs about this specific domain than societal inequality in general. Second, while alternative career paths are open to unsuccessful applicants, they can less easily 'escape' their society's system of stratification, which might lead them to uphold system-justifying beliefs on a general level.

In line with this reasoning, Shane and Heckhausen (2017) show that adverse labor market experiences reduce U.S. graduates' meritocratic beliefs about their own success, but do not substantially affect the general belief in a meritocratic society. Drawing on qualitative interviews, Aronson (2017) confirmed that experiences during the Great Recession did not prompt adolescents to abandon the American dream, as they still saw merit-based education as the key to societal success. Thus, while I expect to find self-serving bias for both domain-specific and societal inequality beliefs, the latter beliefs are likely more stable even after experiencing failure.

Arguments in line with self-serving beliefs theory (Bénabou & Tirole, 2016) may apply to the effects of success and failure on distinct types of meritocratic beliefs (e.g., hard work and abilities beliefs) and of nonmeritocratic beliefs (e.g., fatalistic and structural beliefs), as attributing success to the former and attributing failure to the later has positive effects for one's self-perception.

Previous experiences as a frame for new experiences

So far, my argumentation has focused on the effect that a single experience of success or failure has on inequality beliefs. This focus might, however, be too short-sighted. Previous experiences may provide a frame for perceptions and judgments of new experiences of success or failure.

Cumulative inequality theory (DiPrete & Eirich, 2006) suggests that structural disadvantage and related experiences accumulate over the life course and contribute to growing inequalities. Over the life course, initial differences (e.g., due to family background) grow and for one group opportunities and chances of success become more likely, while for the other group, they become increasingly unlikely. Schafer et al. (2011) expanded on this theory and argued that negative experiences, such as facing adversity in childhood, are not only consequential for chances of success but also for life evaluations. They affect how new experiences are perceived and how individuals react to these new experiences; accumulated past experiences influence how new life experiences are interpreted (Schafer et al., 2011).

If previous experiences influence how new experiences are interpreted, how experiences of success or failure shape inequality beliefs may differ by applicants' previous experiences. In the following, I discuss how long-term experiences of social upbringing as well as short-term experiences in the specific domain of application to medical school (i.e., previous rejections) may influence the effect of (a new) experience of success or failure in admission on applicants' inequality beliefs.

Long-term experiences of social upbringing and belief changes

Parental education may not only be associated with applicants' inequality beliefs but may also influence the effects that success or failure have on these beliefs. Success is less likely to occur for people from disadvantaged backgrounds. However, success against the odds is not impossible, and I propose that for members of less privileged groups, experiencing success may lead to an even greater increase in meritocratic beliefs than for members of privileged groups: People from less privileged groups who managed to overcome structural barriers may believe that other members of their group could achieve the same if they were simply trying hard enough, overlooking the glass ceiling that they themselves had to break through (Cech & Blair-Loy, 2010). For instance, they may neglect or underestimate the role of specific privileges they have enjoyed compared to their peers from formally similar social backgrounds. In line with Bourdieu's (1971) arguments, parental support may also differ within the group of children without college-educated parents, making success for certain members of this group more attainable than for others.

Empirical studies support these theoretical arguments. Qualitative interviews with undergraduates attending elite universities showed that especially first-generation students perceived admission outcomes as meritocratic and their experience of upward mobility as proof of it (Warikoo, 2016, 2018). Furthermore, Mijs et al. (2022) found that subjective social upward mobility is associated with strong meritocratic beliefs, suggesting that people's beliefs are shaped by their experience that merit-based mobility is possible. Another study suggested that women in top-level positions tend to believe that unequal outcomes for men and women were driven mostly by differences in human capital and motivation (Cech & Blair-Loy, 2010). Experiences of success seem to lead members of disadvantaged groups to forget about structural barriers they had to face, reinforcing the positive effect that success has on meritocratic beliefs held within this group.

Whereas Warikoo (2016, 2018) and Cech and Blair-Loy (2010) focused on domain-specific inequality beliefs, I assume that the effect of experiencing success on societal inequality beliefs may also differ by parental education. After all, achieving a desired social position is a crucial step for upward mobility. This reasoning is consistent with Wiederkehr et al.'s (2015) findings, suggesting that the correlation between school-related and general meritocratic beliefs is especially pronounced for disadvantaged groups (i.e., low SES students) and can be explained by the key role that educational success plays in social mobility. For both domain-specific and general inequality beliefs, I thus propose:

H1.4a: Success strengthens meritocratic beliefs and weakens nonmeritocratic beliefs more strongly for less privileged applicants than for their more privileged peers.

How does the effect of failure differ by parental education? Adolescents from disadvantaged family backgrounds may be motivated to keep believing in meritocracy and success through educational efforts, even if they experience failure, as it is their main pathway to upward mobility (Jost & Banaji, 1994; Wiederkehr et al., 2015).

However, previous research suggests that structural disadvantage and related experiences accumulate over the life course and contribute to growing inequalities (DiPrete & Eirich, 2006), which increases affected adolescents' awareness of structural barriers (Mijs, 2017). Due to this higher awareness, a single negative experience might be interpreted as yet another sign of structural barriers by individuals who belong to disadvantaged groups. On the other hand, one single experience of failure may be less consequential for adolescents from privileged backgrounds. I assume that long-term experiences of social upbringing influence the effect of new experiences of failure on inequality beliefs:

H1.4b: Failure weakens meritocratic beliefs and strengthens nonmeritocratic beliefs more strongly for less privileged applicants than for their more privileged peers.

Considering the hypothesized differences in inequality beliefs by parental education (see Chapter 3.2), I suggest that experiencing success as an applicant from a less privileged background may make the applicant's beliefs more similar to the average beliefs of applicants from privileged backgrounds, while experiencing failure may make the applicant's beliefs more different from this group. However, following theories of social reproduction and intergenerational status transmission previously discussed (Boudon, 1974; Bourdieu, 1977; Bourdieu & Passeron, 1990), the latter should be more prevalent, driving aggregate inequality beliefs of applicants from different social backgrounds further apart.

Similar to other educational experiences, social differences in success or failure in admission may contribute to social differences in inequality beliefs. However, I will not formulate a specific hypothesis on this mediation mechanism, as the theoretical arguments rather suggest that the sum of different experiences of success and failure in education (and not only the admission outcome) shape applicants' inequality beliefs—a mechanism that I will examine when testing how inequality beliefs differ by parental education in an exploratory way.

Previous domain-specific experiences and belief changes

I expect that not only long-term experiences of social upbringing may provide a framework for interpreting new experiences of success or failure, but also more recent domain-specific experiences. In the case of application to medical school, previous unsuccessful applications may moderate the effect of the current admission or rejection on inequality beliefs. Previous rejections may influence the effect of success and failure even more strongly than long-term experiences of social upbringing, as these domain-specific experiences are more closely related to the new experience of admission or rejection. Since admission is highly selective, it is important to note that rejection, while correlated with parental education, is a common event across social groups.

As stated in *HI.3*, I expect experiences of success and failure to shape adolescents' inequality beliefs in a self-serving way, with experiences of failure reducing meritocratic beliefs and increasing nonmeritocratic beliefs. There is no reason to believe that this argument should only hold true for the most recent experience but not also for previous experiences of failed attempts to receive an admission: Previous rejections should have influenced inequality beliefs (especially domain-specific ones) in a self-serving way, leading to differences in beliefs between those who apply for the first time (hereafter, first-time applicants) and those who have previously experienced failure in admission (hereafter, repeat applicants).

Nonetheless, eventual success may outweigh previous setbacks: If people kept trying and were rewarded in the end this could likely be interpreted as success through persistence, a meritocratic factor. Furthermore, prior doubts about meritocratic admission due to self-serving mechanisms (Bénabou & Tirole, 2016) could be overcome, leading to a stronger belief change for repeat applicants:

HI.5a: Success strengthens meritocratic beliefs and weakens nonmeritocratic beliefs more strongly for repeat applicants than for first-time applicants.

A single negative experience may be even more consequential for life evaluations if it follows other negative experiences. This assumption cannot only be applied to long-term experiences of social upbringing but also to short-term domain-specific experiences. Self-serving bias in beliefs about factors behind a successful admission, and eventually success in society, may amplify with every failed attempt, while the motivation to justify the admission procedure might decrease (possibly along with the intention to reapply). Hence, I propose:

HI.5b: Failure weakens meritocratic beliefs and strengthens nonmeritocratic beliefs more strongly for repeat applicants than for first-time applicants.

Considering expected differences in inequality beliefs between applicants who have been previously unsuccessful or not, experiencing success as a repeat applicant may make the applicant's beliefs more similar to the average beliefs of first-time applicants, while experiencing failure may make the applicant's beliefs even more different from this group. However, as admission depends on applicants' GPA, which has not changed since the last application attempt, experiencing failure is more likely for repeat applicants than for first-time applicants, driving inequality beliefs between these groups further apart.

3.3 Consequences of inequality beliefs for perceptions of justice and distributive preferences

Inequality beliefs have consequences for (educational) inequality: They may legitimize such inequality and contribute to its persistence, or delegitimize it. While there is a growing academic interest in empirically exploring the inequality-legitimizing consequences of these beliefs (e.g., Batruch et al., 2022; García-Sánchez et al., 2020; Mijs, 2021), previous research often does not address different consequences for perceptions of justice and distributive preferences, as these concepts are often not observed together. Based on theories on the role of meritocratic ideology for the legitimation of inequality (see final subsection of Chapter 3.1) and empirical evidence of previous research, in this chapter, I develop theoretical arguments on a) how inequality beliefs shape distributive preferences through perceptions of justice. I also discuss the specific inequality-(de)legitimizing consequences of distinct types of meritocratic and nonmeritocratic beliefs. Furthermore, I am interested in b) whether the effect of parental education on distributive preferences can be partly explained by social differences in inequality beliefs and their consequences for perceptions of justice.

Figure 3.2: Stylized theoretical model of the relationship between parental education, inequality beliefs, perceptions of justice, and distributive preferences

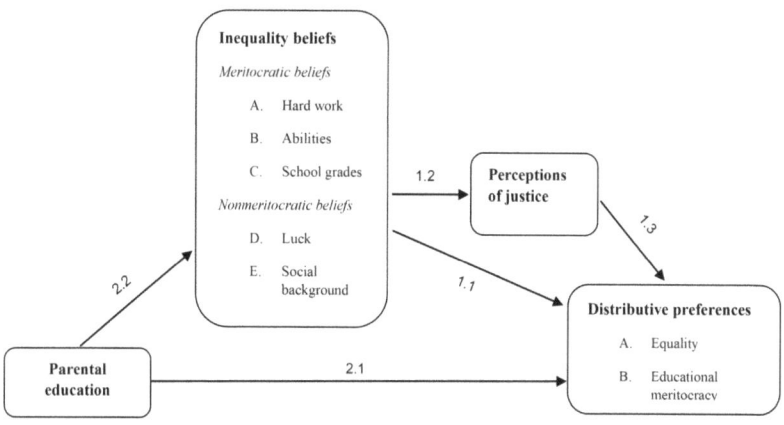

Note. Author's illustration.

As a guide for this chapter, Figure 3.2 displays the relationship between the concepts and the hypothesized paths that will be discussed theoretically. I propose that the effects of inequality beliefs (i.e., meritocratic and nonmeritocratic beliefs) on distributive preferences (Path 1.1) are mediated by perceptions of justice (Path 1.2 + 1.3). The effects of parental education on distributive preferences (Path 2.1) might partly be mediated by social differences in beliefs, as parental education shapes inequality beliefs (Path 2.2). Before I present the theory behind the hypothesized paths, I will introduce and define the concepts of perceptions of justice and distributive preferences.

Perceptions of justice and distributive preferences

Table 3.1 briefly presents definitions and examples of the inequality-legitimizing consequences of inequality beliefs examined in this study: perceptions of justice and distributive preferences. Perception of justice can refer to procedural and outcome-related justice perceptions—perceptions that a procedure or outcome is just (Liebig & Sauer, 2016; Wegener, 1992). Procedural justice perceptions are influenced by how fair selection procedures are perceived to be (e.g., equal treatment of applicants, transparency); outcome-related justice perceptions are influenced by social comparison and the perceived deservingness of rewards and privileges (Batruch et al., 2022; Liebig & Sauer, 2016; Sachweh & Sthamer, 2019). In this dissertation, the domain-specific perception of justice of the admission procedure is a procedural justice perception (i.e., the perception that the admission procedure to medical school is just), and the societal perception of justice represents an outcome-related justice perception (i.e., the perception that societal inequality is just).

Table 3.1: Definitions of perceptions of justice and distributive preferences

Concepts	Definitions	Examples
Perceptions of justice	Perception of a procedure as fair (e.g., equal treatment of applicants, transparency); perception of differences in social positions as appropriate and deserved	Perception of admission procedure to medical school as just; perception of societal inequalities as just
Distributive preferences		
Preference for equal distribution	Preference that resources should be distributed equally between everyone	Preference that medical school places should be distributed equally, preference for equal distribution of income
Preference for distribution based on educational meritocracy	Preference that resources should be distributed based on educational merit	Preference that medical school places should be distributed based on school grades, preference that income should be distributed based on educational credentials

Note. Author's illustration.

Distributive preferences are preferences for distribution based on various justice principles—concepts of what principles of distribution are just (Liebig & Sauer, 2016). Commonly studied justice principles include the principle of equality and equity (Deutsch, 1975; Hülle et al., 2018; van Hootegem et al., 2020)[9]: If resources are distributed based on the equality principle, everyone receives an equal share, whereas if they are distributed based on the equity principle, individuals are rewarded for their contributions to society.

In this dissertation, I focus on preferences for distribution based on the equality principle and the principle of educational meritocracy. The latter principle describes the preference for distribution based on merit attained in the educational setting, a justice principle that is closely connected to the principle of equity (Darnon et al., 2017). I chose these two principles because I aim to test the theory that meritocratic beliefs legitimatize (merit-based) educational inequality while delegitimizing equal distribution of resources (Mijs, 2016; Solga, 2015). Meritocratic beliefs may increase support for the idea that educational success should depend on individual merit and should be rewarded by a higher income. Furthermore, it may counteract support for equal distribution of educational resources, such as access to places in the medical study program, and more general resources, such as income.

How inequality beliefs shape distributive preferences through perceptions of justice

In the last subsection of Chapter 3.1, I discussed the role of meritocratic ideology in the legitimation of educational inequality. As educational inequality and unequal opportunities in the labor market are strongly linked, meritocratic beliefs may not only legitimize educational inequality but inequality in society in general. If people perceive (educational) inequality as solely merit-based, they are likely to perceive inequality as just, and thus to support distributive policies in line with embracing this merit-based inequality, while opposing policies embracing equal distribution. They may view inequality and unequal outcomes as a result of differences in how hard people work and natural differences in abilities that educational institutions objectively assess. Societal success is viewed as a reward for individual achievement, and thus inequality may be regarded as necessary for motivation (Mijs, 2016; Solga, 2015).

---

9 The literature further typically discusses the justice principles of need and entitlement (Deutsch, 1975; Hülle et al., 2018; Miller, 1979): the principle that those most in need should receive more resources and the principle that certain groups are entitled to receive certain benefits (such as inheritance). However, especially regarding the distribution of places in the program, it did not seem feasible to assess these principles, which is why I only focus on the other two justice principles in this study.

Based on the theoretical arguments of meritocracy as an inequality-legitimizing ideology, overall, I propose that meritocratic beliefs increase perceptions of justice and support for distribution based on educational meritocracy, and reduce support for equal distribution, while I expect the opposite for non-meritocratic beliefs. However, before I formulate hypotheses, I will present empirical evidence on the proposed associations, and research gaps regarding the inequality-(de)legitimizing consequences of inequality beliefs.

Path 1.1 (Inequality beliefs → Distributive preferences)

Empirical studies could show that meritocratic beliefs in the importance of hard work for success are negatively associated with support for policies promoting equal redistribution of income (e.g., Alesina & Giuliano, 2011; Kluegel & Miyano, 1995). Using data from the General Social Survey, Alesina and Giulano (2011) showed that in the United States, the belief that hard work rather than luck drives success is negatively associated with support for equal income redistribution. Analyzing data from the International Social Justice Project from the United Kingdom, West Germany, Japan, the Netherlands, and the United States, Kluegel and Miyano (1995) showed that attributing success and failure to the hard work of individuals was negatively associated with the support of government interventions to reduce inequality: minimum income and limitations of high income by the government. Furthermore, in an experimental study, Valero (2022) also showed that people who believed that the income that they received within the experiment depended on work rather than on luck were less likely to redistribute their income to other participants than those who believed that it rather depends on luck than on work.

These studies focused on the effect of believing that hard work is important for success and do not examine how the meritocratic belief that success depends on abilities is associated with this preference. According to the theory of meritocracy as an inequality-legitimizing ideology (Mijs, 2016; Solga, 2015), this belief may also be negatively associated with the preference for equal distribution, as ability-based inequality is seen as natural and thus legitimate. In Germany, the idea of natural differences in academic ability is embedded in the educational system. Despite being criticized for reproducing inequality and contributing to differences in skill development (e.g., Brunello & Checchi, 2007; Dumont et al., 2019; Dumont et al., 2014; Heisig et al., 2020; Traini et al., 2021), ability-based tracking still takes place early in life (usually at the age of 10–12, depending on the federal state). Hence, the idea that there are natural differences in academic ability that should be rewarded by different educational and societal outcomes might be widespread (Kurtz-Costes et al., 2005), and may play a crucial role in legitimizing educational inequality.

The beliefs in both the importance of hard work and abilities for success may legitimize inequality, albeit possibly through different mechanisms. If success is attributed to differences in hard work, an individual may consequently be blamed for their failure (Destin, 2020; Hoyt et al., 2021; Jost & Banaji, 1994). Attributing success to differences in abilities means that less blame is assigned to the individual, but it may make inequalities in outcomes appear inescapable (Friedman et al., 2023; Mijs, 2020; Mulligan, 2018). Which of these beliefs plays a larger role in distributive preferences regarding admission to medical school and regarding the distribution of income more generally remains an empirical question.

Furthermore, Solga (2015) suggests that viewing societal inequality as based on educational credentials may increase its legitimation while neglecting the mechanisms behind educational inequality. Hence, I also expect that the belief that educational merit drives success in society may be negatively associated with the preference for equal distribution, although this has not yet been empirically tested.

How are nonmeritocratic beliefs associated with the preference for equal distribution? Kim and Lee (2018) analyzed data from the International Social Survey Program and found that the belief that social mobility depends on structural factors such as family background and ascriptive characteristics (e.g., gender, race, religion) is positively associated with support of equal income distribution by the government. García-Sánchez et al. (2020) analyzed data from the International Social Survey Program and found that nonmeritocratic beliefs that there are unequal opportunities to succeed in education depending on social background or ethnicity are positively associated with support for equal redistribution of income. Marquis and Rosset (2021) used Eurobarometer data from 27 European countries and examined explanations of poverty and their effects on welfare support. They found that those who attributed poverty to individual factors (i.e., laziness and a lack of willpower) exhibited the lowest support for equal income redistribution through the welfare state. Furthermore, they also examined the effects of structural beliefs. They showed that those who attributed poverty to structural factors exhibited the highest welfare support. Those who attributed poverty to fatalistic factors (i.e., bad luck) showed welfare support levels between these two poles (Marquis & Rosset, 2021).

The opposing principle to equal distribution that I want to examine in this dissertation is the principle of educational meritocracy. Beliefs that (educational) success depends mainly on individual merit and is independent of nonmeritocratic factors may be positively associated with support of distribution based on the presumed status quo: educational meritocracy. So far, the association between inequality beliefs and the preference for educational meritocracy has been scarcely investigated. Previous research by Duru-Bellat and Tenret (2012) using data from the International Social Survey Program only found small correlations between societal meritocratic beliefs and the preference for distribution based on educational meritocracy in the countries included in their study. However, in Germany, strong meritocratic beliefs seem to coexist with a strong preference for educational meritocracy (Duru-Bellat & Tenret, 2012).

Overall, drawing on arguments on the inequality-legitimizing consequences of meritocratic beliefs, I expect that:

HII.1: Meritocratic beliefs are negatively associated with the preference for equal distribution and positively with the preference for distribution based on educational meritocracy, while the opposite is true for non-meritocratic beliefs.

The theories and empirical studies discussed previously seem to explicitly or implicitly assume that inequality beliefs affect distributive preferences through perceptions of justice (e.g., Alesina & Giuliano, 2011; Marquis & Rosset, 2021), albeit without providing a comprehensive theoretical framework or testing this assumption empirically. For example, when explaining the effects of meritocratic beliefs on distributive preferences, Alesina and Giuliano (2011) have stated that "preferences for redistribution may be dictated by a sense of fairness" (Alesina & Giuliano, 2011, p. 121). Hence, in the following, I will discuss the two paths that constitute this mediation mechanism through perceptions of justice (Path 1.2 and Path 1.3 of Figure 3.2) to answer my research question: How do inequality beliefs influence distributive preferences through the perception of justice?

Path 1.2 (Inequality beliefs → Perception of justice)

Empirical research supports theoretical arguments and shows that meritocratic beliefs lead to perceiving inequality as more just (e.g., Batruch et al., 2022; Mijs, 2021): A recently published study by Batruch et al. (2022) found that the belief in school meritocracy, that is, the belief that students get the grades they deserve, is negatively associated with the perceived unfairness of social class inequality (i.e., the perception of discrimination and privileges). Furthermore, another study based on data from the International Social Survey Program found that the belief that differences in hard work drive success is negatively associated with concern about inequality, measured as perceiving income differences in society as too large (Mijs, 2021).

If inequality is perceived as driven by differences in individual merit, this could lead to beliefs that everyone can achieve success through hard work to the extent that their naturally given abilities permit them. Failing to do so becomes an individual responsibility (Hoyt et al., 2021; Jost & Banaji, 1994). Furthermore, qualitative research suggests that elites may also use the narrative of natural abilities to justify their success and make societal inequality seem just and legitimate (Friedman et al., 2023). Hence, all meritocratic beliefs may be positively associated with perceptions of justice, and differences in the extent of these associations for distinct types of beliefs remain unclear. Mijs (2021) only explored the effect of the belief in the importance of hard work, and Batruch et al. (2022) did not disentangle the belief in the importance of hard work and ability but only measured the belief that students get the grades they deserve.

Nonmeritocratic beliefs may also influence perceptions of justice. A study by Mijs (2021) showed that structural beliefs—here measured as beliefs that family background and social networks are important for societal success—increased concerns about inequality. Other studies have found that beliefs that there are unequal opportunities reduce the perception of inequality as just (e.g., Batruch et al., 2022; Sachweh & Sthamer, 2019). The association between the belief that success depends on luck and perceptions of justice has not been explored in the discussed empirical studies. Inequality based on luck may be evaluated as less unjust than inequality based on structural factors since luck is an unstable factor that typically fluctuates throughout a person's life and equally affects everyone (Weiner, 1985). Nevertheless, luck could be seen as contradicting meritocracy in education and luck-based success may be perceived as illegitimate, particularly among the successful (Frank, 2016). Hence, both fatalistic and structural beliefs may be negatively associated with perceptions of justice, even though negative associations with structural beliefs may be stronger. Overall, I expect:

HII.2: Meritocratic beliefs lead to a perception of higher justice, while nonmeritocratic beliefs lead to a perception of lower justice.

I assume this to be true for the effect of domain-specific inequality beliefs about applicants' own admission to medical school on the perception of this procedure as just and for the effect of societal inequality beliefs on the perception of societal inequality in general as just. However, as meritocracy is a widely accepted guiding principle in education—particularly regarding their admission to medical school—people may be motivated to believe that they can achieve educational success through hard work (Jost & Hunyady, 2003). Hence, the effects of beliefs about the participants' own admission to medical school on perceptions of the justice of such admissions may be stronger than effects on perceptions of societal inequalities more generally, as these perceptions are more abstract and less consequential for their own aspirations.

Path 1.3 (Perception of justice → Distributive preferences)

If inequality is perceived as just, policies reducing this inequality may be viewed as unnecessary or even unjust. Indeed, previous research has shown that perceiving inequality as unjust increases support for equal redistribution: Choi (2021) analyzed data from the International Social Survey Program and found that the perception of income inequality as just—here measured as the difference between perceived income inequality and desired income inequality—was strongly positively associated with the preference for equal income redistribution (Choi, 2021).

Furthermore, Lübker (2007) showed that actual inequality only affects distributive preferences if those inequalities are perceived as unjust. Not the extent of inequality itself matters for distributive preferences but rather the extent of inequality that people perceive[10] and especially the justice evaluation of this inequality.

Other research has shown that individuals' perceptions of the injustice of their own salary are negatively associated with support for educational meritocracy (Duru-Bellat & Tenret, 2012), suggesting that perceiving this outcome as unjust leads to doubts that the current system of distribution based on educational meritocracy should be supported. These findings from previous studies support my theoretical expectations, and I hypothesize that:

HII.3: The more applicants perceive inequality as just, the more opposed they will be to equal distribution and the more they will support educational meritocracy.

Path 1.2 + 1.3 (Inequality beliefs → Perceptions of justice → Distributive preferences)

How do meritocratic and nonmeritocratic beliefs influence distributive preferences via perceptions of justice? Despite the frequently made assumption that the effects of inequality beliefs on distributive preferences are mainly driven by effects on the perception of justice, perceptions of justice are often not included in empirical studies on the effects of inequality beliefs on distributive preferences (e.g., Alesina & Giuliano, 2011; Marquis & Rosset, 2021).

Alternative mechanisms are possible. For example, when people perceive unequal educational or social outcomes as merit-based, they may support distribution based on educational meritocracy because they perceive this distributive principle as necessary to organize a society. They may support distribution based on educational merit because they think it enhances people's motivation to develop their skills, even if they do not see inequality arising from this distribution as just. However, meritocratic ideology may legitimize inequality and make it seem just, and lead to neglecting empirical evidence on intergenerational status transmission that opportunities to exhibit the required merit are not equally distributed (Bourdieu, 1977; Mijs, 2016; Solga, 2015), so that non-merit-based distribution may be perceived as unjust. Thus, I expect that perceptions of justice play a crucial role in explaining the association between inequality beliefs and distributive preferences.

Only one empirical study has explicitly tested the mediation mechanism of the belief effect on distributive preferences through perceptions of justice.

---

10 Previous research showed that individuals often misperceive the actual extent of inequality and that those who believe that income inequality is necessary for economic growth seem to perceive less inequality than those who do not (Du & King, 2022).

Batruch et al. (2022) explored the effect of belief in school meritocracy on support for affirmative action policies through the perceived unfairness of social class inequalities (i.e., privileges and discrimination). Their findings support my theoretical expectations: The effect of belief in school meritocracy on support for these policies was indeed mediated by the perception of justice (Batruch et al., 2022). However, as discussed earlier, Batruch et al.'s (2022) study only tested the mediation process for a rather abstract measure of school meritocracy.

This study aims to test whether the finding of a mediation mechanism of the belief effect on distributive preferences through the perception of justice also holds true for more concrete meritocratic and nonmeritocratic beliefs. I hypothesize that the perception of justice mediates the effect of inequality beliefs on a) the preference for equal distribution and b) the preference for distribution based on the principle of educational meritocracy.

HII.4a: Perception of justice mediates the negative relationship between meritocratic beliefs and the preference for equal distribution, and mediates the positive relationship between nonmeritocratic beliefs and this preference.

HII.4b: Perception of justice mediates the positive relationship between meritocratic beliefs and the preference for distribution based on the principle of educational meritocracy, and mediates the negative relationship between nonmeritocratic beliefs and this preference.

Similar mechanisms should be evident in the relationship between domain-specific concepts referring to medical school admission and in the relationship between societal concepts referring to societal inequality. Conversely, distinct meritocratic and nonmeritocratic beliefs may affect distributive preferences differently. For example, the belief that hard work drives success may reduce support for equal distribution because inequality in outcomes is perceived as an important motivator and not only because these inequalities are perceived as just. On the other hand, it is more plausible that the belief that structural factors drive success increases support for equal distribution mainly due to its effect on the perception of justice.

Inequality beliefs as one explanation for social differences in distributive preferences

Path 2.1 (Parental education → Distributive preferences)

People with high levels of education and income, and those who expect to get there, should be more opposed to equal income redistribution than people in less favorable positions. Depending on their own (future) position in society, individuals benefit or might even be economically harmed by equal income redistribution policies, or by distribution based on educational degrees. Individuals from privileged backgrounds can draw on more resources from their parents and are likely to perform better in school, making high social positions more accessible to them (Bourdieu, 1977; Bourdieu & Passeron, 1990).

Hence, one can expect that people from privileged backgrounds are less likely to support distribution following the equality principle. This expectation is supported by empirical research (e.g., Alesina & Giuliano, 2011; Lee, 2023; O'Grady, 2019). Alesina and Giuliano (2011) found that having a father with a college degree is negatively associated with the preferences for equal income redistribution (Alesina and Giulano, 2011). Lee (2023) analyzed data of the General Social Survey and found that people from working-class origins are more likely to support equality-promoting distributive policies than those from middle-class origins. O'Grady (2019) used the Swiss Household Panel Survey and found that being from a family that faced financial hardship during the formative years is positively associated with supporting higher taxation of the rich.

Following this argumentation and the empirical evidence, it can be assumed that applicants from different social backgrounds vary in their distributive preferences:

HII.5: Applicants from privileged backgrounds have a weaker preference for equal distribution and a stronger preference for distribution based on educational meritocracy than their less privileged peers.

Importantly, all discussed studies (Alesina & Giuliano, 2011; Lee, 2023; O'Grady, 2019) found that the effect of social background on the preference for equal distribution can only partly be explained by respondents' current positions (e.g., educational level, class, or income), suggesting that social backgrounds seem to affect distributive preferences beyond people's current position.

Path 2.2 + Path 1.2 + Path 1.3 (Parental education → Inequality beliefs → Perception of justice → Distributive preferences)

Drawing on previous social justice research, Liebig and Sauer (2016) have concluded that "individuals with common traits, the same social background, and similar experiences over their lifespan tend to have the same conception of justice" (Liebig and Sauer, 2016, p. 38), principles for the distribution of resources which they perceive as just. Drawing from Grid-group theory (Douglas, 1973; Liebig & Lengfeld, 2002), Liebig and Sauer (2016) suggest that individuals are embedded in social structures that provide groups with different experiences. People draw from these experiences and form their distributive preferences (Douglas, 1973; Liebig & Lengfeld, 2002; Liebig & Sauer, 2016). I expand on this argument and propose that parental education—and connected socialization and experiences—influences distributive preferences through its effect on inequality beliefs and thus on perceptions of justice. The association between parental education and distributive preferences (Path 2.1) may be partly explained by social differences in inequality beliefs (Paths 2.2)—beliefs that influence distributive preferences (Path 1.1) through perceptions of justice (Path 1.2 + 1.3).

As discussed in Chapter 3.2, I expect people from privileged backgrounds to have stronger meritocratic and weaker nonmeritocratic beliefs due to the transmission of parental beliefs, due to consequences of family background for the social heterogeneity in school, and due to differences in experiences of success and failure that shape inequality beliefs in a self-serving way. These beliefs may lead to a perception of higher justice, opposition to equal distribution, and support for educational meritocracy. Combining the expectation about social differences in inequality beliefs with the expectations of the effects of those inequality beliefs on the perception of justice and distributive preferences, I propose that:

HII.6: Social differences in inequality beliefs, and the resulting perception of justice, partly mediate the relationship between parental education and distributive preferences for equality and educational meritocracy.

The role of the admission outcome for perceptions of justice and distributive preferences

In the case of applying to medical school, another possible factor influencing inequality beliefs, perceptions of justice, and distributive preferences is whether applicants are admitted or rejected. In Chapter 3.2, I argued that differences in experiences of success and failure between social groups are a central mechanism for the association between parental education and inequality beliefs. Accordingly, being admitted may increase meritocratic beliefs and reduce nonmeritocratic beliefs, while being rejected may have the opposite effect.

Furthermore, being admitted or rejected may also influence how just applicants evaluate the procedure. Research has found that the successful—high income-earners and those who are satisfied with their standard of living—consider their own income and the taxation of this income as more just than low-income earners, even though higher income increases their taxation (Liebig & Mau, 2005; Liebig & Schupp, 2008). Furthermore, experimental studies where participants had unequal chances to win showed that winners were more likely than losers to evaluate the games as just and perceive their win as deserved, independent of why they won (Fehr & Vollmann, 2020; Molina et al., 2019). Whether being admitted also influences applicants' perception of societal inequality in general, is less clear, especially because being admitted does not immediately increase their social position and income. Furthermore, previous research suggests that in Germany, the perceptions of societal inequalities as just became increasingly similar between high- and low-income earners between 1994 and 2014 (Sachweh & Sthamer, 2019). Nießen et al. (2023) collected data in Germany and the United Kingdom in 2020 and found no correlation between respondents' income and educational level and their perception of the income distribution as just. They argue that this perception is not shaped by people's position in the income hierarchy but rather by their normative preferences (Nießen et al., 2023).

Finally, the admission outcome may also influence distributive preferences: Those who were admitted are unlikely to wish that others will be admitted based on different selection criteria, while those who were not admitted due to comparatively lower school grades may prefer other selection criteria that are less strongly based on educational merit. Without formulating hypotheses on this, I will consider these arguments in my analyses and examine the role that admission status plays in the relationship between my main concepts of interest.

3.4 Inequality beliefs, persistence in goal pursuit, and educational inequality

Meritocratic beliefs—particularly domain-specific beliefs about one's own success—may not only contribute to the persisting educational inequality by legitimizing it but social differences in meritocratic beliefs may also lead to unequal persistence in goal pursuit between applicants from different social backgrounds. In this chapter, I will discuss how a) persistence in goal pursuit after a first rejection may vary by applicants' parental education, b) beliefs in meritocratic admission may be associated with their persistence, c) social differences in these beliefs may explain social differences in persistence, and d) the effects of these beliefs on persistence may vary by social background. Figure 3.3 displays the proposed relationship between parental education, beliefs in meritocratic admission, and persistence in goal pursuit.

Drawing from motivational theory (Heckhausen et al., 2010) and arguments on the crucial role of social differences in educational decision-making in educational inequality (e.g., Boudon, 1974; Breen & Goldthorpe, 1997), my definition of persistence in goal pursuit entails the mental process of engaging and disengaging from a certain goal (e.g., willingness to invest in this goal and intention to further pursue this goal), as well as the actual behavior to pursue this goal (e.g., reapplying after receiving a rejection).

Figure 3.3: Stylized theoretical model of social differences in beliefs in meritocratic admission and their consequences for persistence in goal pursuit

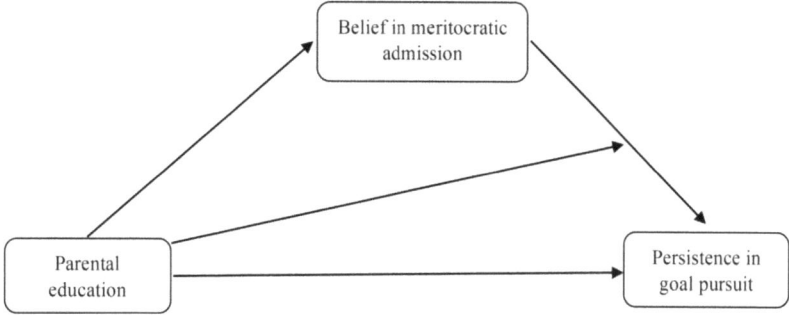

Note. Author's illustration.

Parental education and reapplication behavior after receiving a first rejection

Based on theoretical considerations laid out in Chapter 3.1, applicants with two college-educated parents may show a higher persistence in pursuing HE, or even a selective field of study such as medicine. Their better GPA (primary effects) increases their chances of admission, making persistence more rational (Bourdieu, 1977; Breen & Goldthorpe, 1997). Furthermore, even beyond performance differences, there may be differences in educational choices (secondary effects). Applicants from privileged backgrounds have a high motivation to replicate their parents' status (Breen & Goldthorpe, 1997), and, as more people enter HE, they choose the options with high returns in terms of income and prestige (R. Becker et al., 2010; Finger, 2022)—options that may feel unattainable and as not fitting to less privileged applicants (Bourdieu & Passeron, 2007).

Even after an experience of failure, due to this high motivation and their social capital, applicants from privileged backgrounds may be more persistent in pursuing this goal in comparison to their less privileged peers. A study by Palacios-Abad (2021) confirms differences in persistence (in this case measured as a decline in performance throughout the PISA test) by social background. Furthermore, research suggests that adolescents from privileged backgrounds are less negatively affected by experiences of poor performance and failure, which they explain by compensatory effects of parental financial and cultural resources (Bernardi & Triventi, 2020; Herbaut, 2021). These social differences in persistence may also be explained by a higher perceived need to obtain a high-status occupation and more confidence to be well suited for this selective field of study adolescents from privileged backgrounds (Boudon, 1974; Breen & Goldthorpe, 1997).

Social differences in persistence also show in the case of rejections for university admission. Research using high-quality registry data on university applicants in Finland (Heiskala et al., 2023) found substantial differences in applicants' reapplication behavior after receiving rejections depending on their parental education, whereby applicants with at least one college-educated parent reapply more often after one or more rejections compared to those without college-educated parents. Since typically two-thirds of the applicants receive a first-time rejection, these social differences in reapplication behavior may contribute significantly to socially selective university enrollment. Importantly, some of these social differences in reapplication behavior remained after controlling for school performance, suggesting secondary effects of social background. In sum, the study showed that even among those who initially decided to apply to university, applicants from privileged backgrounds more often continued to reapply. As performance differences were controlled for, it could be that social differences in goal pursuit are the mechanism behind these social differences in reapplication behavior. However, in Heiskala et al.'s (2023) study, goal pursuit is not directly measured but just a potential outcome of it: the reapplication behavior. This research gap can be addressed in this dissertation by examining both self-predicted persistence in goal pursuit and reapplication behavior.

Furthermore, this study examines reapplication behavior for a different context, namely, admission to medical school in Germany. To date, it has not yet been investigated whether the reapplication behavior after a first rejection varies by parental education. As admission to medical school is highly selective, reapplication is an important pathway to enter this field of study with high returns in terms of income and prestige. Thus, social differences in reapplication behavior may contribute to the overrepresentation of adolescents from privileged backgrounds among medical students. However, it could also be possible that there is no variation in persistence by parental education left among those who initially decided to apply to medicine. Applicants from disadvantaged backgrounds who end up applying to medical school may have performed unusually well in school, or have exceptional support, that helps them keep up their persistence even after receiving a first rejection.

Nevertheless, based on my theoretical expectations of secondary effects as mechanisms behind inequality in selective fields of study, I predict that:

HIII.1: Applicants from privileged social backgrounds show a stronger persistence in goal pursuit than their less privileged peers.

University rejections can be crucial in shaping adolescents' future career pathways, and those from less privileged backgrounds seem to be more responsive to these events. Heiskala et al. (2023) propose that potentially this could also be because these rejections negatively affect their meritocratic beliefs—like previously discussed in Chapter 3.2—but do not empirically test this.

Inequality beliefs and persistence in goal pursuit

According to the motivational theory of lifespan development, goal persistence (here: engaging or disengaging from a goal) is adaptive to an individual's perceived control over their goal attainment (Heckhausen & Schulz, 1995; Heckhausen et al., 2010). Different opportunities arise in different stages of life, and goal engagement at the appropriate time points is crucial for success, while it may be detrimental at times when the goal is unattainable. This theory stresses the active role of the individual in selecting, pursuing, and disengaging from a certain goal when pursuing it further becomes too costly. The individual evaluates their own control over the outcome in accessing ways how it can influence the environment to be in line with their own wishes, as well as ways how it can adapt to the environment to achieve the desired goal. If the perceived control over the goal becomes too low, people actively disengage from pursuing this certain goal, and adapt their goal accordingly (Heckhausen et al., 2010).

As already discussed in Chapter 3.2, according to attributional theory, beliefs about the causal factors behind success can (among other dimensions) be classified by how much the individual can control these factors (Weiner, 1985). Typically, the meritocratic factor effort is seen as the one that can be most controlled by the individual, while other factors like abilities, luck, and family background are less or not at all controllable (Skinner et al., 1988; Weiner, 1985). Combining motivational and attributional theory, I expect that the meritocratic belief that success depends on effort is positively associated with goal persistence, as this belief makes the outcome seem controllable and attainable, while other beliefs may be negatively associated with it.

Indeed, these theoretical accounts have partly been tested empirically before. Scholars have examined how meritocratic and nonmeritocratic beliefs affect the persistence of goal pursuit for young adults in school-to-work transitions (e.g., Hu et al., 2020; Shane & Heckhausen, 2013, 2016). Shane and Heckhausen (2013) examined how the meritocratic belief that success in society depends on one's own effort and talent, and the nonmeritocratic belief that it depends on luck are associated with goal engagement (i.e., commitment to pursue one's goal, even when facing obstacles) and goal disengagement (i.e., willingness to change or abandon one's goal). They showed that meritocratic beliefs are positively associated with goal engagement, while the nonmeritocratic belief in the importance of luck for success was negatively associated with goal engagement and positively associated with goal disengagement. In another study, Shane and Heckhausen (2016) examined inequality beliefs about one's own success as well as beliefs about societal success in general.

They found that meritocratic beliefs in terms of effort and talent beliefs are positively associated with goal engagement, while nonmeritocratic beliefs in terms of luck and privileges beliefs are positively associated with goal disengagement. Hu et al. (2020) replicated Shane and Heckhausen's (2013; 2016) studies of American adolescents with Chinese 3rd-year university students. Their study confirmed that meritocratic beliefs about societal success are positively associated with goal persistence and goal clarity (Hu et al., 2020).

The association of goal (dis)engagement and beliefs about one's own success seems to be stronger than the association with beliefs about societal success in general (Shane & Heckhausen, 2016). Feeling in control of one's own success holds importance for persistence, rather than general beliefs about inequality in society. Hence, in this chapter of the dissertation, I will only focus on the belief in one's own (non)meritocratic admission.

These studies combined beliefs in how important effort and talent are for own upward mobility into one meritocratic belief scale (Hu et al., 2020; Shane & Heckhausen, 2016). This decision was justified by the high reliability of the scale. However, according to attributional theory (Weiner, 1985), this may be problematic: If failure is attributed to a lack of one's own innate ability rather than a lack of effort, this may even reduce—rather than increase—motivation and persistence in goal pursuit through feelings of helplessness and limited capability (Försterling, 1985; Skinner et al., 1988; Weiner, 1985). This may be particularly true for people adhering to a fixed mindset (Dweck, 2006), believing that abilities are unalterable. Thus, a combined meritocratic belief scale may be misleading. The belief in the importance of effort may be more strongly associated with persistence than the combined scale, while the belief in the importance of talent may not be associated with persistence or may even be negatively associated with it.

In the context of Australian young adults, Smith and Skrbiš (2017) indeed found divergent associations between beliefs in the importance of effort and ability and educational attainment (Smith & Skrbiš, 2017), and these associations may be driven by differences in persistence in goal pursuit. Their study suggests that beliefs that alterable factors (e.g., hard work or a positive attitude towards school work) drive academic success have a positive effect on educational attainment, while beliefs in the importance of ability and talent have no such effect (Smith & Skrbiš, 2017). The belief that economic family background drives academic success seems to be negatively associated with educational attainment (Smith & Skrbiš, 2017).

The empirical studies described examined self-predicted goal (dis)engagement (Hu et al., 2020; Shane & Heckhausen, 2013, 2016) and educational attainment (Smith and Skrbiš, 2017) but did not measure actual goal persistence behavior. In this dissertation, I combine different aspects of goal persistence and examine the relationship between inequality beliefs and goal (dis)engagement, reapplication intention, and reapplication behavior. Based on considerations of motivational and attributional theory, I expect:

HIII.2: Beliefs in meritocratic admission are positively associated with persistence in goal pursuit, while the opposite is true for the belief in nonmeritocratic admission.

However, there may be only a positive association between persistence in goal pursuit with the meritocratic belief in the importance of effort and not with the meritocratic belief in the importance of talent.

Why is this association between inequality beliefs and persistence in goal pursuit important? In Chapter 3.2, I discussed self-serving beliefs theory (Bénabou & Tirole, 2016) and that I expect experiences of success (e.g., in admission) to increase meritocratic beliefs and reduce nonmeritocratic beliefs, while I expect experiences of failure to reduce meritocratic beliefs and increase nonmeritocratic beliefs. If meritocratic beliefs increase persistence, while nonmeritocratic beliefs reduce persistence, and if experiences of success and failure shape these beliefs in a self-serving way, this could potentially reinforce inequalities.

For example, if success increases the belief in the importance of effort, and this belief increases the persistence in goal pursuit, a "belief-performance cycle" (Skinner, 1998, p. v) emerges. Skinner coined this term and tested how control beliefs—beliefs that are similar but not identical to meritocratic effort beliefs[11]—influence children's academic performance in school and how their performance, in turn, influences their beliefs. Her study followed children from third to seventh grade with a fairly large sample of more than 1,600 children. She found that control beliefs increased children's engagement in the classroom, and, hence, their academic performance (Skinner, 1998). Academic success, which followed this increase in performance, strengthened children's perceived control beliefs. The opposite cycle occurred for attributions to uncontrollable factors. Through this belief-performance cycle, initial differences in children's control beliefs and performance increased over time (Skinner, 1998). Combining self-serving beliefs theory discussed in Chapter 3.2, and research on the role of inequality beliefs for adolescents' persistence in goal pursuit discussed in this chapter, I expect that the effect of inequality beliefs on this persistence may be particularly relevant because persistence, performance, experiences of success and failure, and inequality beliefs may reinforce each other, leading to a widening belief gap between 'winners' and 'losers.'

For the case of highly selective admission in Germany (see Chapter 2), persistence in goal pursuit is particularly relevant. Each semester, about three-

---

11 Skinner (1998) measured control beliefs as beliefs to which extent children can control desired outcomes. As argued before, in line with Weiner's (1985) attributional theory, the meritocratic belief that success depends on effort should be strongly associated with control beliefs.

quarters of all applicants are getting rejected—e.g., in 2018 the admission rate was 25 %. Maintaining persistence in goal pursuit and reapplying at a later point is a common way of eventually being admitted to medical school.[12]

Social differences in inequality beliefs and educational inequality

As argued in Chapter 3.2, parental education shapes inequality beliefs. Beyond the initial differences in inequality beliefs by parental education, receiving a rejection may reduce meritocratic beliefs and increase nonmeritocratic beliefs even more strongly for applicants from less privileged backgrounds than for those from privileged backgrounds, as they interpret their rejection as yet another experience of structural disadvantage (see HI.4b in Chapter 3.2). Hence, weaker meritocratic beliefs (particularly effort beliefs) and stronger nonmeritocratic among applicants from less privileged backgrounds may reduce their persistence in goal pursuit after receiving a rejection, and make them less likely to reapply compared to their more privileged peers. Combining insights from the different theories presented, I propose that:

HIII.3: Social differences in inequality beliefs about admission mediate part of the effect of parental education on persistence in goal pursuit.

Especially social differences in the belief that admission depends on one's own effort may explain social differences in goal pursuit, as I expect this belief to be more strongly associated with goal pursuit than—for example—the belief that it depends on one's own talent.

Social differences in the association between inequality beliefs and persistence

Previous research suggests that the effect of meritocratic beliefs on school performance varies between students from different backgrounds (Darnon et al., 2018; García-Sierra, 2023). Darnon et al. (2018) explored how beliefs in school meritocracy (here, the belief that success in school through hard work is possible for everyone) affected French fifth graders' standardized test performance in French and Mathematics, and how this effect varied by parental occupation (categorized as high and low SES). They found that for low SES students, belief in school meritocracy was negatively associated with test performance, while there was no substantial association for high SES students (Darnon et al., 2018).

12　Looking at the second wave of the weighted medical applicant data supports this expectation: In 2018, 25 % of all applicants were admitted. Of those who were admitted, 45 % stated that they had unsuccessfully applied to medical school before.

Using data from the German Socio-Economic Panel (SOEP), García-Sierra (2023) analyzed how meritocratic beliefs (here, the belief that one must work hard to be successful) are associated with the likelihood of being in a precarious work situation or not being fully employed in one's late twentieths. She found that for low SES individuals, but not for high SES individuals (measured by parental occupation), strong meritocratic beliefs during adolescence were positively associated with both outcomes (García-Sierra, 2023).

Both studies suggest that meritocratic beliefs may have a negative effect on achievement and labor market outcomes for adolescents from disadvantaged family backgrounds, and argue that this may be due to lower self-esteem and frustration about not being able to succeed through hard work (Darnon et al., 2018; García-Sierra, 2023). They believe their own merit is to blame for their failure, and may underestimate the structural reasons that make it harder for them to achieve this merit. I argue that this frustration among socially disadvantaged applicants who believe in meritocracy may lead to a reduction of their persistence in goal pursuit, as they believe that they are not good enough to succeed. This reduction in persistence among the less privileged contributes to unequal achievement and educational inequality.

Contrary to these expectations, other studies found for the group of undergraduate students that the association between societal meritocratic beliefs and self-predicted goal persistence was stronger for students from low SES backgrounds (Hu et al., 2020) than for their more privileged peers, as well as the association between the belief that people get what they deserve and the willingness to invest in long-term goals (Laurin, 2012). The authors argue that these beliefs can compensate for a lower perceived controllability of life outcomes due to previous experiences among the group of low SES students.

However, among the positively selective group of medical applicants from less privileged backgrounds, this compensatory effect may be less important than for more heterogeneous groups. They already managed to obtain the Abitur, and, on average, achieve a very good GPA score, and thus may feel a certain control over their life outcomes. An experience of failure in admission may be particularly frustrating when believing that success depends on merit and underestimating the role of nonmeritocratic factors to achieve such merit: Applicants from disadvantaged backgrounds may believe that they performed just not good enough to be admitted, eventually reducing their persistence. Furthermore, Hu et al.'s (2020) and Laurin's (2012) studies only focused on self-predicted persistence, which may differ from students' actual behavior.

Hence, overall, I propose that beyond differences in inequality beliefs that may lead to social differences in goal pursuit and contribute to educational inequality, it may additionally be possible that inequality beliefs affect applicants' goal pursuit differently depending on their social backgrounds. Precisely, I expect that:

HIII.4: Beliefs in meritocratic admission have a more positive effect on persistence in goal pursuit for applicants from privileged backgrounds than for their less privileged peers.

3.5 Summary of hypotheses

After presenting, discussing, and combining theories and empirical evidence on the formation of inequality beliefs and their consequences for educational inequality, I conclude this section by summarizing my theoretical framework and hypotheses.

In Chapter 3.1, I discussed mechanisms behind educational inequality (Boudon, 1974; Bourdieu, 1977; Bourdieu & Passeron, 1990) and behind inequality in selective fields of study (Lörz, 2012; Lucas, 2001), and hypothesize that applicants from privileged backgrounds are more likely to be admitted than their less privileged peers (*HI.1*). In Chapter 3.2, I discussed how parental education and educational experiences shape inequality beliefs. I argued that inequality beliefs crystallize particularly in early adulthood and that educational institutions and admission procedures play a crucial role in shaping them. Combining arguments of reproduction theory (Bourdieu, 1977; Bourdieu & Passeron, 1990) and Mijs' (2017) framework of socially stratified educational institutions as 'inferential spaces,' I argued that applicants from privileged backgrounds hold stronger meritocratic and weaker nonmeritocratic beliefs than their less privileged peers (*HI.2*) due to transmission of parental beliefs and social homogeneity in educational institutions. Furthermore, these social differences in beliefs may also stem from differences in experiences of success and failure in education—experiences that shape inequality beliefs. I then zoom in on the specific educational experience of success and failure in admission to medical school. Discussing expectations of self-serving beliefs theory (Bénabou & Tirole, 2016) against expectations of system-justification theory (Jost & Banaji, 1994), I argue that in this case, self-serving belief mechanisms are likely to outweigh system-justification mechanisms. Accordingly, success strengthens meritocratic beliefs and weakens nonmeritocratic beliefs, whereas failure weakens meritocratic beliefs and strengthens nonmeritocratic beliefs (*HI.3*).

However, I argued that it is insufficient to look at the effect of a single experience of success or failure, but that previous experiences such as long-term experiences of social upbringing or short-term experiences of previous experiences of failure in admission may moderate the effect of success or failure on inequality beliefs. Drawing on cumulative inequality theory (DiPrete & Eirich, 2006) and Schafer et al.'s (2011) expansion of it, previous experiences may serve as a frame for new experiences, and shape how these experiences are interpreted. I expect that success (failure) strengthens (weakens) meritocratic beliefs and weakens (strengthens) nonmeritocratic beliefs more strongly for less privileged applicants than for privileged applicants (*HI.4a/b*). Furthermore, I expect that success (failure) strengthens (weakens) meritocratic beliefs and weakens (strengthens) nonmeritocratic beliefs more strongly for repeat applicants than for first-time applicants (*HI.5a/b*).

The experience of success against the odds of less privileged applicants may have a particularly positive effect on their meritocratic beliefs, as they view it as proof that merit-based upward mobility is possible. On the other hand, yet another experience of failure may be interpreted as a result of structural disadvantage. In a similar vein, I expect that eventually succeeding through extensive efforts of reapplying may be viewed as a reward for one's merit, while reoccurring experiences of failure may amplify with every failed attempt, and lead to people eventually abandoning their meritocratic beliefs and justification of the admission procedure and societal inequality. Success against the odds is possible (success of those from less privileged backgrounds or those who were previously unsuccessful) and has the potential to outweigh previous doubts about meritocracy. However, overall, I expect experiences of success and failure to further broaden the belief gap between these groups. For applicants from less privileged backgrounds and repeat applicants a rejection is more likely to occur than for the privileged and first-time applicants, and for them experiencing (yet another) experience of failure may reduce meritocratic beliefs and increase nonmeritocratic beliefs even more strongly.

In the last subsection of Chapter 3.1, I discussed the theory of how meritocratic ideology may contribute to the legitimation of (educational) inequality (Mijs, 2016; Solga, 2015). In Chapter 3.3, I returned to the inequality-legitimizing consequences of meritocratic beliefs and proceeded to discuss how inequality beliefs influence perceptions of justice and distributive preferences. Beyond these theoretical arguments, I discussed evidence from previous research on the association between social background, inequality beliefs, perceptions of justice, and distributive preferences (e.g., Alesina & Giuliano, 2011; García-Sánchez et al., 2020; Batruch et al., 2022; Mijs, 2021). I expect that meritocratic beliefs are negatively associated with the preference for equal distribution and positively with the preference for distribution based on educational meritocracy, while the opposite is true for nonmeritocratic beliefs (*HII.1*)—an association that can primarily be explained by perceptions of justice. Meritocratic beliefs lead to the perception of higher justice, while nonmeritocratic beliefs lead to a perception of lower justice (*HII.2*), and the more strongly people perceive inequality as just, the more opposed they are to equal distribution and the more strongly they support educational meritocracy (*HII.3*). Hence, in *HII.4a* and *HII.4b,* I argue that the perception of justice mediates the negative (positive) relationship between meritocratic beliefs and the preference for equal distribution (preference for distribution based on the principle of educational meritocracy) and the positive (negative) relationship between nonmeritocratic beliefs and the preference for equal distribution (preference for distribution based on the principle of educational meritocracy).

Furthermore, drawing on attributional theory (Weiner, 1985), I argue that distinct meritocratic and nonmeritocratic beliefs may have different inequality-(de)legitimizing consequences. While the belief in the importance of hard work and abilities may both legitimize (educational) inequality—although possibly due to different mechanisms—the nonmeritocratic belief that success is based on social background may have stronger inequality-delegitimizing consequences than the belief that it depends on luck, as luck varies throughout a person's lifetime.

Combining expectations from the first and second block of hypotheses, I proposed that social differences in inequality beliefs, and the resulting perception of justice, may partly mediate the relationship between parental education and distributive preferences for equality and educational meritocracy (*HII.5*). Among applicants from privileged backgrounds, strong meritocratic beliefs and weak nonmeritocratic beliefs may lead to perceiving inequality as just, and hence, to an opposition to equal distribution and a preference for distribution based on educational meritocracy—a system that currently reproduces inequality. Additionally, those from less privileged backgrounds who experienced success against the odds may also develop strong meritocratic and weak nonmeritocratic beliefs, and thus share inequality-reproducing distributive preferences despite their background.

Beyond legitimizing educational inequality, meritocratic beliefs also reproduce such inequality by contributing to unequal persistence in goal pursuit. Based on Boudon's (1974) secondary effects and Breen and Goldhorpe's (1997) rational choice model for educational decisions, I propose that applicants from privileged social backgrounds show a stronger persistence in goal pursuit than their less privileged peers (*HIII.1*). Combining motivational and attributional theory (Heckhausen et al., 2010; Weiner, 1985), I expect that beliefs in meritocratic (nonmeritocratic) admission are positively (negatively) associated with persistence in goal pursuit (*HIII.2*). However, there may only be a positive association between persistence and the meritocratic belief in the importance of hard work but not with the meritocratic belief in the importance of abilities. Ascribing an experience of failure to a lack of abilities may even have a demotivational effect if applicants believe that they do not possess the required abilities to succeed even if they try hard enough.

Drawing on theories on how parental education shapes inequality beliefs (Chapter 3.2), and combining them with theories of secondary effects (Chapter 3.1) and motivational and attributional theory (Chapter 3.4), I concluded that social differences in inequality beliefs about admission mediate part of the effect of parental education on persistence in goal pursuit (*HIII.3*). Finally, I proposed that beliefs in meritocratic admission have a more positive effect on persistence in goal pursuit for applicants from privileged social backgrounds than for their less privileged peers (*HIII.4*). Believing that one can succeed through hard work may be frustrating for less privileged applicants who underestimate structural barriers that they are facing and blame themselves for their failure. Overall, stronger beliefs in meritocratic admission—particularly beliefs that it depends on hard work—and weaker beliefs that admission is nonmeritocratic may increase the persistence in goal pursuit after rejections among applicants from privileged backgrounds. Additionally, even if applicants from less privileged backgrounds believe in meritocratic admission, these beliefs may increase their persistence less in comparison to their more privileged peers.

Figure 3.4 illustrates all of my hypotheses and a theoretical framework for the formation of inequality beliefs and their consequences for educational inequality. Hypotheses on educational inequality (Chapter 3.1) and on how parental education and educational experiences shape beliefs (Chapter 3.2) are numbered with I, hypotheses on the inequality-legitimizing consequences of beliefs (Chapter 3.3) are numbered with II, and hypotheses on their consequences for unequal persistence in goal pursuit (Chapter 3.4) are numbered with III. An overview of all hypotheses can also be found in the appendix in Table A3.1.

The case examined in this dissertation, application to medical school in Germany, is an example of a selective procedure to reach desirable social positions. In Chapter 3.1, I discussed that this type of horizontal stratification becomes increasingly important. Even if (more) people from disadvantaged backgrounds enter HE, parental education is associated with the field of study that comes with different returns in terms of income and prestige.

Beyond my expectations regarding this specific case, I argue that inequality beliefs play an important role in educational inequality because a) people from privileged backgrounds and those who are successful form stronger meritocratic and weaker nonmeritocratic beliefs, b) these beliefs contribute to perceptions that inequality is just and to inequality-reproducing distributive preferences especially among the privileged and successful, who are likely to be future decision-makers, and c) these beliefs increase persistence in goal pursuit among the privileged and hinder persistence among the less privileged, thus reproducing inequality.

People from privileged backgrounds are more likely to end up in positions of power due to the mechanism of intergenerational status transmission. One of these mechanisms may be stronger meritocratic beliefs that increase their persistence in goal pursuit. These people make decisions that reproduce inequality, as they view this inequality as based on individual merit, and thus as just. If people from less privileged backgrounds end up being successful against the odds, they may also develop strong meritocratic beliefs and do not question the system of educational meritocracy; if they do not, they may end up questioning the system but are not in a position to change it, and may, additionally, end up giving up on their educational goals due to lower persistence.

Figure 3.4: Hypotheses: The formation of inequality beliefs and their consequences for educational inequality

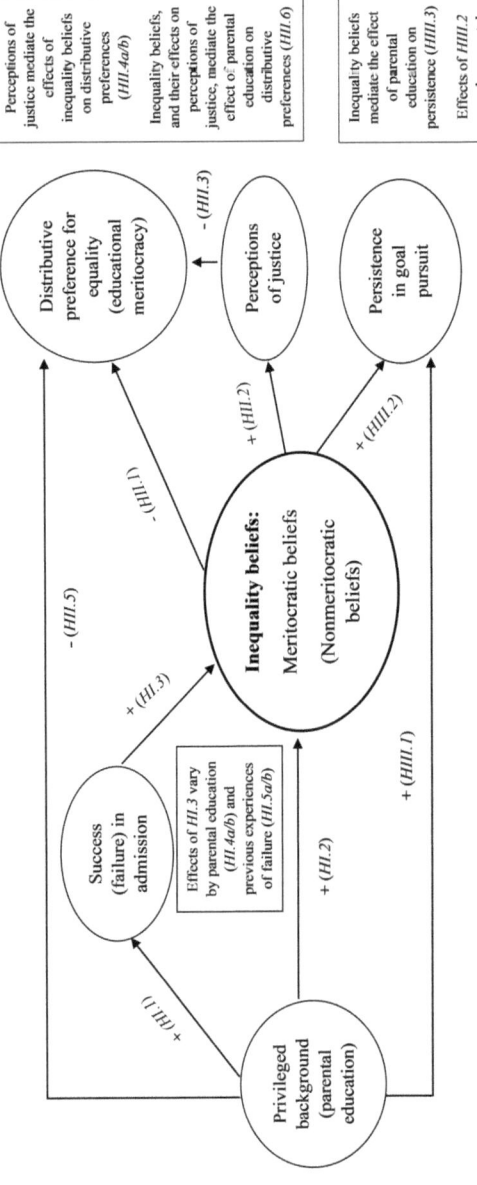

Note. The opposite direction of effect is hypothesized for concepts in brackets. A list of all hypotheses can be found in the appendix in Table A3.1. Author's illustration.

4 Research design

After providing the theoretical framework, this chapter describes the research design of this study. I will describe the data collection of the medical applicant data and discuss the operationalization of variables. As a next step, I will provide an overview of the samples used for each step of the analysis, present the applied weighting strategies, and provide descriptive statistics for each of the respective samples. Subsequently, I will compare the average inequality beliefs of the medical applicant sample to the beliefs of other groups of adolescents in Germany, using data from the National Educational Panel Study (NEPS). Finally, I will present an overview of the methods used through the different steps of the analysis.

4.1 Data collection

In this dissertation I use longitudinal data on medical applicants in Germany (Finger et al., 2023), hereafter called medical applicant data. The three waves of the data were conducted within two projects at the WZB Berlin Social Science Center: One project on social inequality in access to prestigious fields of study, funded by the German Research Foundation (DFG), and another project on meritocratic beliefs, which was internally funded. Waves 1 and 2 were collected within the first project and wave 3 was collected within the second project with the focus on meritocratic beliefs (see Figure 4.1). The medical applicant data has been published online together with the documentation of the data collection, questionnaires, and codebooks for all three waves (Finger et al., 2023).

In cooperation with the central clearinghouse for admission to medical programs in Germany, all applicants for the winter semester of 2018 were invited to participate in the first online survey via email. In the first (and second) survey waves, the respondents could state at the end whether they agree to be contacted again, making it possible to follow up on the applicants. The data collection was approved by the ethics commission of the WZB.

The survey was sent to and filled out by applicants to human medicine, dental medicine, veterinary medicine, and pharmacy, but throughout this dissertation, I only examine applicants to human medicine. Among applicants applying to medical programs, the group of applicants to human medicine, the most selective field of study, is by far the largest (75 %). If I had included applicants to all medical programs in the different steps of the analyses, I would have needed to look at field-specific subgroups that are partly very small in size: The effect of admission or rejection may differ by field as well as the persistence in goal pursuit after a first rejection. However, the focus of this dissertation is not these field-specific differences but the general mechanism of how educational experiences in selective university admission shape inequality beliefs, and how these beliefs contribute to educational inequality. Thus, I decided to only examine applicants to the most selective medical program throughout this dissertation: human medicine.

The first wave was conducted in August 2018, the second wave in November 2018, and the third wave in February 2021. Between the first and second waves, applicants were informed whether they were admitted or rejected, which enabled exploring longitudinally how this educational experience of success or failure changed applicants' inequality beliefs. In the 2.5 years between waves 2 and 3, rejected applicants had up to 4 chances to reapply (see Figure 4.1).

Figure 4.1: Three survey waves of medical applicant data

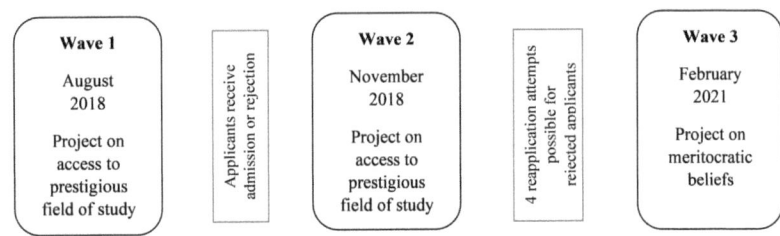

Note. Source: Medical applicant data, author's illustration.

All waves were conducted using the online survey tool LimeSurvey (Limesurvey GmbH, 2006-2020). Before each wave, cognitive pretests of the questionnaire items were conducted in the form of qualitative interviews in which medical students filled out the survey, gave us feedback on the comprehensibility of the variables, and answered additional questions. As an incentive to participate, we offered a lottery with vouchers ranging from 25€ to 350€ in each survey wave. Out of all 43,621 applicants to human medicine in 2018, the first survey was completed by 7,472 applicants (response rate: 17 %[13]); 4,503 applicants completed the second wave, and 2,082 applicants completed the third wave.

---

13 This number is comparable to the response rate of a representative large-scale online survey among German university students (K. Becker et al., 2019).

4.2 Variables

The operationalization of the theoretical concepts was developed based on inspiration from previous research and well-established survey instruments, as well as one's own ideas, and implemented into the survey waves. While the focus in the first two waves was on the selective admission process, it also included applicants' beliefs about inequality. The third wave had a stronger focus on meritocracy and included an extended version of this inequality belief scale as well as items on perceptions of justice and distributive preferences. The list of the translated questionnaire wording for all main variables can be found in the appendix in Table A4.1, the original questionnaire can be found online (Finger et al., 2023).

Inequality beliefs

In line with the theoretical arguments discussed in Chapter 3.2, the main distinction made in this dissertation is the one between meritocratic beliefs and nonmeritocratic beliefs. Furthermore, the questionnaire and analyses distinguish between different (non)meritocratic beliefs, and between domain-specific inequality beliefs and societal inequality beliefs. Domain-specific inequality beliefs measure the importance that respondents attribute to different meritocratic and nonmeritocratic factors of being successful in their own admission, while societal inequality beliefs measure how important they believe that these factors are generally for being successful in society. The scales were inspired by Shane and Heckhausen's (2013, 2017) scale of causal attributions for SES attainment. Table 4.1 displays the translated wording of the inequality belief scales.

The items represent the five distinct types of inequality beliefs discussed theoretically: hard work beliefs, abilities beliefs, educational merit beliefs, luck beliefs, and social background beliefs (see Chapter 3.2). In waves 1 and 2, applicants were asked how much they agree that their own admission depends on a) hard work and effort, b) talent and intelligence, c) subject-specific skills, d) school grades, e) endurance, and f) luck (domain-specific beliefs). Furthermore, applicants were asked how much they agree that being successful and climbing up the social ladder in Germany depends on a) hard work and effort, b) talent and intelligence, c) subject-specific skills, d) educational degrees e) initiative, f) endurance, g) family background, h) money and assets, i) connections, and j) gender (societal beliefs). All items were measured on a 5-point scale from 1 "totally disagree" to 5 "totally agree," where only the endpoints of the scale are labeled.

Table 4.1: Translated inequality beliefs scales in waves 1-3, and additional scale in wave 3

Domain-specific inequality beliefs	Societal inequality beliefs
1 (totally disagree) – 5 (totally agree)	
Scales implemented in waves 1 - 3	
An admission can depend on several factors. How much do you agree to the following statements: An admission depends on … a) **how much effort I put in and how hard-working I am.** b) **how talented and intelligent I am.** c) how good my subject-specific skills are. d) how good my school grades are. e) how strong my endurance is. f) **how lucky I am.**	On what does it actually depend in Germany whether someone is successful and climbs up the social ladder? a) **One must put in effort and be hard-working.** b) **One must be talented and intelligent.** c) One must have good subject-specific skills in one's area. d) One must have a good educational degree. e) One must be dynamic and show initiative. f) One must possess endurance. g) **One must be from the right family.** h) **One must possess money and assets.** i) One must have connections to the right people. j) One must have the right gender; men have better opportunities for upward mobility.
Scales additionally implemented in wave 3	
How much do you agree to the following statements: An admission depends on … a) how much initiative I show. b) from which family I am. c) how much money and assets I have. d) whether I have connections to the right people. e) which gender I have.	On what does it, furthermore, depend on whether someone is successful and climbs up the social ladder in Germany? a) One must be lucky. b) One must be born in Germany. People who were born in Germany have better opportunities.

Note. Items in bold were selected for the analyses for research objectives I and III. For research objective II, all items (except gender and being born in Germany, see Chapter 6) are included in the analyses. Original question-wording in German can be found in the published questionnaires (Finger et al., 2023). Author's translation.

Initially, in waves 1 and 2, applicants were not asked how much they agreed that their own admission depends on structural factors because admission to medical school is a strongly standardized and performance-related process that is only indirectly affected by structural factors. However, for wave 3—the wave with a stronger focus on meritocracy—we decided to include these items to make the list of inequality beliefs more comprehensive and the domain-specific and societal beliefs more comparable. Thus, in wave 3, additional questions were added asking 1) how much they agree that their own admission depends on a) initiative, b) family background, c) money and assets, d) connections, and e) gender, and 2) how much they agree that being successful and climbing up the social ladder in Germany depends on a) luck, and b) being born in Germany.

For the empirical chapter that uses inequality beliefs measured in wave 1 or wave 2 (research objectives I and III), I decided to only include a selection of inequality beliefs representing different types of meritocratic and nonmeritocratic beliefs. For domain-specific beliefs, the following beliefs were selected: the meritocratic belief that one's own admission depends on a) hard work and effort, b) talent and intelligence, and the nonmeritocratic belief that it depends on c) luck. For societal inequality beliefs, these beliefs were selected: the meritocratic belief that success in society depends on a) hard work and effort, and b) talent and intelligence, and the nonmeritocratic belief that it depends on c) family background and d) money and assets.

The item effort and hard work beliefs (hereafter referred to as effort belief), and talent and intelligence belief (hereafter referred to as talent belief) were selected because they represent the common definition of merit, and are measured both for domain-specific and societal beliefs.[14] The luck belief item was selected as the only item representing a domain-specific nonmeritocratic belief, while the societal item family background and money beliefs[15] were selected as a typical representation of structural factors related to the social background effects discussed in this dissertation.

For research objective II, I conduct factor analysis for the extended inequality belief scales measured in wave 3 to confirm the 3 meritocratic types of beliefs, and 2 nonmeritocratic types of beliefs, and implement them in my structural equation models.

Parental education

Throughout this dissertation, I operationalize having a more or less privileged social background by applicants' parental education. For that purpose, I use information on parents' highest educational level, distinguishing between three social groups: applicants with no parents with a college degree (i.e., university degree or university of applied science degree), applicants with one parent with a college degree, and applicants with two parents with a college degree (hereafter called college-educated parents).

---

14 The importance of endurance is also measured for both domain-specific and societal beliefs and is conceptionally close to item a. Including both variables in one model (in analyses for research objective III) may lead to multicollinearity, but it did also not seem feasible to combine these items into one index (Cronbach's alpha: 0.53), especially as item a more closely reflects the common meritocratic belief discussed in the literature.

15 As societal beliefs measured in waves 1 and 2 were not included together in one model, the issue of multicollinearity such as discussed in Footnote 14 did not occur here.

As discussed in Chapter 3.1, I decided to focus on parental education as it has been found to be the strongest predictor of educational success among other social background characteristics (Bourdieu, 1984; Hällsten & Thaning, 2018; Thaning, 2021). Thus, I am interested in how it influences applicants' admission likelihood, inequality beliefs, distributive preferences, and persistence in goal pursuit.

Success and failure in admission

Between waves 1 and 2, all applicants were informed whether they were admitted (i.e, success) or rejected (i.e., failure)—a variable measured in wave 2. Furthermore, in wave 3, rejected applicants were asked again whether and when they were admitted.

Grade point average (GPA)

GPA ranges from the best score of 1.0 to the worst score of 4.0 and is the final grade that students receive for their Abitur, their university entrance certificate obtained at an upper-secondary school. It is calculated based on their grades in the last two years in school and their grades in the final exams. This variable was used for analyses regarding research objective I as mediator in some analyses, and for subgroup analyses in other analyses.

First-time vs. repeat applicants

In wave 1, applicants were asked whether they previously applied to medical school in Germany. I use this variable to distinguish between first-time and repeat applicants.

Perceptions of justice

In wave 3, perceptions of justice and distributive preferences were added to the survey. Perceptions of justice were measured on a five-point scale based on a question that asked respondents how just they perceive the admission procedure and how just they perceive inequalities in society more generally. The latter question wording was taken from the German General Social Survey (Allerbeck et al., 2017), the ALLBUS, while we developed the question wording regarding the perception of the admission procedure as just in a similar manner.

There has been some criticism in research on social justice that measuring the perception of justice of societal inequality in the described way does not consider that individuals often misperceive the extent of actual inequalities (Nießen et al., 2023). People may be biased in their perceived level of inequality, whereby those who believe that income inequality is necessary for economic growth seem to perceive less inequality than those who do not (Du & King, 2022). While this argument should be considered in the interpretation of findings, I am interested in the effect of inequality beliefs on the general perception of justice of societal inequalities (including potential misperception of the extent of such inequalities), and in the effect of this perception of justice on distributive preferences, which is why this general scale seemed appropriate.

Distributive preferences

Distributive preferences were measured for the hypothetical distribution of vacant places in the program and income distribution. A list of several items was included, representing distribution based on the common justice principles of equality, equity, need, and entitlement. For preferences for the distribution of vacant places in the program, we designed the item ourselves, while the preference for income distribution scale was taken from the questionnaire of the International Social Justice Project (Wegener, 2006), adding one item representing educational meritocracy. This dissertation examines how meritocratic beliefs legitimize (merit-based) educational inequality. Hence, as discussed in Chapter 3.3, I chose to only focus on two principles: equality and educational meritocracy. I will now present the items measuring preferences for distribution based on these two principles. However, a list of all items can be found in the appendix (Table A4.1).

We asked respondents to rate on a 5-point scale, if there were 100 medical school places left after the current round of admissions, how much would they support a) equal admission through a lottery, b) admission purely based on school grades. We designed this item carefully to follow the concept of equal distribution without completely abandoning the current merit-based admission procedure. As the item specified, only the remaining medical school places would be distributed through a new procedure. To assess distributive preferences regarding inequality in society generally, we asked respondents how much they supported a) equal income distribution (i.e., income should be distributed equally), and b) income distribution based on educational credentials (i.e., those with high educational credentials should earn more).

Growth vs. fixed mindset

Dweck (2006) suggests that not everyone views abilities as unalterable, but that some people view abilities as stable (i.e., 'fixed mindset'), while others may view them as alterable (i.e., 'growth mindset'). Following up on academic debates discussed in Chapter 3.3, I explore whether the inequality-legitimizing effect of abilities beliefs differs depending on whether people adhere to a growth or fixed mindset. For that purpose, I conduct a subgroup analysis using a binary variable asking whether applicants believe that abilities and intelligence are rather innate and determined at birth or rather alterable by the individual. This variable is part of a scale on whether different (non)meritocratic beliefs are innate or alterable (see Table A4.1).

Persistence in goal pursuit

In this dissertation, persistence in goal pursuit is defined as applicants' mental process of engaging and disengaging from the goal to study medicine after receiving a first rejection, as well as their actual behavior to pursue this goal. Four dimensions of goal pursuit are examined: goal engagement, goal disengagement, reapplication intention, and reapplication behavior. While the first three concepts measure self-predicted persistence in wave 2 (right after receiving a rejection), the last concept measures their actual reapplication behavior between wave 2 and 3 (operationalized as conditional likelihood to reapply and number of reapplication attempts).

The goal engagement and goal disengagement scales are an adapted version of Wrosch et al.'s (2000) primary and secondary control scales. To measure applicants' goal engagement, they were asked how much they agree that in terms of securing a place for their preferred study field, they a) are prepared to do everything necessary, b) will try even harder if it proves to be difficult, c) make sure nothing distracts them from their goal, and d) will keep telling themselves that they will succeed. As the last item slightly deviates from the other items conceptionally (which also shows empirically), I decided to only combine the first three items into a goal engagement index (Cronbach's alpha: .83). To measure their goal disengagement, they were asked how much they agree that they are willing to a) move to a place that is not their preferred choice to study their preferred study field, b) take up another subject that is easier to achieve, c) take a different career path. The first item slightly deviates from the other two, and thus, I decided to only combine the latter two into a goal disengagement index (Cronbach's alpha: .76). All items were measured on a 5-point scale, and the indices were generated by dividing the sum of all items by the number of items.

Reapplication intention was measured on a 5-point scale asking rejected applicants how likely they were to reapply. In wave 3, we collected information on rejected applicants' reapplication behavior between waves 2 and 3, including whether and when they eventually were admitted, and for which semesters they applied before their admission or before wave 3. Between waves 2 and 3, there were up to 4 time points when applicants could reapply. The number of highest possible reapplication attempts is conditional on when and whether applicants were admitted, which is accounted for in the analysis.

Control variables

Depending on the applied method, control variables were included in the analyses. Regarding research objectives I and III, some analyses include gender (measured as a binary variable) and age[16], and regarding research objective I, some analyses include applicants' GPA. In wave 3, half of the respondents participated in an experimental survey part before the main survey. To ensure that responses were not biased by this participation, all analyses using data from wave 3 include a binary dummy of participation in this experiment as a control variable (research objectives II and III).

Treating ordinal variables as continuous

Many of the main variables of interest (e.g., inequality beliefs, perceptions of justice, distributive preferences, goal engagement, goal disengagement, and reapplication intention) were (based on the original scales) measured on 5-point scales. There has been a long-standing debate on whether, and if at all, under which conditions, ordinal scales can be treated as continuous variables to allow for parametric analyses (Bauer & Sterba, 2011; Carifio & Perla, 2007; Harpe, 2015). Under some conditions, treating ordinal variables as continuous may not be as problematic. Traditionally, Likert scales comprise a set of variables that are summarized into an index to measure the latent construct behind the scale. Likert (1932) himself proposed that the distances between the numbers in the response set should be equal, suggesting an interval rather than an ordinal scale (Harpe, 2015; Likert, 1932). Thus, Harpe (2015) proposes that aggregated rating scales may be treated as continuous variables if they are normally enough distributed.

However, while I use indices generated from traditional Likert scales in some analyses (e.g., goal engagement and disengagement, and latent inequality beliefs in the structural equation models), I also analyze single items (e.g., distinct inequality beliefs, perceptions of justice, and reapplication intention). Harpe (2015) suggests that individual rating items with numerical response formats of at least five categories in length may also be treated as continuous variables. Drawing on previous research (D. Cohen & Blanc-Goldhammer, 2011), he argues that when presented with numbers, people think of a mental number line with equal intervals between the numbers (Harpe, 2015). The variables conducted in the medical applicant data fit this description: They range from 1 to 5, and only the extremes are labeled (e.g., 1 "totally disagree" - 5" totally agree"), while the numbers between are not labeled.

---

16 As only the birth year and not the birth month were collected, age was generated considering the month of the survey, and (for simplicity) assuming that births are distributed equally across the months of the year.

Most of my analyses include a variety of different concepts, and hence, to facilitate interpretations, I decided to treat the indices derived from Likert scales as well as the single items measured on a 5-point scale as continuous variables. However, I am aware of recommendations to only use this approach if variables are normally distributed and have at least seven values (Bauer and Sterba 2011). Thus, I will provide some robustness checks with analyses accounting for the ordinal nature of the scales in the appendix, when examining the single items.

4.3 Samples

In this dissertation, I include different subgroups of the medical applicant data in the analyses for each research objective. Figure 4.2 illustrates the relationship between these subsamples and their respective case numbers. Respondents with missing values on any variables included in the respective analyses are excluded.

My first research objective is to examine how parental education and educational experiences shape inequality beliefs, whereby I am interested in the change in beliefs. Thus, subsample I only comprises respondents who also participated in wave 2, and do not have any missing values on the variables of interest (N = 4,138). For the second research objective, I used variables that are only included in wave 3, and hence subsample II includes only a subgroup of subsample I: those who also participated in W3 (N = 1,725).

For the third research objective, I only examined a specific subgroup of medical applicants: first-time[17] rejected applicants who still stated medicine to be their preferred field of study. To illustrate the selection of this subgroup, and how the selection changes the sample characteristics, I also included the group of first-time applicants (N = 1,992) in Figure 4.2, and Table 4.2 (Chapter 4.5). I used two different subsamples to examine self-predicted persistence in W2 and reapplication behavior between waves 2 and 3. Subsample IIIa comprises first-time rejected applicants who participated in waves 1 and 2 (N = 594); subsample IIIb includes only those of subsample IIIa who also participated in wave 3 (N = 190).

---

17 I decided to include only first-time applicants in the main analyses, as I expect previous experiences of rejection to affect applicants' persistence in goal pursuit and inequality beliefs. For the group of repeatedly rejected applicants in 2018, it is unclear when and how many times they applied previously, and therefore it would not be possible to properly account for previous experiences in admission—experiences potentially confounding the relationship between the observed variables.

Figure 4.2: Samples of medical applicants used in analyses for three research objectives

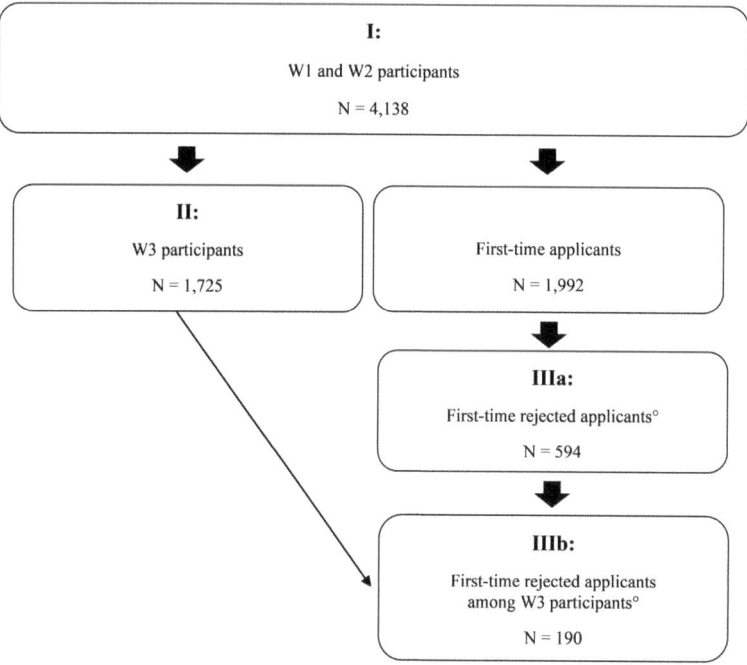

Note. Only respondents without missing values on any of the variables were included in the respective analyses. ° Only those who still stated medicine to be their preferred field of study were included. Source: Medical applicant data, author's illustration.

4.4 Weighting

A common problem of survey-based research is that initial participation and panel attrition are not random. However, based on the rich information included in the application register data provided by the SfH (such as applicants' GPA, gender, age, and admission status), I constructed a sampling weight for wave 2 (for sample I and IIIa) to reduce bias due to selective survey participation and attrition, and a panel weight for wave 3 (for sample II and IIIb) to additionally account for nonrandom attrition between waves 2 and 3.

Sampling weight for wave 2

Selection for participation in the medical applicant survey is not random, as demonstrated—for instance—by the overestimated unweighted admissions rate of 46 % among applicants to human medicine in the sample (compared to 25 % in the overall population). To reduce this source of bias, I constructed a sampling weight based on the application register data provided by the central clearinghouse. This data covers the whole population of medical school applicants for the winter term of 2018. Following recommendations on how to create and apply weights in Stata (Dupraz, 2013), the weight was constructed using the distributions of gender, age, high school GPA, and the state (*Bundesland*) in which the university entrance certificate was acquired, all interacted with admission status.[18]

After applying the cross-sectional sampling weight, the weighted admission rate amounts to 25 %, which is precisely the admission rate in the overall population, confirming that the applied weighting strategy seems to be appropriate. Because I apply the weight to wave 2 participants, it accounts for both selection and attrition bias, which is connected to the weighting variables. The weighted sample represents the overall applicant population in the respective variables. The interaction with admission status allows subgroup analyses of admitted and rejected applicants. When looking at admitted applicants, applying the sampling weight makes the sample representative of the overall population of admitted applicants (in terms of the variables used to construct the weight); when looking at rejected applicants, applying the sampling weight makes the sample representative of the overall population of rejected applicants.[19]

Alternatively, I considered applying a panel weight by multiplying a wave 1 sampling weight (based on distributions of the variables mentioned above except for admission status) with 1 divided by the predicted likelihood

---

18 Considering the distribution of the variables in the register data, gender was coded as binary, age was recoded into 4 categories, GPA was recoded into 11 categories, and state was recoded into 10 categories. The weight was created using the Stata command '*ipfweight.*' For this purpose, the share of people in each category interacted with admission status for all variables was specified, and used to generate the weight. The interaction with admission status is included, as it can be expected that the distribution of variables (particularly GPA) substantially differs between admitted and rejected applicants. For instance, for the gender variable four shares were specified: admitted men, rejected men, admitted women, and rejected women.

19 Even though for other subsamples (e.g., applicants from different social backgrounds, first-time vs. repeat applicants), the weighted distribution in the sample may not perfectly represent distribution in the respective subpopulation, applying weights still partly reduces selection and attrition bias.

of wave 2 participation. This predicted likelihood was estimated by running a logistic regression with wave 2 participation as the dependent variable and gender, age, GPA, and state, as well as the variable parental education (not included in the register data) as the independent variable, and predicting the probability of wave 2 participation for each respondent based on these characteristics. This strategy accomplishes that those with a lower likelihood to participate in wave 2 (but still did) gain more weight, accounting for nonrandom attrition between waves 1 and 2. Despite this advantage to consider attrition between waves 1 and 2 (that may also differ by parental education), it has one major disadvantage, namely that the admission decision only took place after wave 1, and thus different distributions of the variables between the group of later admitted or rejected applicants could not be considered. As this is a central variable for my analysis, I decided to apply the sampling weight to analyses using the wave 2 data (even though robustness checks with alternative weighting strategies will be provided where appropriate).

Panel weight for wave 3

To reduce selection and attrition bias in wave 3, I constructed a panel weight by multiplying the previously described W2 sampling weight with 1 divided by the predicted likelihood of participation in wave 3. This predicted likelihood of W3 participation was created similarly to the likelihood of W2 participation described before. The only difference is that, furthermore, admission status was included as a predictor in the logistic regression. Although admission status is already accounted for with the W2 sampling weight, attrition between waves 2 and 3 may be influenced by applicants' admission status in wave 2.

4.5 Descriptive sample statistics

Table 4.2 provides descriptive statistics for the different samples described in Chapter 4.3, weighted according to the weighting strategy described in Chapter 4.4. For sample I (whole W2 sample), the admission rate is 25 %. Women are overrepresented among applicants (67 %). The average age of applicants is 21.31 years old, and the average GPA is 1.92. As the sample is weighted based on these characteristics from the register data, these characteristics are representative of the overall population of applicants to medicine in 2018. Among the sample, the share of applicants with two college-educated parents (42 %) is larger than the share of those with no college-educated parent (29 %) or only one college-educated parent (29 %). 52 % of the sample have already previously applied to medical school in Germany. The characteristics of sample I (the whole W2 sample) and sample II (the whole W3 sample) do not differ substantially from each other, supporting the applied weighting strategy. The panel weight reduces bias due to attrition between waves 2 and 3.

Table 4.2: Descriptive statistics for different samples

	W2 sample			W3 sample	
	Sample I: All applicants	First-time applicants	Sample IIIa: First-time rejected applicants°	Sample II: All applicants	Sample IIIb: First-time rejected applicants°
N	4,138	1,992	594	1,725	190
	% or mean (sd)				
Admitted	25 %	29 %	-	25 %	-
Woman	67 %	70 %	70 %	66 %	70 %
Age	21.31 (3.15)	19.61 (2.20)	19.53 (2.12)	23.58 (3.06)	21.59 (2.00)
GPA (1.0–4.0)	1.92 (0.61)	1.72 (0.58)	1.94 (0.53)	1.92 (0.62)	1.92 (0.52)
Parental education					
No college-educated parent	29 %	28 %	31 %	30 %	31 %
One college-educated parent	29 %	27 %	27 %	29 %	26 %
Two college-educated parents	42 %	45 %	42 %	41 %	43 %
Repeat (vs. first-time) applicant	52 %	-	-	54 %	-

Note. ° Only those who still stated medicine to be their preferred field of study were included. Sampling weight applied to W2 sample; panel weight applied to W3 sample (absolute numbers (N) not weighted). Source: Medical applicant data, author's calculations.

For analyses regarding research objective III, I examine first-time rejected applicants. How does this group differ from all applicants? To illustrate how the selection of a specific sample changes the sample characteristics, I first compare all applicants (sample I) to first-time applicants. Among first-time applicants, the admission rate is higher, the share of women is higher, they are younger, they have a better GPA score, and the share of applicants with two college-educated parents is larger compared to the overall applicant sample. Those who previously applied unsuccessfully are likely to have a worse GPA (which is associated with parental education and admission likelihood), explaining differences between the samples.

However, sample IIIa and sample IIIb only include specific subgroups of first-time applicants: those who were rejected (and still state medicine to be their preferred field of study). Among sample IIIa (W2 first-time rejected applicants) the gender and age distribution are similar to all first-time applicants

(W2), although the sample differs in respect of certain characteristics: Rejected first-time applicants have a worse GPA, and a larger share of applicants without college-educated parents than all first-time applicants. The characteristics of sample IIIa (W2) and of sample IIIb (W3) do not differ substantially between each other.

At the center of this dissertation are applicants' inequality beliefs. Thus, Table 4.3 displays the average inequality beliefs for sample I. As analyses for the different research objectives include inequality beliefs measured in different waves (and for research objective II an extended belief scale), it does not seem sensible to compare the inequality beliefs across the samples. At this point, I rather aim at providing a general idea of how much applicants to medical school believe that their own admission as well as societal success in general depends on meritocratic and nonmeritocratic factors.

Table 4.3: Average inequality beliefs (W1 beliefs)

	Domain-specific beliefs: University admission depends on my own ...	Societal beliefs: Societal success depends on ...
	mean (sd)	mean (sd)
Meritocratic Beliefs		
Effort	3.17 (1.37)	4.05 (0.94)
Talent	2.80 (1.25)	3.47 (0.91)
Nonmeritocratic Beliefs		
Luck	3.44 (1.28)	-
Family	-	3.36 (1.26)
Money	-	3.15 (1.24)

Note. Scale of beliefs in the importance of different factors for success: 1 – 5. N = 4,138. Sampling weight applied. Source: Medical applicant data, author's calculations.

Applicants believe that success in their own admission as well as societal success in general depends on both meritocratic and nonmeritocratic factors. However, they seem to have stronger domain-specific nonmeritocratic beliefs than meritocratic beliefs about their own admission. On the 5-point scale, the average agreement that their own admission depends on luck is 3.44, while the average agreement that it depends on effort is 3.17, and that it depends on talent only 2.80. By contrast, about societal success in general, applicants seem to have slightly stronger meritocratic beliefs than nonmeritocratic beliefs. The average agreement that societal success depends on effort it 4.05, and the agreement that it depends on talent is 3.47, while the agreement that it depends on family background is 3.36, and the agreement that it depends on money is 3.15. Applicants seem to be slightly more convinced that societal success in general depends on meritocratic factors than their own admission to medical school.

4.6 Representativeness of beliefs of medical applicants for adolescents in Germany

Applicants to medical schools are a specific group of adolescents in Germany in terms of their aspirations, qualifications, and social background. As discussed in Chapter 3.2, educational experiences in early adulthood shape inequality beliefs. Hence, the question arises of how similar the inequality beliefs of applicants to medical school are to the inequality beliefs of other groups of adolescents in Germany.

To address this question, I draw on data from the 11th wave of the 3rd cohort of the German National Educational Panel Study (NEPS Network, 2021)—a panel of adolescents who were surveyed since the 5th grade. In the 11th wave, when respondents were about 19 years old, they were asked about their domain-specific inequality beliefs about factors that determine whether they are successful at their work, and about their societal inequality beliefs about factors that determine societal success in Germany more generally. The sample includes respondents with and without university entrance certificate, the so-called Abitur, and further includes some respondents who state that they aspire to become doctors of human medicine[20]. This design enables comparing inequality beliefs of different groups of adolescents within the NEPS data to gain an idea about possible differences between the inequality beliefs of the sample observed in this dissertation—medical applicants—and other groups of adolescents in Germany.

Table 4.4 displays the weighted[21] average inequality beliefs in the different samples in the NEPS data, and whether the mean difference to the respective

---

20 In the NEPS data, idealistic and realistic occupational aspirations are measured. Conceptionally, those with a realistic aspiration to become doctors (i.e., expectations to hold this occupation in the future) should be closest to the group of medical applicants. However, this group only comprises 57 respondents. Hence, I decided to select the sample on the idealistic aspiration measure: 166 respondents stated that they aspire to become doctors if they had the opportunity to become whatever they desire.

21 For the NEPS analyses, I applied the cross-sectional design weight for wave 11, as recommended by Schnapp (2021). For the medical applicant data analyses, I applied the previously described sampling weight.

reference category (i.e., respondents without Abitur, or respondents who do not aspire to become doctors) is statistically significant. Furthermore, the average inequality beliefs in the medical applicant data are displayed in this table, which will be compared to the beliefs in the NEPS samples at a later point.

Comparing the three NEPS samples, among respondents with Abitur, and among respondents who aspire to become doctors the average belief that one's own success at work depends on effort seems to be stronger than among the whole sample (4.44 / 4.42 vs. 4.34). The belief of respondents with Abitur that one's own success at work depends on talent is stronger than this belief among the whole sample (3.79 vs. 3.71), but this belief seems to be weaker among those who aspire to become doctors than among the whole sample (3.63 vs. 3.71). However, the average belief that one's own success at work depends on luck is also stronger among respondents with Abitur, and those who aspire to become doctors, compared to the whole sample (3.35 / 3.36 vs. 3.14). When asked about societal success in general, the meritocratic beliefs that success in society depends on effort and talent are stronger among respondents with Abitur and among those who aspire to become doctors, compared to the whole sample. The nonmeritocratic beliefs that it depends on family background and money are stronger among respondents with Abitur, compared to the whole sample. However, among the sample of respondents who aspire to become doctors, the belief that success depends on family background is similar to this belief among the whole sample, and the belief that it depends on money is stronger among this group than among the whole sample, but weaker than among respondents with Abitur.

Regarding meritocratic beliefs, these descriptive findings are in line with self-serving beliefs mechanisms discussed in Chapter 3.2: the group of adolescents with an Abitur and the group that aspires to become doctors are likely to have made more positive educational experiences compared to other groups of adolescents. These differences in experiences—experiences that vary by parental education—may lead to a stronger belief that one's own success at work depends on effort and hard work among these samples compared to the overall sample. Regarding nonmeritocratic beliefs, these descriptive findings illustrate that both self-serving mechanisms and system-justification mechanisms may shape inequality beliefs (as also discussed in Chapter 3.2): In line with expectations of system-justification, the group of respondents without Abitur have weaker structural beliefs (i.e., beliefs that success depends on family background and money) than those who do not, but, in line with expectations of self-serving beliefs, respondents who aspire to become doctors—a group with potentially even more positive experiences—seem to have weaker structural beliefs than the sample of all respondents with Abitur. While a higher educational level may be associated with a higher awareness of structural inequality—as suggested by research on beliefs about racial inequality (Wodtke, 2012)—those who are very successful such as applicants to medical school may nevertheless underestimate these structural barriers due to the self-serving beliefs mechanism.

Table 4.4: Average inequality beliefs in different samples of the NEPS data and the medical applicant data

	NEPS data			Medical applicant data	
	Whole sample (N = 2,111)	Respondent with Abitur (N = 1,408)	Respondents who aspire to become doctors (N = 166)	Applicants to medical school (N = 4,138)	
	mean (sd)			mean (sd)	
Inequality Beliefs					
Domainspecific beliefs					
	1 (disagree) – 5 (agree)			1 (totally disagree) – 5 (strongly agree)	
Effort	4.34	4.44 **	4.42	3.17	
	(0.94)	(0.85)	(0.87)	(1.37)	
Talent	3.71	3.79 **	3.63	2.80	
	(0.92)	(0.89)	(0.85)	(1.25)	
Luck	3.14	3.35 **	3.36 **	3.44	
	(1.00)	(1.01)	(0.96)	(1.28)	
Societal beliefs					
	1 (total disagree) – 4 (strongly agree)			1 (total disagree) – 5 (strongly agree)	Scale equivalent (1-4)
Effort	3.40	3.49 **	3.44	4.05	3.24
	(0.67)	(0.57)	(0.59)	(0.94)	
Talent	2.91	2.97 **	2.97	3.47	2.78
	(0.65)	(0.62)	(0.61)	(0.91)	
Family background	2.47	2.61 **	2.46	3.36	2.69
	(0.88)	(0.84)	(0.97)	(1.26)	
Money	2.25	2.36 **	2.32	3.15	2.52
	(0.85)	(0.83)	(0.96)	(1.24)	

Note. For medical applicant data, means of inequality beliefs measured in wave 1 are displayed. Question-wording, reference points, and labels of the scale differ between the NEPS data and the medical applicant data (see Table A4.1). Statistically significant group mean difference to the reference category: Respondents without Abitur / respondents who do not aspire to become doctors: ** p < .01 * p < .05. Sampling weight applied. Source: NEPS data (11th wave of 3rd cohort) and medical applicant data, author's calculations.

While there are certain differences between samples within the NEPS data, it is important to consider their magnitude. Overall, the findings suggest that the differences between the inequality beliefs of adolescents who aspire to become doctors and the inequality beliefs of adolescents in Germany who aspire to other career goals are rather similar. Only the group difference in the belief that one's own success at work depends on luck is statistically significant, and the size of this group difference is only one-fifth of a standard deviation, which is considered a small difference (J. Cohen, 1992).[22]

But how do these inequality beliefs in the NEPS compare to the beliefs in the medical applicant data? The characteristics of the respondents who aspire to become doctors may come closest to the characteristics of the sample I observe for this dissertation (see Footnote 20). Table 4.5 shows how comparable the NEPS samples and the medical applicant sample are in terms of characteristics such as GPA and parental background. For each sample, means and standard deviations are displayed, and it is shown whether the mean difference to the respective reference category (i.e., respondents without Abitur, or respondents who do not aspire to become doctors) are statistically significant.

Respondents who aspire to become doctors in the NEPS data have a mean GPA score of 2.06 (that is better than the GPA of those who do not aspire to become doctors), while respondents in the medical applicant data have a mean GPA score of 1.92. Comparing the three NEPS samples, the share of respondents with two college-educated parents is the largest among those who aspire to become doctors (31 %). The share of respondents with two college-educated parents is statistically significant between those who do and those who do not aspire to become doctors. However, in the medical applicant data, the share of respondents with two college-educated parents is even larger (42 %). While the later NEPS sample may be not as representative due to small case numbers (N = 166), there may also be conceptual differences between the group of those who (idealistically) aspire to become doctors and those who apply to medical school. Indeed, previous research shows that aspirations do not always translate into actual application behavior and that there are social differences in this process (Finger, 2022).

These sample differences need to be considered when comparing adolescents' inequality beliefs. Furthermore, comparing inequality beliefs in the NEPS samples to beliefs in the medical applicant data is challenging since the beliefs are measured similarly but not identically. For domain-specific inequality beliefs, the reference point differs between the sample (success at own work vs. success in admission to medical school); for the more comparable societal inequality beliefs, the scale differs between the survey (4-point scale in NEPS data vs. 5-point scale in the medical applicant data). The translated question wording and scales of inequality belief in the NEPS data and the medical applicant data are displayed in Table A4.2 in the appendix.

---

22 Cohen (1992) suggests the following benchmarks for the magnitude of effects: One-fifth of a standard deviation is a small effect size, one-half of a standard deviation is a medium effect size, and four-fifths of a standard deviation is a large effect size. Standard deviations are calculated by dividing the mean differences between groups (effect) by the standard deviation of the variable (of the whole sample).

Table 4.5: Average GPA and distributions of parental education in different samples of the NEPS data and the medical applicant data

	NEPS data			Medical applicant data
	Whole sample (N = 2,111)	Respondent with Abitur (N = 1,408)	Respondents who aspire to become doctors (N = 166)	Applicants to medical school (N = 4,138)
		mean (sd)		mean (sd)
GPA	2.25 (0.65)	2.25 (0.65)	2.06 ** (0.62)	1.92 (0.61)
		%		%
Parental education				
No college-educated parent	51 %	43 % **	51 % *	29 %
One college-educated parent	28 %	31 % **	17 % *	29 %
Two college-educated parents	21 %	26 % **	31 % *	42 %

Note. Statistically significant group mean difference to the reference category: respondents without Abitur / respondents who do not aspire to become doctors: ** $p < .01$ * $p < .05$. Sampling weight applied. Source: NEPS data (11th wave of 3rd cohort) and medical applicant data, author's calculations.

Despite these limitations, in Table 4.4, I also report the average inequality from the medical applicant data to at least give some suggestions about differences between inequality beliefs measured in the medical applicant data, and the comparison group of respondents who aspire to become doctors in the NEPS data. Following suggestions made by Coleman et al. (1997), for societal inequality beliefs of medical applicants, I display a naive scale equivalent to account for the different scales between the data sets, simply dividing the mean by five and then multiplying it by four.

Comparing the inequality beliefs of the NEPS respondents who aspire to become doctors to the inequality beliefs of respondents in the medical applicant data, the means of domain-specific beliefs are rather different, while the (equivalent) means of societal beliefs are more similar. Group differences in domain-specific beliefs are likely primarily caused by the different reference points. Respondents in the NEPS data think about their own success at work even beyond their aspiration to become doctors, while respondents in the medical applicant data think about their admission to medical school specifically. Meritocratic beliefs that one's own success in admission depends on effort and talent seem to be substantially weaker than meritocratic beliefs that one's own success at work generally depends on these factors. Furthermore, the belief that one's own success in admission depends on luck may be slightly stronger than the belief that one's own success at work depends on luck. These findings suggest that admission to medical school is regarded as less meritocratic than occupational success generally.

Societal inequality beliefs, which have the same reference point in both data sets, seem to be more similar among the NEPS respondents who aspire to become doctors and respondents in the medical applicant data when looking at the naive scale equivalent. However, meritocratic beliefs seem to be weaker, and nonmeritocratic beliefs seem to be stronger in the medical applicant data. However, this may mostly be caused by the different scales, as the choice of scale may influence the response behavior, and scales without a neutral response option may generate more polarized responses (Coleman et al., 1997).

Figure A4.1 the appendix indeed shows that the distribution of the exemplary societal effort variable with a 4-point scale in the NEPS data is more left-skewed than this variable with a 5-point scale in the medical applicant data, and the exemplary societal family background variable with a 4-point scale in the NEPS data is more right-skewed than this variable with a 5-point scale in the medical applicant data.

Overall, while there are slight differences in inequality beliefs between different groups of adolescents, the inequality beliefs of respondents who aspire to become doctors do not largely differ from the inequality beliefs of other groups of adolescents in Germany. In this chapter, I have argued that this can partly be explained by contradictory effects of educational level, self-serving beliefs mechanism, and system-justification mechanism on inequality beliefs. Differences may rather arise between successful and unsuccessful applicants to medicine: a group that obtained the Abitur, a high educational level, and may generally be aware of structural inequality. However, the experiences of success and failure in selective admission to medical school—an important event to achieve their career goal—may crucially shape their inequality beliefs in a self-serving way.

4.7 Overview of methods

In each empirical chapter of this dissertation, I chose the methods that seemed the most appropriate to answer the respective research questions. Table 4.6 provides an overview of these methods and the rationale behind using them. The methodological approaches will be described more precisely in the respective empirical chapters (Chapters 5, 6, and 7).

The first empirical chapter starts by exploring patterns in inequality beliefs using cluster analysis. Subsequently, the chapter examines how parental education and educational experiences shape inequality beliefs. For that purpose, I use cross-sectional and longitudinal methods such as group mean comparison, linear and logistic regression models, and individual fixed-effect models. I conducted subgroup analyses to estimate heterogeneity in the effects of success and failure in admission between applicants from different social backgrounds and between first-time and repeat applicants, and heterogeneity in the effects of being admitted via different quotas. I also conducted analyses including only a sample following the logic of a fuzzy regression discontinuity design (only applicants close to the fuzzy GPA cut-off point of being more or less likely to be admitted).

Table 4.6: Overview of methods

Research objective	Data	Methods	Rationale to use this method
I: Chapter 5	Waves 1 - 2: cross-sectional and longitudinal methods	Cluster analyses	Explore patterns in inequality beliefs
		Group mean comparison (Bonferroni post-hoc tests + t-tests)	Comparison of admission likelihood and inequality beliefs by parental education, and comparison of pre and post beliefs: easy illustration of results as figure possible
		Regression models (linear and logistic)	Estimate associations and mediation mechanisms
		Individual fixed-effects models (with interaction terms)	Causal effect of being admitted vs. being rejected; fixed-effects control for differences in prior inequality beliefs between individuals and for all time-constant unobserved heterogeneity between them
		Fuzzy regression discontinuity design approach	Causal effect of being admitted vs. rejected beyond different development paths of winners and losers
II: Chapter 6	Waves 1 - 3: cross-sectional methods	Factor analyses	Test expectations about distinct types of beliefs and determine which variables to use to measure latent constructs in SEMs
		Structural equation modeling (SEM)	Include observable and latent variables and test for direct and indirect paths between concepts
III: Chapter 7	Waves 1 - 3: longitudinal methods	Survival analysis (discrete-time hazard models)	Estimate conditional likelihood to reapply considering the temporal dimension of events
	Wave 1 - 3: cross-sectional methods	Regression models (linear and logistic)	Estimate associations, and mediation and moderation mechanisms

Note. All methods will be described more extensively in the respective empirical chapters. Weights were applied to analyses conducted with all methodologies, except for SEMs (here only weighted robustness checks). Author's illustration.

The second empirical chapter examines the complex relationship between parental education, inequality beliefs, perceptions of justice, and distributive preferences. It starts by estimating distinct types of inequality using factor analysis. Subsequently, I use the method of structural equation modeling (SEM) to explore direct and indirect paths between these concepts and include observable variables as well as latent variables reflecting these distinct types of inequality beliefs.

The third empirical chapter explores the association between parental education, inequality beliefs, and persistence in goal pursuit after receiving a first rejection. I conducted survival analyses to examine and illustrate social differences in the conditional reapplication likelihood, considering the temporal dimension of events. Subsequently, I conducted (linear and logistic) regression models to examine the effect of parental education and inequality beliefs on different measurements of persistence. As including latent constructs is not required in this analysis, conducting regression models seemed more feasible than conducting SEMs, as this method enables including more control variables also with relatively low case numbers

5 Changes and persistence of inequality beliefs by educational experiences[23]

In this empirical chapter, I test the hypotheses for research objective I, examining how the educational experience of success or failure in admission to medical school shapes inequality beliefs, and how this belief change contributes to differences in inequality beliefs between applicants from different social backgrounds and between winners and losers.

More precisely, the analyses presented aim at answering the following research questions: Do success in admission and inequality beliefs differ by parental education? How do experiences of success and failure shape inequality beliefs? I will further explore whether the effects of success and failure differ depending on applicants' previous experiences.

5.1 Descriptive statistics: Patterns in inequality beliefs

To explore the effect of success or failure in admission I use information on whether applicants were admitted or rejected. As this information was included in wave 2 of the survey, I look at sample I: all wave 1 and 2 participants. Descriptive sample statistics on admission rate, gender, age, GPA, parental education, and share of repeat applicants were already provided in Chapter 4.5 (Table 5.2). Furthermore, I briefly reported applicants' mean inequality beliefs (Table 5.3). Applicants believe that both meritocratic and nonmeritocratic factors are important for their own admission as well as for societal success in general. On average, domain-specific meritocratic beliefs about their own admission were slightly weaker than domain-specific nonmeritocratic beliefs. By contrast, their societal meritocratic beliefs about societal success in general were slightly stronger than their societal nonmeritocratic beliefs.

Inequality belief patterns

As discussed in Chapter 3.2, previous research suggests that meritocratic and nonmeritocratic beliefs are not mutually exclusive and that most people believe that an interplay of meritocratic and nonmeritocratic factors determines success (Kreidl, 2000). However, there may be different patterns in applicants'

---

23 Parts of this chapter, particularly the results presented in Chapter 5.4 and Chapter 5.5 have been published in a co-authored article with Claudia Finger (Wetter & Finger, 2023).

inequality beliefs. To explore these belief patterns, I conducted cluster analyses using Ward's linkage approach to identify the main clusters in beliefs.

Figure 5.1 displays dendrograms based on these cluster analyses illustrating how similar the top 10 clusters of domain-specific belief patterns as well as of societal belief patterns are to each other. For both domain-specific and societal beliefs, the dendrograms suggest that individuals can be grouped into three main clusters concerning their beliefs. In the dendrogram on the left, the first cluster comprises groups 1, 2, and 3, the second cluster comprises groups 4 and 5, and the third cluster comprises groups 6 to 10. In the dendrogram on the right, the first cluster comprises groups 1 and 2, the second cluster comprises groups 3 to 7, and the third cluster comprises groups 8, 9, and 10.

Figure 5.1: Dendrograms of belief patterns

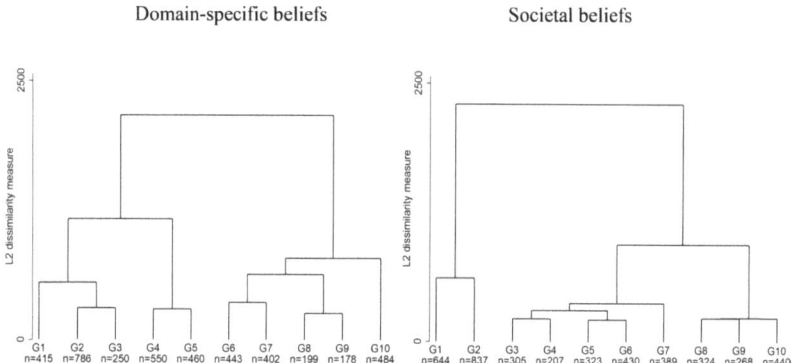

Note. Cluster calculated using Ward's linkage approach. L2 = squared Euclidean distance. Display limited to the top 10 branches. N = 4,128. Source: Medical applicant data, author's calculations.

How can the three main clusters of inequality belief patterns be described? Table 5.1 shows the weighted means of the inequality beliefs in wave 1 for each cluster. For domain-specific beliefs, the belief pattern in cluster 1 can be described as mixed beliefs. In this cluster, applicants believe that their own admission depends similarly on effort (3.46) and talent (3.74), but most strongly on luck (4.21). Cluster 2 can be described as applicants with strong meritocratic beliefs. They believe that their admission primarily depends on their own effort (4.27) and talent (3.74), and that luck plays only a minor role in their own admission (2.17). By contrast, cluster 3 can be described as applicants with weak meritocratic beliefs, whereby they believe that luck plays the most important role in their own admission (3.44), and they rather disagree that it depends on their own effort (2.41) and especially their own talent (1.62).

Table 5.1: Average beliefs in domain-specific belief cluster and societal belief cluster

	Cluster 1: Mixed belief pattern	Cluster 2: Meritocratic belief pattern	Cluster 3: Nonmeritocratic belief pattern
Domain-specific belief pattern			
N	1,443	1,001	1,694
Domain-specific beliefs:		mean (sd)	
Effort	3.46	4.27	2.41
	(1.16)	(0.82)	(1.28)
Talent	3.74	3.74	1.62
	(0.78)	(0.66)	(0.85)
Luck	4.21	2.17	3.44
	(0.74)	(0.74)	(1.32)
GPA	1.84	1.70	2.08
(1.0 – 4.0)	(0.60)	(0.59)	(0.59)
Societal belief pattern			
N	1,650	1,024	1,464
Societal beliefs:		mean (sd)	
Effort	4.18	4.59	3.55
	(0.81)	(0.53)	(1.03)
Talent	3.45	3.57	3.42
	(0.86)	(0.90)	(0.96)
Family background	3.27	1.74	4.56
	(0.72)	(0.75)	(0.52)
Money	2.90	1.79	4.35
	(0.74)	(0.75)	(0.68)
GPA (1.0 – 4.0)	1.85	1.98	1.92
	(0.59)	(0.62)	(0.63)

Note. Cluster calculated using Ward's linkage approach. Sampling weight applied. Source: Medical applicant data, author's calculations.

Similar clusters of belief patterns can be found for applicants' societal beliefs. Therefore, the clusters of societal belief patterns in Table 5.1 are ordered according to the domain-specific belief patterns.[24] In the cluster of applicants with the mixed belief pattern, the belief that societal success depends on effort is the strongest belief (4.18) and the belief that it depends on money is the weakest (2.90). This suggests that the societal mixed belief pattern is different from the domain-specific mixed belief pattern, where the belief that one's own admission depends on effort is the weakest. Applicants with the societal meri-

---

24 Originally, like clusters are illustrated in Table 5.1, cluster 1 represented the nonmeritocratic belief pattern, cluster 2 represented the mixed belief pattern, and cluster 3 represented the meritocratic belief pattern.

tocratic belief pattern strongly believe that societal success depends on effort (4.59) and talent (3.57), and believe that structural factors such as family background (1.74) and money (1.79) play only a minor role in success. Applicants with the societal nonmeritocratic belief pattern believe that societal success depends more on nonmeritocratic factors such as family background (4.56) and money (4.35) than on meritocratic factors such as effort (3.55) and talent (3.42).

The results from this cluster analysis indeed confirm, in line with theoretical expectations, that meritocratic and nonmeritocratic beliefs are not mutually exclusive, but that there are certain patterns in beliefs that vary across individuals. Regarding domain-specific beliefs about one's own admission, the nonmeritocratic belief pattern is the most common one ($N = 1,694$) and the meritocratic belief pattern is the least common one ($N = 1,001$) in the medical applicant sample. Regarding societal beliefs about success in society in general, the mixed belief pattern is the most common one ($N = 1,650$) and the meritocratic belief pattern is the least common one ($N = 1,024$). However, it is important to note that applicants in the societal mixed belief pattern lean more towards believing that meritocratic factors are important for societal success than towards believing that structural factors are important for it, and applicants in the domain-specific belief pattern lean more towards believing that luck is important for their own admission than believing that meritocratic factors are important for it.

The description of the belief pattern also reveals that in line with my theoretical expectations based on attributional theory (Weiner, 1985), the meritocratic belief in the importance of effort and talent are two distinct concepts. Even within the clusters, the means of these beliefs substantially differ. Correlations between the inequality beliefs confirm that effort and talent beliefs are distinct types of meritocratic beliefs (see Table A5.1 in the appendix). The domain-specific belief that admission depends on one's own effort is weakly to moderately correlated with the belief that it depends on talent (Pearson's correlation = .51, $p < .01$), and the societal belief that success in general depends on effort is only weakly correlated with the belief that it depends on talent (Pearson's correlation = .33, $p < .01$).

As a brief exploration, I further examined whether applicants' GPA varies between the cluster of belief patterns. The results from this exploration suggest that, on average, applicants with the meritocratic belief pattern have, the best GPA score (1.70), applicants with the nonmeritocratic belief pattern have the worst GPA score (2.08), and applicants with the mixed belief pattern fall in the middle of these groups in terms of their GPA (1.84). These differences in group means are statistically significant ($p < .01$). The differences in GPA between applicants with different societal belief patterns are less substantial. The average GPA of applicants with the meritocratic belief pattern (1.92) is slightly better than the GPA of applicants with the nonmeritocratic belief pattern

(1.98), but this difference slightly misses the common threshold of statistical significance (p = 0.05). Regarding societal beliefs, applicants with the mixed belief pattern have the best GPA score (1.85). This difference in average GPA is statistically different from applicants with the two other belief patterns (p < .01).

These findings provide first insights into the relationship between inequality beliefs and experiences of success and failure. Domain-specific belief patterns about one's own admission seem to be more strongly associated with applicants' own experiences of success and failure than societal belief patterns. In this chapter, I will examine in further depth how parental education and experiences of success and failure shape domain-specific and societal inequality beliefs.

5.2 Methodological approach

In this chapter, a mix of bivariate methods, cross-sectional multivariate methods, and longitudinal methods is used to answer my research questions regarding how parental education and the experience of success and failure in admission to medical school shape applicants' inequality beliefs.

First, group means in admission rates and inequality beliefs between applicants with no, one, and two college-educated parents are compared. Whether these group differences are statistically significant is determined by Bonferroni post-hoc tests. Beyond these group mean comparisons, linear regression models were used to confirm that the association between parental education with admission rate and inequality beliefs is not confounded by other variables, and to examine possible mediation mechanisms. The mediation of the effect of parental education on inequality beliefs is illustrated by displaying the regression results as coefficient plots. To account for the ordinal scale of inequality beliefs, I also conducted ordered logistic regression models with inequality beliefs as the dependent variable as a robustness check.

To examine how the experience of success and failure in admission shapes applicants' inequality beliefs, I make use of the longitudinal nature of the data. Domain-specific inequality beliefs about one's own admission as well as societal beliefs about success in society in general were measured in wave 1 (August 2018) before applicants learned about their admission decision and in wave 2 (November 2018) immediately after they were either admitted or rejected. As a first step of the analysis, I compare average inequality beliefs before and after the admission decision, separately for admitted and rejected applicants. These average beliefs pre and post the admission decision are displayed in a bar graph, while also showing the average change in beliefs following admission and rejection.

Subsequently, I conducted individual linear fixed-effects models with the interaction term between change and admitted vs. rejected and inequality beliefs as dependent variables. These individual fixed-effects models control for differences in prior inequality beliefs between individuals and for all time-constant unobserved heterogeneity between them and allowed me to examine whether the belief change among admitted applicants differs significantly from the belief change among rejected applicants. As a robustness check to account for the ordinal scale, I also conducted ordered logit fixed-effects models. Even though the individual fixed-effects models control for all time-constant heterogeneity between individuals, they cannot rule out the possibility that heterogeneity in belief trends between the group of to-be-admitted and to-be-rejected applicants explain the differences in belief changes rather than the actual event of success or failure in admission. Thus, I also compared pre and post group means in inequality beliefs and conducted fixed-effects models for a smaller sample following the logic of a fuzzy regression discontinuity design (RDD). These analyses only included applicants close to the fuzzy RDD cut-off-point with the highest drop in admission likelihood: those with a GPA score between 1.3 and 1.4. As a brief excursus, I also examined whether changes in beliefs after admission varied depending on the quota through which applicants were admitted.

Finally, in order to examine whether the effect of admission and rejection varies by previous long-term experiences of social upbringing and short-term domain-specific experiences of failure in admission to medical school, subgroup analyses were conducted separately for applicants with no, one, and two college-educated parents and separately for first-time and repeat applicants. Interaction terms between change and social background as well as repeated application were added to test whether differences in changes after admission and rejection between groups were statistically significant

5.3 Social differences in inequality beliefs are shaped by educational experiences

In Chapters 3.1 and 3.2, I discussed my expectations that applicants from privileged backgrounds are more likely to be admitted to medical school than their less privileged peers (*HI.1*) and that those applicants hold stronger meritocratic and weaker nonmeritocratic beliefs than their less privileged peers (*HI.2*). I argued that those social differences in inequality beliefs arise due transmission of parental beliefs, differences in the heterogeneity of the social environment in which they grow up, and differences in experiences of success and failure in education.

To test the first expectation of differences in admission chances by applicants' social background (*HI.1*), I compare the weighted admission rates by parental education (Table 5.2). I chose this bivariate approach to test hypothesis *HI.1*, as I am interested in the total difference in admission chances by parental education, including differences in admission chances resulting from performance differences (primary effects) such as social differences in high school GPA.

Table 5.2: Weighted admission rates and GPA by parental education

Parental education	No college-educated parent (N = 1,150)	One college-educated parent (N = 1,203)	Two college-educated parents (N = 1,785)
Admission rate	22 %	24 %	28 % **
GPA	2.05 (0.63)	1.92 ** (0.59)	1.82 ** (0.59)

Note. Statistically significant differences to the reference category (no college-educated parent): ** p < .01. Sampling weight applied. Source: Medical applicant data, author's calculations.

Table 5.2 shows that the admission rate among applicants with no college-educated parent is the lowest (22 %), the admission rate among applicants with one college-educated parent is slightly higher (24 %), and the admission rate among applicants with two college-educated parents is the highest (28 %).[25] The results of Bonferroni post-hoc tests showed that the difference in admission rate between applicants with two college-educated parents and those with no college-educated parent (+ 6 percentage points) is statistically significant (p < .01).[26] The difference in admission rate between applicants with one and no college-educated parent is not statistically significant. However, overall these findings support *HI.1* that applicants from privileged backgrounds are more likely to be admitted than their less privileged peers.

Furthermore, Table 5.2 shows that applicants with two college-educated parents have a substantially better GPA score than applicants with no college-educated parent (0.23 on the grade scale ranging from the best score of 1.0 to the worst score of 4.0). As an additional analysis, to ensure that the effect of parental education on admission chances is not driven by possible differences in age and gender, I additionally conducted logistic regression models including these control variables (see Table A5.2 in the appendix). Furthermore, I

---

25 As expected, the unweighted admission rate in the sample is substantially higher (43 %) than when applying the sampling weight, but similar differences in admission rates by parental admission can be observed. Applying a panel weight instead of the sampling weight neither substantially changes the level of the admission rate nor social differences in admission likelihood (see Table A5.3 in the appendix).
26 The difference in admission rate is relatively small in size, amounting to one-seventh of a standard deviation.

ran models including applicants' GPAs. As expected, controlling for age and gender did not influence the effect of parental education on admission chances, while including GPA in the model substantially reduced the effect of having two college-educated parents (in comparison to having none) by more than half. Primary effects are the main mechanism behind unequal admission chances between applicants from different backgrounds.[27]

To test the second expectation of differences in inequality beliefs by social background, I first compared the weighted means of the inequality beliefs by parental education, before I conducted step-wise regression models to examine the mechanism of different educational experiences behind the effect of parental education on inequality beliefs.

The group mean comparison presented in Table 5.3 suggests that those from privileged backgrounds believe more strongly that their own admission depends on effort than their less privileged peers. Furthermore, applicants from privileged backgrounds seem to hold stronger meritocratic beliefs about society generally as well as weaker nonmeritocratic beliefs: Applicants with one or two college-educated parents believe more strongly that societal success depends on effort than those with no college-educated parent, applicants with two college-educated parents believe less strongly that societal success depends on family background than those with no college-educated parent, and applicants with one or two college-educated parents believe less strongly that societal success depends on money than those with no college-educated parent. All of these social differences in inequality beliefs are relatively small in size, ranging from one-eighth to one-fourth of a standard deviation. The domain-specific beliefs that one's own admission depends on talent or luck do not differ by parental education, nor does the belief that societal success depends on talent.[28]

---

27 As less than half of all respondents participated in the voluntary admission tests, I did not include admission test scores as a mediator in the model. Findings by Finger et al. (2024) showed that social differences in admission likelihood are entirely driven by performance differences in GPA and test scores, suggesting that the remaining effect of parental education in Table A5.2 is caused by differences in test scores.
28 Applying different weighting strategies (e.g., no weights or applying a panel weight) does not change the findings of social differences in beliefs substantially (see Table A5.4 in the Appendix).

Table 5.3: Average inequality beliefs by parental education (W1 beliefs)

	Domain-specific beliefs: University admission depends on my own ...			Societal beliefs: Societal success depends on ...		
	No college-educated parent (N = 1,150)	One college-educated parent (N = 1,203)	Two college-educated parents (N = 1,785)	No college-educated parent (N = 1,150)	One college-educated parent (N = 1,203)	Two college-educated parents (N = 1,785)
	mean (sd)			mean (sd)		
Meritocratic Beliefs						
Effort	3.09 (1.40)	3.12 (1.33)	3.26** (1.33)	3.97 (0.97)	4.10** (0.92)	4.08** (0.91)
Talent	2.76 (1.26)	2.73 (1.25)	2.86 (1.23)	3.42 (0.90)	3.48 (0.92)	3.49 (0.90)
Non-meritocratic Beliefs						
Luck	3.43 (1.31)	3.47 (1.28)	3.42 (1.24)	-	-	-
Family	-	-	-	3.46 (1.34)	3.34 (1.24)	3.29** (1.21)
Money	-	-	-	3.35 (1.32)	3.15** (1.22)	3.02** (1.18)

Note. Scale of inequality beliefs: 1 – 5. Sampling weight applied. Mean substantially different from the mean of applicants with no college-educated parent: ** $p < .01$ * $p < .05$. Source: Medical applicant data, author's calculations.

Overall, *HI.2*—claiming that applicants from privileged backgrounds have stronger meritocratic and weaker nonmeritocratic beliefs than those from less privileged backgrounds—can be supported concerning the meritocratic belief in the importance of effort for success and the nonmeritocratic beliefs in the importance of family background and money for success. However, *HI.2* cannot be supported concerning the meritocratic belief in the importance of talent and the nonmeritocratic belief in the importance of luck for success.

As discussed earlier, one mechanism behind group differences in inequality beliefs by parental education may be differences in educational experiences. Following theories on transgenerational status transmission (Bourdieu & Passeron, 1990), applicants with two college-educated parents may have an advantage in adapting to the school setting in comparison to those from less privileged backgrounds, leading to more positive experiences in school as well as better school grades, which increases their admission chances and influences their inequality beliefs in a self-serving way (see Chapter 3.1 and 3.2).

To explore this mechanism, I calculate linear regression models[29] with inequality beliefs as dependent variables and parental education as the independent variable. In all models, gender is included as a control variable. Age is not included, as in the sample of medical applicants, it is related to educational experiences. Among older applicants, many may have experienced (multiple) failures in admission. However, age is only an unsharp proxy for these experiences, and hence I decided to only include more direct measures of educational experiences, without controlling away the effects of parental education on beliefs by including age.

Using a step-by-step approach, in the other models, I added further mediating variables as a proxy for experiences that may differ by parental education. Thus, the base model only includes parental education and gender, the second model additionally includes a dummy variable of whether applicants experienced rejection in admission in the past (repeat vs. first-time applicants), and the third model additionally includes applicants' GPA.[30] While the dummy variable repeat vs. first-time applicants directly represents an educational experience, GPA can be seen as a proxy for educational experiences in high school. I conducted the models with wave 1 beliefs as well as with wave 2 beliefs to explore whether the experiences of receiving the admission outcome (admission or rejection)—an event unequally distributed between the groups as previously shown—increases social differences in inequality beliefs.

Figure 5.2 displays the coefficients of parental education in these three models for each of the domain-specific inequality beliefs about one's own admission: the base model, the model controlled for repeat application, and the model controlled for repeat application as well as GPA. In the base model, the only statistically significant effect is the effect of having two college-educated parents (in comparison to none) on the belief that own admission depends on effort (.16). Effects on the beliefs that it depends on talent or luck are not significant. As already suggested by the descriptive statistics displayed in Table 5.3, applicants with two college-educated parents believe more strongly that their admission depends on effort compared with their less privileged peers already prior to receiving their admission decision.

---

29 To account for the ordinal scale of the belief variables, as a robustness check, I conducted ordered logistic regression models Figure A5.1 and Figure A5.2 in the Appendix). The findings do not substantially differ from findings using the linear approach, confirming the arguments made in Chapter 4.2 that items with numerical response formats of at least five categories may be treated as continuous variables.
30 Indeed, only 48 % of applicants with two college-educated parents experienced prior rejections in admission in comparison to 55 % of applicants with no college-educated parent, and on average applicants with two college-educated parents had better school grades than their less privileged peers (Mean GPA of 0 coll.-ed. parent = 2.05; Mean GPA of 1 coll.-ed. parent 1 = 1.92; Mean GPA of 2 coll.-ed. parent = 1.82).

Figure 5.2: Effects of parental education on domain-specific inequality beliefs

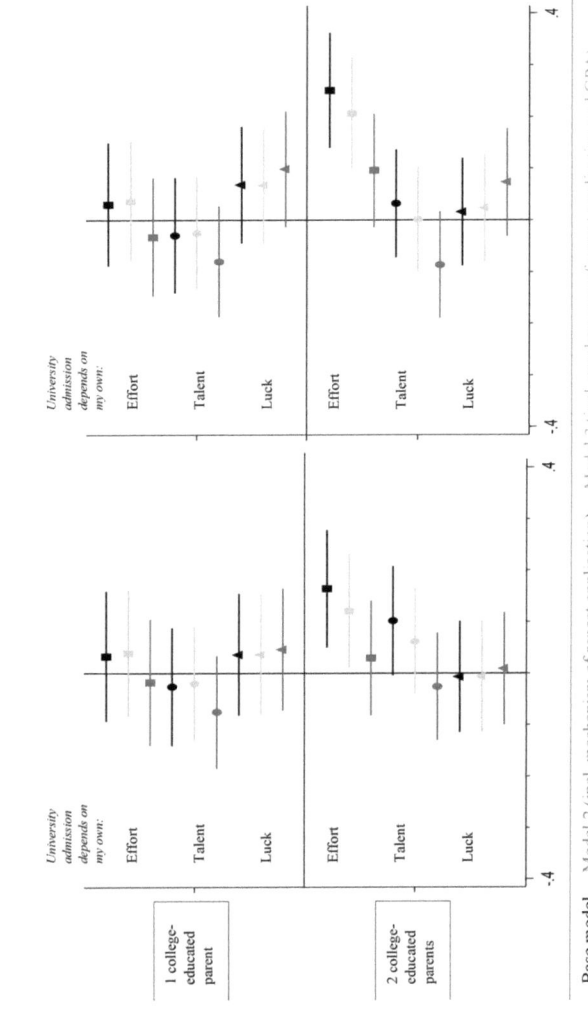

Note. Linear regression model results. Reference for 1 / 2 college-educated parents: no college-educated parent. N = 4,138. Sampling weight applied. Source: Medical applicant data, author's calculations.

Comparing the left to the right panel of Figure 5.2, it becomes visible that the difference in the effort belief by parental education increases from wave 1 to wave 2 (base model: .16 to .25), from the time before applicants learned about the admission outcome to the time after.

Including the mediators (previous experience of rejection and GPA) reduces the effect of parental education substantially. Differences in the effort belief conducted in wave 1 by parental education seem to be fully mediated by social differences in previous experiences of rejection and GPA (model 3), while small social differences in the effort belief conducted in wave 2 seem to remain beyond these previous experiences, even though they slightly miss the common threshold of statistical significance (model 3: .10, p = .09). Overall, these findings suggest that the experiences of learning about the admission outcome (i.e., being admitted or rejected) may increase differences in the belief that own admission depends on effort by parental education. This widened gap in beliefs could be driven by the higher share of applicants with two college-educated parents being admitted (and the discussed self-serving effect of being admitted vs. being rejected) or by heterogenous effects of admission and rejection on inequality beliefs by parental education. Self-serving belief effects after success and failure (*HI.3*) and heterogeneity in these beliefs by parental background (*HI.4a/b*) will be tested in the next chapters (Chapters 5.4 and 5.5).

Figure 5.3 displays the results from the regression models with societal beliefs as dependent variables. Similar to the domain-specific belief that own admission depends on effort, the belief that societal success depends on effort differs by parental education. Applicants with one or two college-educated parents believe more strongly that societal success depends on effort than those with no college-educated parent (base model: .11)—an effect that is partly mediated by differences in experiences (i.e., prior experiences of rejection in admission and GPA). However, a slight effect of having two college-educated parents on this belief seems to remain when controlling for these experiences, even though this effect slightly misses the common threshold of statistical significance (model 3: .07, p = .08).

Comparing the right to the left panel of Figure 5.3, social differences in the societal effort belief do not seem to substantially differ between waves 1 and 2, suggesting that learning about the admission outcome (i.e., being admitted or rejected) does not increase social differences in this belief.

Figure 5.3: Effects of parental education on societal inequality beliefs

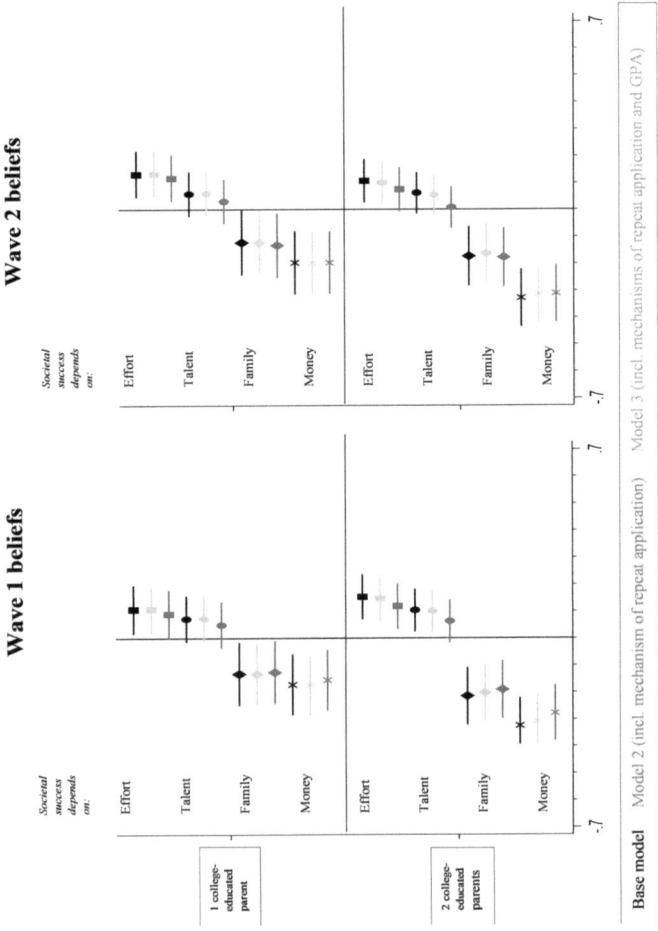

Note. Linear regression model results. Reference for 1 / 2 college-educated parents: no college-educated parent. N = 4,138. Sampling weight applied. Source: Medical applicant data, author's calculations.

Furthermore, Figure 5.3 shows social differences in structural beliefs—beliefs that societal success depends on family background and money. Applicants with one and two college-educated parents believe less strongly in the importance of family background than those with no college-educated parent (base model: -.12 / -.17), and applicants with one and two college-educated parents believe less strongly in the importance of money than those with no college-educated parent (base model: -.20 / -.32). These effects of parental education on structural beliefs do not become substantially smaller when controlling for differences in experiences (model 3). Furthermore, social differences in structural beliefs do not substantially differ between wave 1 to wave 2.

Overall, the findings presented in this chapter partly support *HI.2* that applicants from privileged backgrounds have stronger meritocratic and weaker nonmeritocratic beliefs than those from less privileged backgrounds, by showing that having two college-educated parents is associated with stronger beliefs that the own admission as well as societal success generally depends on effort and with weaker beliefs that societal success depends on family background and money. Furthermore, the findings suggest that social differences in the domain-specific belief that one's own admission depends on effort can be explained by differences in educational experiences such as previous experiences of failure in admission to medical school and experiences of success and failure in high school (proxied as GPA). The (new) experiences of success or failure in admission further widen the social gap in this belief. On the other hand, differences in societal beliefs cannot substantially be explained by these differences in experiences. These findings suggest that these differences rather result from other mechanisms related to socialization such as transmission of parental beliefs or differences in the heterogeneity of the social environment in which adolescents grow up.

5.4 Influence of experiences of success and failure on inequality beliefs

In Chapter 3.2, I argued that, in the case of application to medical school, experiences of success and failure shape applicants' inequality beliefs in a self-serving way. Accordingly, success strengthens meritocratic beliefs and weakens nonmeritocratic beliefs, whereas failure weakens meritocratic beliefs and strengthens nonmeritocratic beliefs (*HI.3*).

Admission to medical school is not a random event but depends on applicants' qualifications. Hence, applicants who were admitted and those who were rejected differ in certain characteristics (see Table 5.4). Unsurprisingly, the most pronounced is the difference in GPA between admitted and rejected applicants (1.47 among admitted applicants vs. 2.07 among rejected applicants).

In line with the expectation that performance in school, and rewarded school grades connected to it, are influenced by social background (Bourdieu and Passeron 1977). Among applicants who were admitted and, on average, have a better GPA, the share of applicants with two college-educated parents is higher than among those who were rejected (47 % vs. 40 %).

Already prior to the admission decision, the groups of to-be-admitted and to-be-rejected applicants likely differ in their (partly socialization-based) experiences in high school, which is reflected in the group differences in GPA. These difference in prior experiences may shape their inequality beliefs, leading to belief differences between to-be-admitted and to-be-rejected applicants.

Table 5.4: Descriptive statistics of admitted and rejected applicants

	Admitted applicants % or mean (sd)	Rejected applicants % or mean (sd)	Group differences (admitted/rejected)
N	1,764	2,374	
Woman	67 %	66 %	1 %
Age	21.19	20.90	0.29 **
	(3.79)	(2.90)	
GPA (1.0–4.0)	1.47	2.07	-0.60 **
	(0.58)	(0.55)	
Parental education			
No college-educated parent	26 %	31 %	-5 % **
One college-educated parent	28 %	29 %	-1 % **
Two college-educated parents	47 %	40 %	7 % **
Repeat applicant (vs. first-time applicant)	45 %	55 %	-10 % **
Admission through			
GPA quota	13 %	-	-
Waiting-period quota	17 %	-	-
University-specific quota	66 %	-	-
Other quotasa	5 %	-	-

Note. a 3 % wait-listed applicants, 1 % lottery, 1 % hardship cases. ** $p < .01$. Sampling weight applied (absolute numbers (N) not weighted. Source: Medical applicant data, author's calculations.

Indeed, Figure 5.4 suggests that average inequality beliefs differ already prior to the admission decision between the groups of admitted and rejected applicants. Applicants who will be admitted believe more strongly that their own admission depends on effort (.56) and talent (.44) than those who will be rejected, and less strongly that it depends on luck (-.22). Group differences in societal beliefs are less pronounced but still substantial, whereby applicants who will be admitted believe more strongly that societal success depends on effort (.13) and talent (.15) than those who will be rejected, and less strongly that it depends on money (-.13). The belief that societal success depends on family background does not substantially differ between to be admitted and to be rejected applicants. However, overall the findings suggest that to-be-admitted applicants have stronger meritocratic and weaker nonmeritocratic beliefs than to-be-rejected applicants, particularly in terms of their domain-specific beliefs about their own admission.

Figure 5.4: Average inequality beliefs pre and post admission decision and belief changes

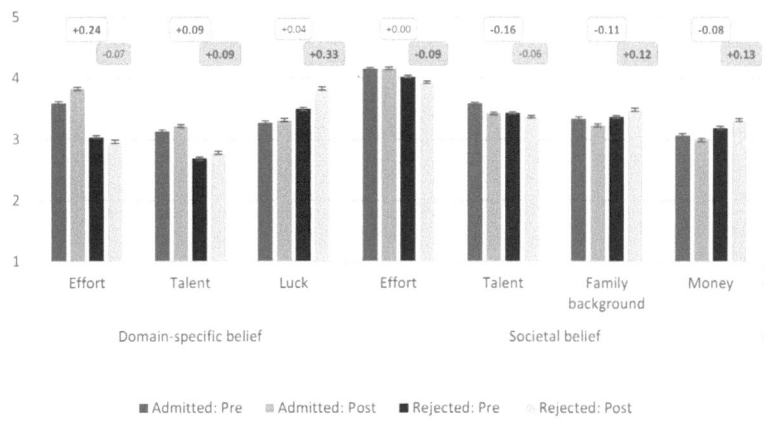

Note. Belief changes after admission displayed in white boxes; changes after rejection displayed in grey boxed. Significant changes displayed in bold. $N = 1,764$ admitted applicants; 2,374 rejected applicants. Sampling weight applied. Source: Medical applicant data, author's calculations.

These differences in prior beliefs amplify through the admission decision. Comparing pre and post beliefs suggests that individual experiences indeed change prior inequality beliefs. Regarding domain-specific beliefs, being successful strengthens the meritocratic belief in the importance of one's own effort for admission by .24 points on a 5-point scale. The nonmeritocratic luck belief is strengthened by experiencing failure (.33) but is not affected by experiencing success. However, there is only a slight decrease in effort belief after failure (-.07) and even a very slight increase in luck belief (.04) after success. Finally, the belief in the importance of talent for one's own admission increases similarly after both admission and rejection (.09).

To test whether the effects of admission and rejection differed significantly from each other, individual fixed-effects models with interaction terms (belief change*admission/rejection) were conducted. The first column of Table 5.5

replicates the belief change for rejected applicants displayed in Figure 5.4. For instance, domain-specific effort belief slightly reduces by .07 points for rejected candidates. The second row shows the difference in this change for admitted versus rejected applicants. The change in effort belief following admission (.24, see Figure 5.4) significantly differs by .31 points from the change following rejection. Furthermore, the increase in luck belief following rejection (.33) is statistically different (-.29, $p < .01$) from its stability following admission (.04, Figure 5.4).

Table 5.5: Linear fixed-effects models with interaction term: Belief change*admission

	Belief change of rejected applicants (reference group)	Belief change*admission (ref. rejection)
	b (se)	
Domain-specific beliefs:		
University admission depends on my own ...		
Effort	-.07 * (.03)	.31 ** (.05)
Talent	.09 ** (.03)	-.00 (.04)
Luck	.33 ** (.03)	-.29 ** (.04)
Societal beliefs:		
Societal success depends on ...		
Effort	-.09 ** (.02)	.09 ** (.03)
Talent	-.06 ** (.02)	-.10 ** (.03)
Family	.12 ** (.03)	-.23 ** (.04)
Money	.13 ** (.03)	-.21 ** (.04)

Note. ** $p < .01$ * $p < .05$. N = 4,138. Sampling weight applied. Source: Medical applicant data, author's calculations.

Regarding changes in societal inequality beliefs, individual experiences affect the belief in nonmeritocratic factors as expected, with success slightly weakening their perceived importance (-.11 and -.08, respectively) and failure strengthening it (.12 and .13, respectively). The pattern looks less clear regarding meritocratic factors. Whereas failure weakens effort beliefs as expected (-.09), success is not related to it. One explanation for admittance's null effect on effort beliefs might be their fairly high baseline level of this belief, which could lead to a ceiling effect. Finally, the belief in how important talent is for societal success decreases after admission (-.16) as well as after rejection (-.06) suggesting again that this belief might be affected differently than predicted by self-serving beliefs theory. Diverging findings for talent beliefs will be further discussed in the summary at the end of this chapter. Fixed-effects models (Table 5.5), show that the effects of admission and rejection are statistically different from each other for all societal beliefs.

Overall, *H1.3* that success strengthens meritocratic beliefs and weakens nonmeritocratic beliefs, whereas failure weakens meritocratic beliefs and strengthens nonmeritocratic beliefs is partly supported. Success increases the domain-specific effort belief, and failure increases the domain-specific luck belief. Furthermore, success reduces nonmeritocratic societal beliefs, and failure both reduces meritocratic (effort-based) and increases nonmeritocratic beliefs. However, success only increases the domain-specific effort belief but does not extend to societal effort beliefs. As expected, changes in societal inequality beliefs are weaker than those for domain-specific beliefs. After receiving the admission outcome, total differences in domain-specific beliefs between winners and losers are medium in size, and total differences in societal beliefs are small in size.

As robustness checks, I additionally conducted the linear fixed-effects models with different weighting strategies (see Chapter 4.4) such as no weights and applying a panel weight (Table A5.5 in the appendix), and conducted ordered logit fixed-effects models[31] (Table A5.6 in the appendix) to consider the 5-point-likert scale of the dependent variables. The main results do not substantially change, supporting the robustness of the findings.[32]

Besides (partly) supporting *HI.3*, these findings suggest diverging paths for the successful and the unsuccessful group: the 'winners' and 'losers.' Differences that are already observable prior to admission amplify after the admissions decision is received.

5.4.1 Causal effect of being admitted or rejected?

As previously described, already prior to the admission decision, the differences in inequality beliefs between those who will be admitted and those who will be rejected are quite substantial—likely due to differences in GPA that are tied to experiences (of success or failure) adolescents make in high school—experiences that shape inequality beliefs. Admission to medical school is a further experience of success and failure which is crucial for applicants and their future social positioning. Does this experience change inequality beliefs beyond the preexisting paths of winners and losers? Using a fuzzy regression discontinuity design (RDD) allows to examine whether admission itself has a causal effect on inequality beliefs that is not solely driven by different paths.

Due to the quota system for admission to medical school in Germany, no clearly definable cut-off point decides whether people will be admitted or re-

---

31 Fixed-effects ordered logit models, were conducted using the Stata package 'feologit,' written by Baetschmann et al. (2020). Margins resulting from the models were estimated, as they are comparable to the linear fixed-effects coefficients.
32 As applying different weighting strategies and using ordinal approaches of analyses did not change the main results for testing *HI.1, HI.2,* and *HI.3,* suggesting that the sampling weighting strategy and linear approach are appropriate, from now onwards no further robustness checks regarding these issues will be displayed.

jected, although GPA is still a rather good predictor of admission likelihood. Therefore, a standard RDD is not feasible but a fuzzy RDD can be applied (Angrist & Pischke, 2015).

Figure 5.5: Fuzzy cut-off point of drop in admission likelihood

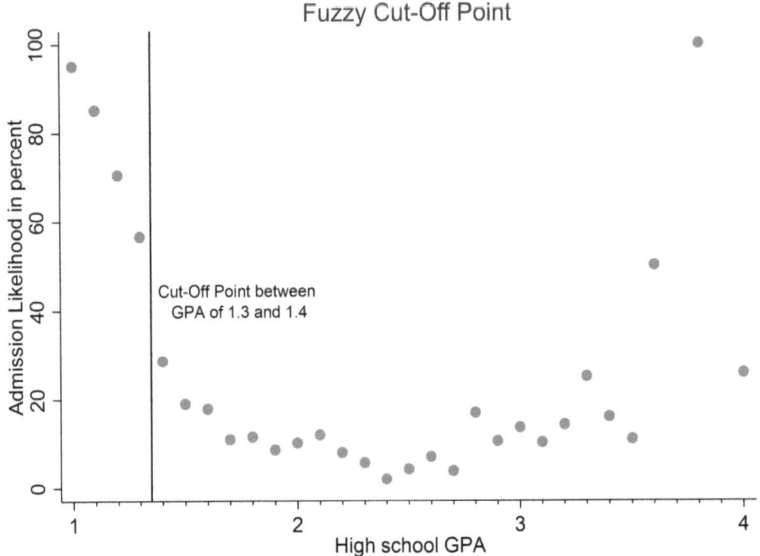

Note. Admission likelihood calculated as weighted group means. N = 4,138. Source: Medical applicant data, author's calculations.

Looking at weighted group means of admission rates by GPA (Figure 5.5), the fuzzy cut-off point is identified to be between a GPA of 1.3 and 1.4 where admission likelihood drops most substantially. Hence, the same steps of analysis conducted for the whole sample of applicants were conducted for those close to this cut-off point, who are rather similar in their GPA score and related experiences but differ in their admission likelihood: applicants with a GPA of 1.3 and 1.4.

Figure 5.6: Average inequality beliefs pre and post admission decision and belief changes for applicants close to the fuzzy admission likelihood cut-off: GPA 1.3 – 1.4

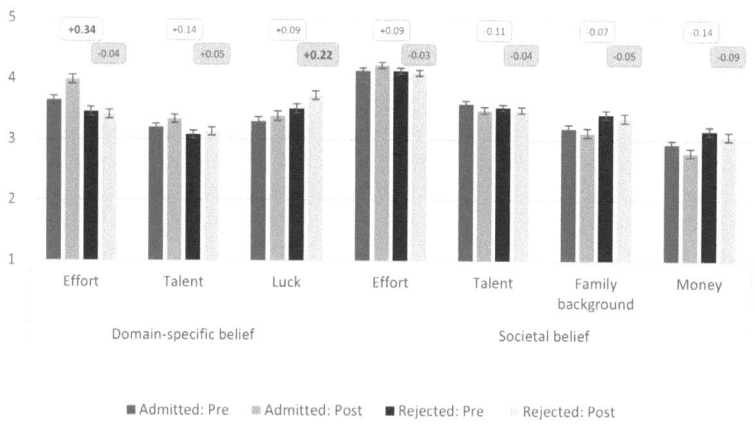

Note. Belief changes after admission displayed in white boxes; changes after rejection displayed in grey boxed. Significant changes displayed in bold. N = 329 admitted applicants; 279 rejected applicants. Sampling weight applied. Source: Medical applicant data, author's calculations.

In Figure 5.6, applicants' inequality beliefs before and after receiving the admission decision, as well as belief changes are displayed for this subgroup. As expected, differences in meritocratic beliefs about admission between to be admitted and to be rejected applicants prior to the admission decision are substantially smaller in the group of applicants with a 1.3-1.4 GPA than in the whole sample.[33] Applicants who will be admitted believe more strongly that their own admission depends on effort (.20) and talent (.12) than those who will be rejected, and less strongly that it depends on luck (-.21). However, these differences are about half the size of prior belief differences in the whole sample. The goal of the fuzzy RDD to make the admitted and rejected group more comparable seems to be achieved.

However, even in this more homogenous group, receiving an admission increases the belief that admission depends on effort substantially (.34), and this belief change substantially differs from the change after receiving a rejection (see Table A5.7 in the appendix). A rejection increases the belief that admission depends on luck (.22), even though the difference in effect of admission and rejection does not reach statistical significance. However, this occur-

---

[33] Regarding their societal beliefs, applicants who will be admitted believe less strongly that societal success depends on family background (-.22) and money (-.21); differences in societal meritocratic beliefs are not substantial.

rence could mainly be caused by low case numbers. Overall, receiving an admission or rejection decision changes beliefs about admission similarly for the RDD group as for the overall sample; there seems to be a (causal) self-serving effect of the decision also for a rather homogenous group of applicants.

In contrast, the changes in societal beliefs partly differ for the group of applicants with a GPA of 1.3-1.4 from the overall sample, especially changes after receiving a rejection. While the belief changes after being admitted are rather similar for the RDD sample and the whole sample (even though they fail to reach statistical significance), being rejected does not substantially reduce the belief that success depends on effort and tentatively reduces rather than increases structural beliefs. When examining applicants with a GPA of 1.3 or 1.4, the group becomes even more selective than it is the case when observing the whole sample. Rejected applicants with such good school grades are likely to be disappointed and self-serving mechanisms might bias beliefs about admission. However, they are not real 'losers': They achieved far above-average GPAs and many other career paths are open to them, which might explain why being rejected does not change their societal inequality beliefs.

This fuzzy RDD analysis explores the local effect of the admission decision for the group of applicants who are similarly likely to be admitted or rejected. It supports the idea that admission or rejection to medical schools indeed has a causal effect on inequality beliefs—particularly on domain-specific beliefs—that is not only driven by diverging paths of winners and losers prior to receiving the admission outcome.

5.4.2 Effect of merit-based success or success in general?

For the cohort of applicants in 2018, places in the program at public medical schools in Germany were mainly allocated via three quotas: (a) 20 % by GPA, (b) 20 % by waiting-period, and (c) 60 % by university-specific criteria. For the university-specific quota, GPA is also the most important criterion, while other factors like work experience or civic engagement are also considered. Hence, the GPA quota and the university-specific quota can be regarded as merit-based quota. In contrast, 20 % of the places were allocated by the waiting-period—a nonmeritocratic criterion.

When receiving a positive admission decision, applicants are informed through which quota they were admitted. This enables exploring whether it is only the experience of merit-based success that shapes inequality beliefs in a self-serving way or the experience of success in general: whether the change in beliefs varies by admission quota. As discussed in Chapter 3.2, results from previous experimental game studies (Fehr & Vollmann, 2020; Molina et al., 2019) suggest that winners are likely to attribute their success to meritocratic beliefs, regardless of the conditions of the game. Does this also hold true for the real-life experience of being admitted to medical school?

Figure 5.7: Average inequality beliefs pre and post admission and belief changes for admitted applicants through different quotas

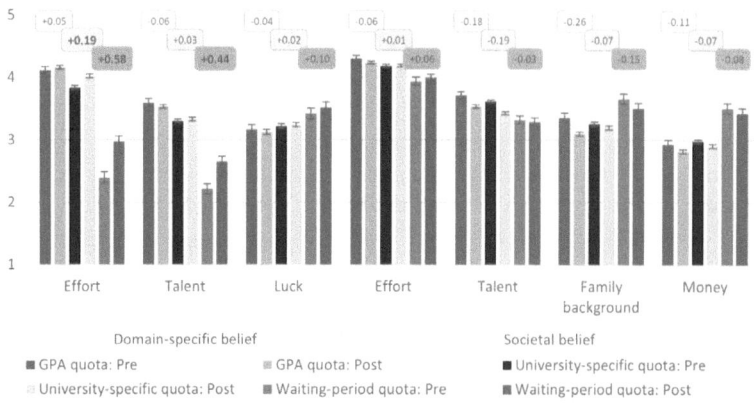

Note. Belief changes after admission through GPA quota displayed in white boxes, through university-specific quota in light grey boxed, and through waiting-period quota in dark grey boxes. Significant changes (p < .05) displayed in bold numbers. N = 1,663 admitted applicants through three main admission quotas (244 admitted through GPA quota, 1,194 through university-specific quota, 225 through waiting-period quota). Sampling weight applied. Source: Medical applicant data, author's calculations.

Figure 5.7 shows that prior to being admitted, meritocratic beliefs about one's own admission differed substantially between those who will be admitted through one of the merit-based quotas and those who will be admitted through the waiting-period quota. This finding is unsurprising as applicants are aware through which quotas they applied and based on which qualifications (GPA or waiting-period) they are likely to be admitted. However, receiving an admission increases beliefs that own admission depends on effort and talent for admission via all quotas—even more strongly for being admitted through the waiting-period quota than through the GPA or university-specific quota. Group differences in belief changes are even statistically significant (see Table A5.8 in the appendix).

For societal inequality beliefs, waiting-period applicants have weaker meritocratic and stronger nonmeritocratic beliefs prior to receiving the admission decision than applicants who will be admitted through merit-based quotas. This may be the case because the group of waiting-period applicants has worse school grades (the average GPA of waiting-period quota applicants is 2.47, while it is 1.01 for GPA quota applicants and 1.27 for university-specific quota applicants) and possibly believes less in upward mobility through academic performance. Differences in societal belief changes between the admission quotas do not seem to follow any specific pattern. Overall, success seems to shape inequality beliefs in a self-serving way, regardless of whether the success was actually based on one's own merit or not.

5.5 The role of previous experiences as a frame for new experiences

In Chapter 3.2, I discussed that previous experience may influence the effects of the (new) experience of being admitted or rejected to medical school on inequality beliefs—an expectation that will be examined in this chapter.

Parental education and belief changes

Regarding social differences in effects, I expect that success strengthens meritocratic beliefs and weakens nonmeritocratic beliefs more strongly for less privileged applicants than for their more privileged peers (*HI.4a*), while failure weakens meritocratic beliefs and strengthens nonmeritocratic beliefs more strongly for less privileged applicants than for their more privileged peers (*HI.4b*).

Against this expectation of heterogenous belief changes across social groups, the self-serving belief changes in inequality beliefs are rather homogenous for the three observed groups. The results from linear fixed-effects models including interaction terms (see Table A5.9 in the appendix) suggest that the belief changes do not substantially differ by applicants' parental education.

However, to explore tentative patterns, Figure 5.8 displays the average inequality beliefs pre and post admission decision, as well as changes in beliefs by parental education. Regarding the effect of success (*HI.4a*), group differences in belief changes after admission do not seem to follow a specific pattern. Regarding the effect of failure (*HI.4b*), the findings potentially suggest a pattern with effort beliefs seeming to be most resistant to failure among applicants with two college-educated parents (both for domain-specific and societal beliefs: -.02; -.04), the most privileged group. Furthermore, the increase in structural beliefs is the weakest among this group (.08; .11). This is generally in line with the idea that failure weakens meritocratic beliefs and strengthens nonmeritocratic beliefs more strongly for applicants from privileged backgrounds than for their less privileged peers. However, group differences are small and do not reach statistical significance. Thus, both *HI.4a* and *HI.4b* cannot be confirmed by the findings.

Figure 5.8: Average inequality beliefs pre and post admission decision and belief changes by parental education

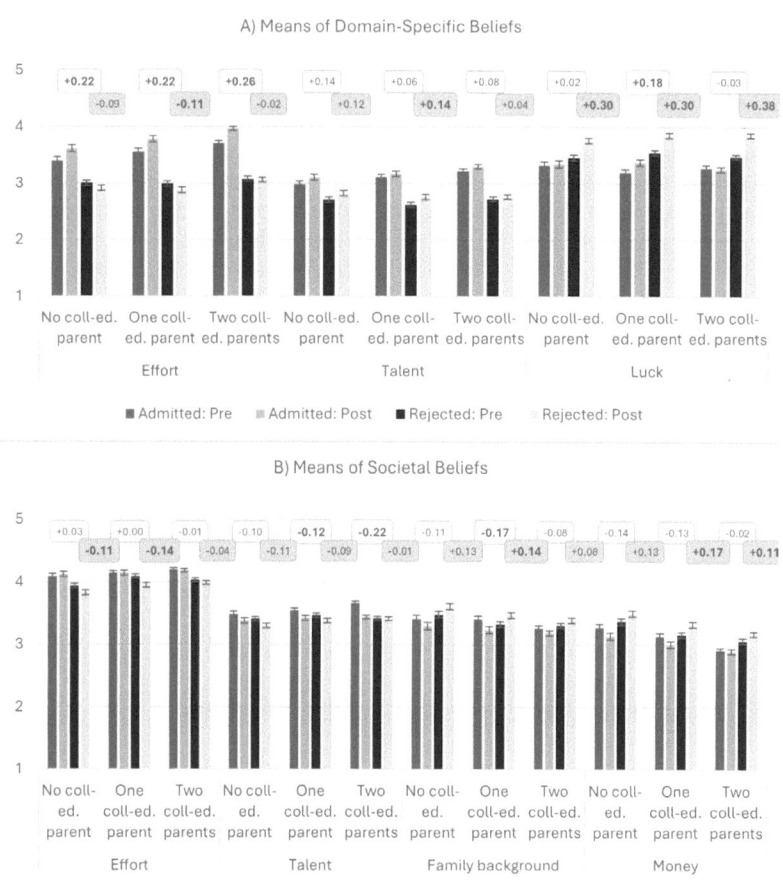

Note. Belief changes after admission displayed in white boxes; changes after rejection displayed in grey boxed. Significant changes (p < .05) displayed in bold. N = 1,764 admitted applicants (421 no college-educated parent, 491 one college-educated parent, 852 two college-educated parents); 2,374 rejected applicants (729 no college-educated parent, 712 one college-educated parent, 933 two college-educated parents). Sampling weight applied. Source: Medical applicant data, author's calculations.

The results displayed in Figure 5.8 also reveal that within the group of admitted and rejected applicants there remain social differences in inequality beliefs as observed in Chapter 5.3 for the whole sample. After receiving the admission decision, admitted applicants with two college-educated parents more strongly believe in the importance of effort and talent for their own admission than admitted applicants with no college-educated parent (.35). However, among rejected applicants, social differences in domain-specific effort beliefs are not statistically significant, and social differences in societal effort beliefs are also not substantial within the group of admitted, but within the group of rejected applicants. Rejected applicants with two college-educated parents more strongly believe that success in society depends on effort than rejected applicants with no college-educated parent (.16). Furthermore, admitted as well as rejected applicants with two college-educated parents believe less strongly in the importance of money for success in society than those with no college-educated parent (-.25 and -.33), and to a lesser extent also less strongly in the importance of family background (-.15 and -.22).

Overall, in line with expectations, these findings suggest that social differences in success or failure in admission explain only a small part of social differences in inequality beliefs. As Figure 5.2 and Figure 5.3 have already shown, differences in effort beliefs can partly be explained by social differences in (previous) experiences of failure in admission, but to a larger extent by differences in GPA (a proxy of an accumulation of educational experiences). Even though GPA is an important selection criterion, it still varies within the groups of admitted and rejected applicants. Furthermore, social differences can only be explained by educational experiences (such as in admission to medical school) to a limited extent, and beyond these experiences, applicants from privileged backgrounds hold stronger social background beliefs and are more aware of structural barriers than their more privileged peers.

Previous domain-specific experiences and belief changes

Regarding differences in effects between applicants who previously experienced failure in admission to medical school and those who did not, I expect that success strengthens meritocratic beliefs and weakens nonmeritocratic beliefs more strongly for repeat applicants than for first-time applicants (*HI.5a*), while failure weakens meritocratic beliefs and strengthens nonmeritocratic beliefs more strongly for repeat applicants than for first-time applicants. (*HI.5b*).

Figure 5.9 (Panel A) shows that prior to admission, those who had previously experienced a rejection of their application (i.e., repeat applicants) have substantially weaker beliefs in meritocratic admission than those who had not (i.e., first-time applicants). Prior differences in societal beliefs (Panel B) are less pronounced suggesting, in line with the main findings, that prior self-serving belief biases following previous rejection to medical school are stronger for domain-specific beliefs than for societal beliefs. However, regarding nonmeritocratic beliefs, structural societal beliefs of repeat applicants are slightly stronger than those of first-time applicants, while no differences in terms of domain-specific luck belief can be observed.

Figure 5.9: Average inequality beliefs pre and post admission decision and belief changes for first-time and repeat applicants

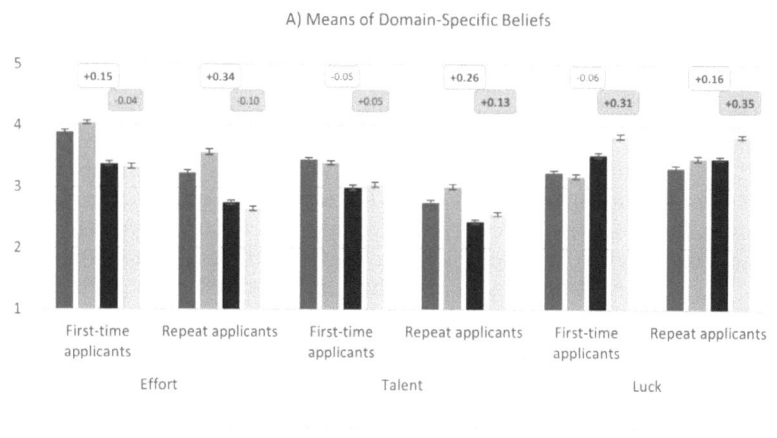

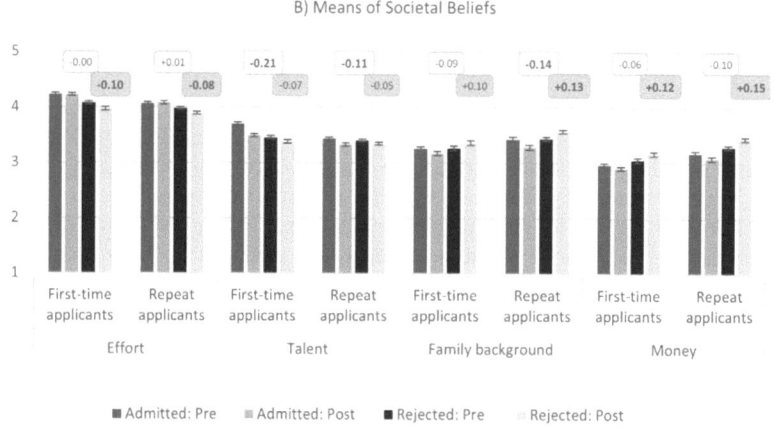

Note. Belief changes after admission displayed in white boxes; changes after rejection displayed in grey boxed. Significant changes (p < .05) displayed in bold. N = 1,764 admitted applicants (1,014 first-time applicants, 750 repeat applicants); 2,374 rejected applicants (978 first-time applicants, 1,396 repeat applicants). Sampling weight applied. Source: Medical applicant data, author's calculations.

HI.5a suggesting a stronger increase in meritocratic beliefs and stronger decrease in nonmeritocratic beliefs following success for repeat applicants can partly be supported: Success strengthens meritocratic beliefs in effort- and talent-based admission more strongly for repeat applicants (Panel A: .34; .26) than for first-time applicants (.15; -.05). The potential decrease in meritocratic beliefs about admission through past experiences, as expressed in lower beliefs prior to receiving the admission decision, is at least partly outweighed by the experience of success. However, the same pattern is not observable for societal beliefs (Panel B).

Regarding belief change in nonmeritocratic beliefs, for repeat applicants, the belief in the importance of luck for admission increases after admission (.16), different than for first-time applicants (-.06), driving both groups further apart regarding nonmeritocratic beliefs. Those who are finally successful after several attempts seem to have consolidated their belief that admission to highly prestigious university programs is also a lottery and they are among the lucky ones. At the same time, they seem to have reconsidered prior doubts about meritocratic procedures and to have recognized merit as a necessary condition for success.

Regarding societal beliefs, the decrease in structural beliefs after admission is slightly stronger for repeat applicants (family background: -.14; money: -.10) than for first-time applicants (-.09; -.06). However, Table A5.10 (see appendix) shows that all of these group differences in belief changes are statistically insignificant.

HI.5b—suggesting a stronger decrease in meritocratic beliefs and a stronger increase in nonmeritocratic beliefs following failure for repeat applicants—can also not be supported as group differences are rather small and statistically insignificant. Nevertheless, in relative terms, the negative effect that a rejection has on the belief in the importance of effort for university admission is twice as large for repeat applicants (-.10) as for first-time applicants (-.04), a finding in line with *HI.5b*. This finding is particularly interesting when considering the group differences prior to the new admission decision. Experiencing failure repeatedly weakens the belief in meritocratic admissions procedures even further. Furthermore, the increase in fatalistic beliefs about admission after experiencing failure is slightly stronger for repeat applicants (.13) than for first-time applicants (.05).

Overall, as group differences in belief changes are not significant, neither *HI.5a* nor *HI5b* can be supported by the findings but tentatively some differences in effects are in line with the expectations.

5.6 Summary: Diverging paths in inequality beliefs

I will now briefly summarize and discuss the main findings presented in this chapter. A systematic summary of the results regarding the hypotheses can be found in Table 5.6 at the end of this chapter.

Previous research has examined the relationship between social position and inequality beliefs cross-sectionally (e.g., Kluegel & Smith, 1986; Kreidl, 2000), examined the effect of experiences with experimental methods (e.g., Fehr & Vollmann, 2020; Molina et al., 2019), and focused on changes in inequality beliefs among the winners (e.g., Warikoo, 2016). The relationship between social origin and meritocratic beliefs remains empirically less explored, even though there has been research on the effect of social position dependent on social origin (e.g., Mijs et al., 2022).

This dissertation contributes to this research by investigating how parental education is associated with inequality beliefs, how educational experiences of success or failure affect inequality beliefs, and how differences in these experiences (such as social differences in admission) contribute to social differences in inequality beliefs. To this end, I first tested the basic assumption that admission chances vary by applicants' parental education, and then estimated differences in inequality beliefs by parental education. Subsequently, I estimated the changes in beliefs following the real-life event of admission or rejection to medical school, thereby approximating its causal effect. Additionally, I conducted a subgroup analysis following the logic of a fuzzy RDD (only including applicants with a GPA of 1.3 – 1.4) and a subgroup analysis to explore heterogeneity in the effect of being admitted via different quotas. Finally, I conducted subgroup analyses to examine whether the effect of success and failure on inequality beliefs varies by previous experiences: accumulated experiences related to social upbringing as well as recent domain-specific experiences in admission.

The findings confirm that the admission likelihood indeed differs by parental education. In line with the results of Finger et al. (2024), I find that applicants with two college-educated parents are 6 percentage points more likely to be admitted than applicants with no college-educated parent—an effect that seems to be mostly driven by differences in GPA.

Furthermore, the findings partly support the expectation that people from privileged backgrounds have stronger meritocratic and weaker nonmeritocratic beliefs than those from less privileged backgrounds. Applicants with two college-educated parents have stronger beliefs that their own admission as well as societal success generally depends on effort and have weaker beliefs that societal success depends on family background and money, suggesting that they are less aware of structural barriers than their less privileged peers. However, these differences are small in size. The analyses indicate that social differences in inequality beliefs can partly be explained by differences in experiences such as social differences in the likelihood of previous experiences of failure in admission, and in experiences in high school, which translated into higher grades.

Regarding changes in beliefs, findings suggest that individual experiences of success or failure in admission influence inequality beliefs in a mostly self-serving way. Being admitted increases applicants' domain-specific belief in how important one's own effort is for the admission outcome and reduces the societal belief in how important family background and money are for societal success. Being rejected reduces domain-specific and societal beliefs in the importance of effort and increases beliefs in the importance of nonmeritocratic (structural and fatalistic) factors for success. The changes observed in inequality beliefs are more pronounced for domain-specific beliefs than for societal beliefs, but the experience in admission indeed shapes inequality beliefs also beyond the admission procedure.

The analyses also revealed some notable patterns regarding the concept and measurement of inequality beliefs. The results of the cluster analysis as well as the correlations between the inequality beliefs suggest that—in line with my expectation discussed in Chapter 3.2 based on attributional theory (Weiner, 1985)—meritocratic beliefs in effort and talent are distinct concepts. This finding implies that the belief about effort and belief about talent should be examined separately rather than summarized in an index, as is common in previous research (e.g., Shane and Heckhausen 2013; Hu et al. 2020).

While changes in beliefs about the importance of effort confirm the theoretical assumptions based on self-serving beliefs theory, the belief in the importance of talent partly points in opposite directions: For instance, the belief that admission depends on talent increases among rejected applicants. One reason for this finding could be that applicants may believe that intelligence—and thus talent—is a given, unalterable trait. Being rejected may be frustrating, strengthening the idea that especially innate talent rather than effort is important, which one might simply not have enough of. This belief may be a justification for the rejection that takes the blame away from the applicant. Based on these considerations, I argue that experiences may have a self-serving effect only on beliefs about the role of merit-based factors that lie within the individual's control but not on beliefs about factors like talent which could be considered stable and uncontrollable (Skinner et al., 1998; Weiner, 1985).

Moreover, the findings clearly show group differences in inequality beliefs between to-be-admitted applicants and to-be-rejected applicants already before they learned about their admission outcome. This suggests diverging paths in inequality beliefs for 'winners' and 'losers.' On average, those who will be admitted have better school grades than those who will be rejected, and they likely have accumulated more positive experiences in high school than those who will be rejected. These experiences may have increased their meritocratic beliefs and reduced their nonmeritocratic beliefs through continuous self-serving belief mechanisms. New experiences of success or failure, such as the admission outcome (an outcome that is crucially influenced by prior educational merit, measured as GPA), amplify these differences in inequality beliefs. After receiving the admission decision, the differences in domain-specific beliefs between winners and losers are medium in size, and differences in societal beliefs are small in size.

However, the change in inequality beliefs is not merely caused by different paths in beliefs of winners and losers: Analyses applying a fuzzy RDD and observing changes in beliefs only for applicants with a GPA between 1.3 and 1.4 provide confidence that receiving the admission outcome indeed influences domain-specific inequality beliefs in a self-serving way. Testing for differences in the effects of admission through different quotas, also reveals that success shapes inequality beliefs in a self-serving way, regardless of whether the success is based on one's own merit or was based on applicants' waiting-period.

Furthermore, the findings tentatively suggest a widening belief gap between groups differing in their previous long-term experiences related to their social background as well as short-term domain-specific experiences. As applicants with two college-educated parents are more likely to experience success in admission than their less privileged peers, this (slightly) amplifies differences in beliefs by social background, particularly in effort beliefs. Additionally, the findings tentatively suggest that meritocratic effort beliefs seem to be most stable and resistant to failure among members of the most advantaged group. Even if they happen to be rejected, this single experience of failure does not reduce their effort beliefs: They may have internalized beliefs that effort led to their previous success and stick to this belief. However, group differences in belief changes are small and statistically insignificant, suggesting that effect moderation through parental education does not play a major role in the belief gap between applicants from different social backgrounds. Parental education seems to affect inequality beliefs rather via social differences in educational experiences (e.g., admission chances and particularly differences in GPA) and their consequences for inequality beliefs.

Regarding domain-specific experiences, I find that repeat applicants have weaker meritocratic beliefs and mostly stronger nonmeritocratic beliefs than first-time applicants prior to the admission decision—a finding consistent with the idea that previous experiences shaped the beliefs of repeat applicants in a self-serving way. Additionally, experiences of failure in previous admission rounds indeed moderate the effect of the new experience of success. For repeat applicants, eventual success has a greater positive effect on the belief in the importance of effort in admissions than it does for first-time applicants, partly outweighing differences in beliefs prior to receiving the admission decision.

Table 5.6: Systematic illustration of results of hypotheses testing I

Hypotheses	Domain-specific beliefs about admission				Societal beliefs			
	Effect of Success		Effect of Failure		Effect of Success		Effect of Failure	
	Meritocratic Beliefs	Non-meritocratic Beliefs	Meritocratic Beliefs	Non-meritocratic Beliefs	Meritocratic Beliefs	Non-meritocratic Beliefs	Meritocratic Beliefs	Non-meritocratic Beliefs
HI.1: Applicants from privileged backgrounds are more likely to be admitted to medical school than their less privileged peers.	+ (Admission likelihood is significantly higher for applicants with two than for applicants with no college-educated parent; difference between applicants with one and no college-educated parent points in the same direction)							
HI.2: Applicants from privileged backgrounds hold stronger meritocratic and weaker nonmeritocratic beliefs than their less privileged peers.	(+) (people from privileged backgrounds have stronger effort beliefs)				(+) (people from privileged backgrounds have stronger effort beliefs and weaker family and money beliefs)			
HI.3: Success strengthens meritocratic beliefs and weakens nonmeritocratic beliefs, whereas failure weakens meritocratic beliefs and strengthens nonmeritocratic beliefs.	+ (for effort but not for talent)	-	(+) (for effort but not for talent)	+	-	+	+ (for effort but not for talent)	+
HI.4a: Success strengthens meritocratic beliefs and weakens nonmeritocratic beliefs more strongly for less privileged applicants than for their more privileged peers.	- (homogenous effects)	- (no systematic pattern)			- (homogenous effects)	- (homogenous effects)		
HI.4b: Failure weakens meritocratic beliefs and strengthens nonmeritocratic beliefs more strongly for less privileged applicants than for their more privileged peers.			(+) (for effort but not for talent)	- (homogenous effects)			(+)	- (homogenous effects)
HI.5a: Success strengthens meritocratic beliefs and weakens nonmeritocratic beliefs more strongly for repeat applicants than for first-time applicants.	+	(difference in the opposite direction)			- (homogenous effects)	(+)		
HI.5b: Failure weakens meritocratic beliefs and strengthens nonmeritocratic beliefs more strongly for repeat applicants than for first-time applicants.			(+) (for effort but not for talent)	- (homogenous effects)			- (homogenous effects)	- (homogenous effects)

Note. + Hypothesis supported by findings: belief change $p < .05$ and belief change substantially different from belief change of reference group; (+) Findings tentatively point in the expected direction of hypothesis but either belief change $p > .05$ or/and belief change does not substantially differ from belief change of reference group; - Findings do not support the hypothesis. Author's illustration.

Diverging paths in inequality beliefs of winners and losers can be redirected if eventual success occurs for those who had previously experienced failure, strengthening the argument that such experiences directly affect inequality beliefs on top of (and sometimes against the direction of) winners' and losers' diverging paths in inequality beliefs.

However, the eventual success of the previously unsuccessful is not the most likely event, which might contribute to a downward spiral in meritocratic beliefs of a nonnegligible number of applicants. In the case of failure, I expected a stronger negative impact on meritocratic beliefs for those applicants who were repeatedly rejected. I could not find strong evidence for this, since differences in belief changes after being rejected do not significantly differ between first-time and repeat applicants, but the difference in the belief change in effort-based admission points in the expected direction. New experiences of failure seem to reduce meritocratic beliefs even further, driving beliefs of winners and losers apart.

6 The complex relationship between parental education, inequality beliefs, perceptions of justice, and distributive preferences

In this empirical chapter, I test hypotheses for research objective II by examining what consequences inequality beliefs have for perceptions of justice and distributive preferences, and how social differences in inequality beliefs contribute to differences in distributive preferences by parental education.

More precisely, the analyses presented aim to answer the following research questions: How do inequality beliefs influence distributive preferences through perceptions of justice? Do social differences in inequality beliefs, and the resulting perception of justice, partly explain the association between parental education and distributive preferences? As discussed in Chapter 3.3, I chose to focus on two distributive preferences: the preference for distribution based on the principle of inequality and the preference for distribution based on the principle of educational meritocracy.

6.1 Descriptive statistics: Perceptions of justice and distributive preferences

As applicants' perceptions of justice and distributive preferences were only included in wave 3, my analysis for research objective II only includes applicants who participated in all three waves. Wave 3 furthermore includes an extended scale of inequality beliefs, which enables identifying distinct types of inequality beliefs as discussed in Chapter 3.2, as well as their different consequences for perceptions of justice and distributive preferences as discussed in Chapter 3.3. The sample examined here (subsample II) comprises 1,725 applicants to medical school.[34] Descriptive statistics on admission rate, gender, age, GPA, parental education, and share of repeat applicants were provided in Chapter 4.5 (Table 4.2). As a panel weight is applied, regarding these characteristics the sample does not substantially differ from the sample observed in the previous chapter (subsample I).

---

34 All respondents applied at least once in 2018. In wave 3 (conducted in February 2021), some respondents were admitted (at first or further attempt) and are now studying medicine, and other respondents were unsuccessful in their application attempt(s). The role of the outcome of their own admission for (social differences in) the variables of interest will be examined in Chapter 6.4.3.

My main variables of interest are applicants' domain-specific inequality beliefs about their own admission as well as their societal beliefs about success in society in general, their perceptions of the admission procedure as just as well as the perception of inequalities in society as just, and their distributive preferences for the distribution of places in the program as well as their preferences for income distribution: preferences for equal distribution and those for distribution based on educational merit.

Table 6.1 shows the weighted average perceptions of justice and distributive preferences in the sample.[35] On a scale from 1 (very unjust) to 5 (very just), respondents evaluate the admission procedure to medical school as rather unjust than just (2.43) and societal inequalities in society as even less just (2.10). Regarding their preferences for distribution of places in the program, respondents were asked if there were 100 medical school places remaining after admission through the current procedure, as how just would they evaluate a) equal admission through a lottery and b) admission purely based on school grades (see Chapter 4.2). Furthermore, they were asked how just they evaluate equal income distribution and distribution of income based on educational degrees. On average, respondents stated that they would evaluate equal admission through a lottery as rather just (3.20), but equal income distribution as rather unjust (1.92). The distribution of remaining places in the program after the current admission procedure based on school grades was evaluated as rather unjust (2.14), while the distribution of income based on educational degrees was evaluated as rather just (3.69).

Table 6.1: Average perceptions of justice and distributive preferences

	Domain-specific variables on admission	Societal variables on inequality and income distribution
	mean (sd)	mean (sd)
Perceptions of justice	2.43	2.10
	(1.01)	(0.92)
Distributive preferences		
Equality	3.20	1.92
	(1.46)	(1.02)
Educational meritocracy	2.14	3.69
	(1.08)	(1.01)

Note. Scale 1 (very unjust) – 5 (very just). N = 1,725. Panel weight applied. Source: Medical applicant data, author's calculations.

Respondents seem to (moderately) support the idea that at least a small share of applicants to medical school are admitted equally through a lottery but it

---

35 Average inequality beliefs are displayed later, as first distinct types of inequality beliefs are identified.

should be considered that the questionnaire item suggests that the majority of places in the program are still admitted through the current procedure that is (primarily) based on educational merit. In this scenario, they evaluate it as rather unjust to distribute remaining places in the program also based on school grades. Overall, their average perceptions and distributive preferences related to admission to medical school suggest that they see the current procedure, which is based on the principle of educational meritocracy, critically. On the other hand, while they do not seem to evaluate societal inequalities in society as just, they are also rather not supportive of equal income distribution and rather supportive of income distribution based on educational degrees. This suggests that in a broader and less competitive context than admission to medical school, they generally evaluate inequality based on educational meritocracy as just but are rather concerned about social inequalities that are not based on differences in educational merit or about the extent of such inequalities.

6.2 Methodological approach

Before testing my main hypothesis for this research objective, I first conducted principal-component factor analyses to identify distinct types of inequality beliefs among the 11 domain-specific belief items and the 11 societal belief items. The number of factors was determined by applying Jolliffe's (1986) criterion of a suggested cut-off for eigenvalues. Only factors with an eigenvalue greater than 0.7 should be considered as distinct factors. The distinct types derived were then used in the consecutive analyses.

To examine the complex relationship between parental education, inequality beliefs, perceptions of justice, and distributive preferences, and test proposed relations as presented in Figure 3.2 (Chapter 3.3), I used structural equation modeling (SEM). Two separate models were conducted: One model (the domain-specific model) examines the effects of applicants' domain-specific beliefs about their own admission on their preferences for the distribution of places in the program, and how these effects may be mediated by perceiving the admission procedure as just. The other model (the societal model) examines the effects of applicants' societal beliefs about success in society on their preferences for income distribution, and how these effects may be mediated by perceiving societal inequality in Germany as just. Furthermore, both models examine the effects of parental education on distributive preferences, and how these effects may be mediated by social differences in inequality beliefs and perceptions of justice.

Besides the variables of interest, the SEMs included the error term's correlation of the inequality beliefs of how important different factors are for success, as they are theoretically and empirically related. Models were estimated using maximum-likelihood estimation (Iacobucci, 2010). One main limitation of SEM is that it does not permit researchers to include many control variables. The inclusion of too many variables in the SEMs requires the specification of numerous different parameters, resulting in overly complex models that are hard to fit and interpret. Hence, I only included one control variable in my main analysis, namely a dummy variable whether applicants participated in the experimental survey before the wave 3 questionnaire (see Chapter 4.2).

Furthermore, the application of weights to account for possible bias due to selective survey participation and attrition would lead to problems in calculating model fits. Theoretically, there are no strong reasons to believe that self-selection into survey participation would confound the theorized relationships; after all, the goal of this study is to explore the relation between the concepts and not to be representative of the beliefs of applicants to medical school. Hence, the method is a suitable way of testing whether the complex theory of the relationship between parental education, inequality beliefs, perception of justice, and distributive preferences properly fits the data, while allowing me to estimate direct and indirect paths between latent and observable variables.

6.3 Distinct types of meritocratic and nonmeritocratic beliefs

For the analyses presented in Chapter 5, selected inequality beliefs were examined representing theorized distinct types of beliefs. In line with the theoretical considerations discussed in Chapter 3.2 based on attributional theory (Weiner, 1985), correlations between beliefs (see Table A5.1 in the appendix) already suggested that the meritocratic belief in the importance of effort for success and the meritocratic belief in the important of talent for it are distinct types of beliefs. Furthermore, findings showed that success and failure in admission had diverging effects on these beliefs. For instance, while it (tentatively) reduced applicants' belief that their own admission depends on effort, being rejected increased their belief that it depends on (lack of) abilities.

In waves 1 and 2, applicants were only asked whether their own admission depends on luck and not whether it depends on structural factors, and were only asked whether success in society in general depends on structural factors and not whether it depends on luck. Hence, the theoretical consideration that fatalistic and structural beliefs are distinct concepts (Weiner, 1985) could not be tested with data from waves 1 and 2. The extended belief scale implemented in wave 3 allows a more thorough investigation of distinct types of inequality beliefs.

To identify distinct types of domain-specific beliefs as well as of societal beliefs, the method of principal-component analysis was used, and items on beliefs on how important 11 meritocratic and nonmeritocratic factors are for success were included in the factor analyses.[36] The results of the factors analysis for domain-specific beliefs suggest a 6-factor solution applying Jolliffe's (1986) criterion (eigenvalue > 0.7), while the results for societal beliefs suggest a 5-factor solution.

The results for domain-specific beliefs are displayed in Table 6.2, and the results for societal beliefs are displayed in Table 6.3. Overall, the factor solutions are fairly similar. The only substantial difference is that the domain-specific results suggest that the belief item that one's own admission depends on gender is a distinct type of beliefs, while the societal results suggest that the belief that societal success depends on gender is included in the social background belief factor. Why the belief in the importance of gender for success is a distinct domain-specific belief but not a distinct societal belief can be explained by the gender distribution among medical students. In contrast to the structural disadvantage of women in many other areas of society, women are overrepresented among medical students. This may explain why 74 % of applicants totally disagree that success in one's own admission depends on gender. To make the distinct types of inequality beliefs comparable between the domain-specific and the societal models, I decided to not include the items on the importance of gender for success in the subsequent analyses.

Excluding the gender belief, the results of the factor analyses support the theoretical consideration of five distinct types of inequality beliefs in both domain-specific and in societal beliefs. The meritocratic hard work belief type (factor loadings < .5 with effort, endurance, and initiative beliefs), the meritocratic abilities beliefs type (factor loadings < .5 with talent and skills beliefs), the meritocratic educational merit belief type (factor loadings < .5 only with school grades / educational degree belief), the nonmeritocratic luck belief type (factor loadings < .5 only with luck belief), and the nonmeritocratic social background belief type (factor loadings < .5 with family background, money, and connections beliefs).

Hence, in the SEMs, I combine the items effort, endurance, and initiative in the latent construct hard work belief (i.e., the belief that success depends on hard work), the items talent and skills in the latent construct abilities belief, and the items family background, money, and connections in the latent construct social background belief. I further included beliefs in the importance of educational merit (school grades and educational degrees) and luck as distinct observable variables in the models (i.e., educational merit belief and luck belief).

---

36 As it was only measured how important the factor of being born in Germany is for societal success but not for one's own admission, this belief was not included in the factor analyses, as I aimed to identify distinct types that are comparable between domain-specific and societal beliefs.

Table 6.2: Factor analysis results for domain-specific inequality beliefs

University admission depends on my own ...	Factor 1: Social background belief	Factor 2: Hard work belief	Factor 3: Abilities belief	Factor 4: Luck belief	Factor 5: Gender belief	Factor 6: Educational merit belief	Uniqueness
Effort		0.58					0.34
Talent			0.81				0.26
Skills			0.87				0.23
School grades						0.96	0.06
Endurance		0.92					0.28
Luck				0.98			0.10
Initiative		0.77					0.36
Family background	0.90						0.23
Money	0.89						0.23
Connections	0.70						0.29
Gender					1.00		0.01
Cronbach's Alpha	0.79	0.67	0.56	0.25	-	-	

Note. Principal-component factor analysis: rotated factor loadings. Factors with Eigenvalue < 0.7. Factor loadings < 0.50 not displayed. N = 1,725. Panel weight applied. Source: Medical applicant data, author's calculations.

Table 6.3: Factor analysis results for societal inequality beliefs

Societal success depends on ...	Factor 1: Social background belief	Factor 2: Hard work belief	Factor 3: Luck belief	Factor 4: Abilities belief	Factor 5: Educational merit belief	Uniqueness
Effort		0.54				0.43
Talent				0.84		0.24
Skills				0.75		0.32
Educational degree					0.94	0.10
Endurance		0.85				0.26
Luck			0.96			0.05
Initiative		0.81				0.31
Family background	0.84					0.21
Money	0.85					0.21
Connections	0.80					0.31
Gender	0.70					0.47
Cronbach's Alpha	0.84	0.68	-	0.53	-	

Note. Principal-component factor analysis: Rotated factor loadings. Factors with Eigenvalue < 0.7. Factor loadings < 0.50 not displayed. N = 1,725. Panel weight applied. Source: Medical applicant data, author's calculations.

Table 6.4 shows the weighted average beliefs of what factors respondents in the sample (wave 3) believe success in their own admission as well as in societal inequality depends on. For this descriptive analysis, indices were generated (by dividing the sum of belief items by the number of items) for the beliefs that will be included as latent constructs in the SEMs. Similar as suggested by applicants' average inequality beliefs measured in wave 1, which only included one representative belief item for each type (see Table 4.3), respondents believe that their own success (or failure) in admission depends similarly on hard work (3.33) and luck (3.38), but less on their abilities (2.34). As GPA is the most important admission criterion, it is unsurprising that respondents strongly agree that admission depends on their school grades (4.81). Furthermore, on average, they slightly rather disagree than agree that admission depends on their social background. However, that they do not strongly disagree that it plays a role shows that they seem to be aware of structural barriers related to social background to some extent.

Table 6.4: Average distinct types of inequality beliefs

	Domain-specific beliefs about own admission	Societal beliefs about success in society
	mean (sd)	mean (sd)
Success depends on ...		
Hard work 1	3.33	4.17
	(1.01)	(0.64)
Abilities 2	2.34	3.67
	(0.96)	(0.72)
Educational merit	4.81	3.45
	(0.64)	(0.98)
Luck	3.38	3.41
	(1.26)	(1.16)
Social background	2.78	3.50
	(1.14)	(1.01)

Note. Scale 1 (strongly disagree) – 5 (strongly agree). 1 Index out of belief in the importance of effort, endurance and initiative; 2 Index out of belief in the importance of talent and skills; 3 Index out of belief in the importance of family background, money, and connections. N = 1,725. Panel weight applied. Source: Medical applicant data, author's calculations.

Regarding societal success in general, they agree even more strongly that success depends on social background (3.50) but also that it depends on hard work (4.17) and abilities (3.67). That educational merit is important for societal success but less important than for application to medical school specifically, is reflected in respondents' beliefs (4.81 vs. 3.45), and they evaluate the role of luck for admission (3.38) and for success in society similarly (3.41).

As in sample I (wave 1), respondents in sample II (wave 3) believe that their own success in admission and societal success in general depends both on meritocratic and nonmeritocratic factors. However, belief patterns vary between individuals, and the goal of this chapter is to examine the consequences of (differences in) these inequality beliefs for perceptions of justice and distributive preferences.

6.4 The complex relationship: Structural equation model results

In Chapter 3.3, I hypothesized that inequality beliefs influence distributive preferences through differences in perceptions of justice and that parental education influences distributive preferences through differences in inequality beliefs, and their consequences for perceptions of justice (see Figure 3.2 for illustration). I expect meritocratic beliefs to be positively associated with perceptions of justice and preferences for distribution based on educational meritocracy but negatively with preferences for equal distribution, and expect the opposite for nonmeritocratic beliefs. Furthermore, I expect privileged parental education to be negatively associated with the preferences for equal distribution and positively associated with the preference for educational meritocracy, and this association to be partly explained by social differences in beliefs—differences that were already confirmed in Chapter 5.

Table 6.5: Direct and total effects of parental education, inequality beliefs, and perceptions of justice on distributive preferences, and mediation mechanisms

	Domain-specific model: University admission			Societal model: Social inequalities		
	Direct effect	Total effect	% of total effect via mediation	Direct effect	Total effect	% of total effect via mediation
Path 1.1: Inequality beliefs → Distributive preference (incl. mediation via perception of justice) & Path 1.3: Perception of justice → Distributive preference & Path 2.1: Parental education → Distributive preference (incl. mediation via inequality beliefs and perception of justice)						
DV: Equality preference – Equal admission through lottery				Equal distribution of income		
Inequality beliefs						
Hard work	-.05 (.08)	-.06 (.08)	14	-.17 (.07)	-.17 (.10)	-2
Abilities	-.08 (.11)	-.09 (.11)	10	-.10 (.11)	-.16 (.11)	40
Educational merit	-.04 (.06)	-.04 (.06)	3	.04 (.03)	.03 (.03)	-12
Luck	.10** (.03)	.10** (.03)	2	-.01 (.02)	-.01 (.02)	60
Social background	.01 (.04)	.02 (.04)	28	.08* (.03)	.12** (.03)	33
Perception of justice	-.03 (.04)	No ind. path	-	-.21** (.03)	No ind. path	-
1 col.-ed. parent	-.00 (.09)	-.01 (.09)	85	-.07 (.06)	-.10 (.06)	29
2 col.-ed. parents	-.24** (.09)	-.27** (.09)	12	-.14** (.06)	-.18** (.06)	24

	Domain-specific model: University admission			Societal model: Social inequalities		
	Direct effect	Total effect	% of total effect via mediation	Direct effect	Total effect	% of total effect via mediation
DV: Educational Meritocracy Preference – Admission based on grades				Income distribution based on degrees		
Inequality beliefs:						
Hard work	.07 (.06)	.13* (.06)	50	.07 (.10)	.06 (.10)	-6
Abilities	.30** (.08)	.37** (.08)	21	.29** (.11)	.36** (.11)	21
Educational merit	.00 (.04)	.01 (.04)	73	.01 (.03)	.01 (.03)	36
Luck	-.07** (.02)	-.08** (.02)	20	.06** (.02)	.07** (.02)	15
Social background	-.07* (.03)	-.10** (.03)	37	-.02 (.03)	-.06 (.03)	70
Perception of justice	.29** (.03)	No ind. path	-	.24** (.03)	No ind. path	-
1 col.-ed. parent	-.03 (.06)	.02 (.07)	258	.09 (.06)	.12 (.06)	26
2 col.-ed. parents	.11 (.06)	.20** (.07)	45	.19** (.06)	.23** (.06)	16
Path 1.2: Inequality beliefs → Perception of justice & Parental education → Perception of justice (incl. mediation via inequality beliefs)						
DV: Perception of admission as just				Perception of inequalities as just		
Inequality beliefs:						
Hard work	.23** (.05)	No ind. path	-	-.02 (.09)	No ind. path	-
Abilities	.27** (.07)	No ind. path	-	.23* (.10)	No ind. path	-
Educational merit	.03 (.04)	No ind. path	-	.02 (.02)	No ind. path	-
Luck	-.06** (.02)	No ind. path	-	.04* (.02)	No ind. path	-
Social background	-.14** (.03)	No ind. path	-	-.18** (.03)	No ind. path	-
1 col.-ed. parent	.08 (.06)	.11 (.06)	34	.00 (.06)	.05 (.06)	100
2 col.-ed. parents	.10 (.06)	.18** (.06)	45	.05 (.05)	.08 (.05)	42
Path 2.2: Parental education → Inequality beliefs						
DV: Hard work						
1 col.-ed. parent	.06 (.08)	No ind. path	-	-.02 (.05)	No ind. path	-
2 col.-ed. parents	.17* (.07)	No ind. path	-	.06 (.04)	No ind. path	-
DV: Abilities						
1 col.-ed. parent	-.01 (.07)	No ind. path	-	.08 (.05)	No ind. path	-
2 col.-ed. parents	-.02 (.06)	No ind. path	-	.05 (.04)	No ind. path	-
DV: Educational merit						
1 col.-ed. parent	-.04 (.04)	No ind. path	-	-.06 (.06)	No ind. path	-
2 col.-ed. parents	-.01 (.04)	No ind. path	-	-.06 (.06)	No ind. path	-
DV: Luck						
1 col.-ed. parent	-.03 (.08)	No ind. path	-	-.08 (.07)	No ind. path	-
2 col.-ed. parents	-.14 (.07)	No ind. path	-	-.03 (.07)	No ind. path	-
DV: Social background						
1 col.-ed. parent	-.21** (.07)	No ind. path	-	-.15* (.07)	No ind. path	-
2 col.-ed. parents	-.30** (.06)	No ind. path	-	-.11 (.06)	No ind. path	-
Goodness-of-fit-statistics						
CFI		.914			.915	
RMSEA		.064			.067	
SRMR		.037			.040	

Note. Standardized coefficients. All path models controlled for participation in experiment dummy. Reference for 1 / 2 coll.-ed. parent(s): no college-educated parent. Hard work, abilities, and social background are latent constructs. Percentage of total effect via mediation calculated based on nonrounded coefficients. N = 1,725; ** p < .01 * p < .05. Source: Medical applicant data, author's calculations.

To examine this complex relationship between my variables of interest, I conducted SEMs. Table 6.5 displays their results and the associations between all concepts, following the paths 1.1 to 2.2 illustrated in Figure 3.2: It shows direct and total effects (including mediation) as standardized coefficients and the percentages of total effects explained by the mediation mechanism.

I calculated goodness-of-fit (GoF) statistics to assess how well the theorized model fits the data, which are displayed at the bottom of the table. Commonly, a comparative fit index (CFI) above .90 is desired, along with a root mean square error of approximation (RMSEA) close to the upper bound of .05 and the standardized root mean square residual (SRMR) below the recommended cut-off of .05 (Acock, 2013). All of the GoF statistics are within or very close to the recommended thresholds, suggesting an acceptable fit of the theorized models. As a robustness check, weighted models (albeit for which CFI and RMSEA could not be calculated, see Chapter 6.2) are displayed in Table A6.1 in the appendix. The results do not substantially differ from those of the main analysis.

6.4.1 Associations between inequality beliefs and distributive preferences, and the role of perceptions of justice

As illustrated in Figure 3.2 (Chapter 3.3), I hypothesized that inequality beliefs influence distributive preferences through differences in perceptions of justice (*HII.4a/b*). However, the findings of the SEMs (see Table 6.5) suggest no or only weak mediation mechanisms through perceptions of justice. They clearly show that there are remaining direct effects of inequality beliefs on distributive preferences.

Even though the results did not confirm the hypothesized mediation mechanism, they provide partial support for the hypothesized path 1.1 (*HII.1*), 1.2 (*HII.2*), and 1.3 (*HII.3*) constituting the mediation (paths displayed in Figure 3.2). Regarding the magnitude of effects, all effects are rather small in size. I start by discussing the findings for paths 1.1 to 1.3 in further detail.

Path 1.1 (Inequality beliefs → Distributive preferences)

In the SEMs, the total effects[37] of inequality beliefs (including the mediation through perceptions of justice) were estimated, as well as the indirect effects through justice perception and the remaining direct effects. I will start by re-

---

37 When reporting SEM, researchers commonly talk about direct and total effects. Hence, I adopted the wording of 'effects' when reporting the findings. However, in this chapter, I do not intend to make strong causal claims due to the limitations of cross-sectional data analysis (e.g., possible reverse direction of causality).

porting the total effects to test the general assumption of *HII.1* that meritocratic beliefs are negatively associated with the preference for equal distribution and positively with the preference for distribution based on educational meritocracy, while the opposite is true for nonmeritocratic beliefs.

As shown by total effects on path 1.1 (displayed at the top of Table 6.5), most domain-specific beliefs about admission do not seem to have substantial effects on the preference for equal admission through a lottery. However, in line with expectations of *HII.1,* the nonmeritocratic belief in the importance of luck has a positive effect on this preference (.10). Regarding the preference for admission based on school grades, effects were more in line with the expectations of *HI.1*. The beliefs in the importance of hard work and abilities have a positive effect on this preference (.13 and .37), and beliefs in the importance of luck and background have negative effects on it (-.08 and -.10).

The results of the societal model (right side of Table 6.5), suggest that, in line with *HII.1*, the belief in the importance of social background has a positive effect on the preference for equal income distribution (.12), and suggest tentatively that hard work belief and abilities beliefs have a negative effect on the preference for equal income distribution (-.17 and -.16), although they slightly miss the threshold of statistical significance. Furthermore, the abilities belief is positively associated with the preference for income distribution based on educational degrees (.36). Contrary to *HII.1*, the belief in the importance of luck is also positively associated with this preference (.07).

Overall, these findings partly support *HII.1*, although they reveal notable differences in the effects of distinct types of inequality beliefs on distributive preferences. Regarding preferences for equal distribution, the nonmeritocratic belief in the importance of luck for success seems to be more important for the preference for the equal distribution of places in the program than the social background belief, and the nonmeritocratic belief in the importance of social background seems to be more important for the preference for equal income distribution than the luck belief. For preferences for distribution based on the principle of educational meritocracy (both for distribution of places in the program and income distribution), the meritocratic belief in the importance of abilities for success seems to be more important than the belief in the importance of hard work. The belief that success in admission or society in general depends on educational merit is not associated with distributive preferences.

Path 1.2 (Inequality beliefs → Perception of justice)

HII.2 proposes that meritocratic beliefs lead to a perception of higher justice, while nonmeritocratic beliefs lead to a perception of lower justice. The results of the SEMs partly confirm *HII.2* (displayed in the middle section of Table 6.5): Meritocratic beliefs in the importance of hard work and abilities in one's own medical-school admission have positive effects on the perception of the admission procedure as just (.23 and .27), while nonmeritocratic beliefs in the importance of luck and background for one's own admission have negative effects on it (-.06 and -.14).

When evaluating societal inequality generally, *HII.2* was less clearly supported. Not all distinct types of inequality beliefs are related to perceiving social inequalities as just in the expected way: While the abilities belief has a positive effect on the perception of existing inequalities as just (.23), the hard work belief has no substantial effect on it. The nonmeritocratic social background belief has a negative effect on the perception of justice (-.18), while— contrary to expectations—the nonmeritocratic belief in the importance of luck has a weak positive effect on it (.04). Referring to admission and societal inequality, the belief that success depends on educational merit is not associated with perceptions of justice.

Path 1.2 (Perception of justice → Distributive preferences)

I will now discuss findings regarding expectations of *HII.3* that the more people perceive inequality as just, the more opposed they will be to equal distribution and the more they will support educational meritocracy. Effects can be found at the top of Table 6.5.

While people's perception of how just the admission procedure is does not seem to have a substantial effect on their preference for the allocation of remaining medical school places through a lottery, it has a positive effect on preference for allocation mechanisms similar to those currently in operation, namely admission based on school grades (.29). Respondents' perceptions of societal inequalities as just has a negative effect on the preference for equal income distribution (-.21) and a positive effect on the preference for educational meritocracy (.24). Overall, the findings partly support *HII.3* that the more people perceive inequality as just, the greater will be their opposition to equal distribution and support for educational meritocracy.

Mediation of path 1.1 (Inequality beliefs → Perceptions of justice → Distributive preferences)

I will now test *HII.4a* (i.e., whether the perception of justice mediates the negative relationship between meritocratic beliefs and the preference for equal distribution and the positive relationship between nonmeritocratic beliefs and this preference) and *HII.4b* (i.e., whether the perception of justice mediates the positive relationship between meritocratic beliefs and the preference for distribution based on educational meritocracy, and mediates the negative relationship between nonmeritocratic beliefs and this preference).

For that, I will refer to the percentages of the total effects of the inequality beliefs mediated by the respective perception of justice (of the admission procedure or societal inequalities), which are displayed at the top of Table 6.5. Overall, these percentages suggest that, for most inequality beliefs, only a small part of the effect of these beliefs on distributive preferences can be explained by differences in perceptions of justice.

Of the statistically significant total effects of inequality beliefs on distributive preferences, 2 % to 50 % are mediated by perceptions of justice. Regarding the preferences for equal distribution, luck belief increases the preference for equal admission through a lottery directly (only 2 % of the total effect mediated by perception of justice), while social background belief increases the preference for equal income distribution directly and indirectly (33 % mediated).

Regarding the preference for distribution based on educational merit, abilities belief increases the preference for distribution of places in the program and income based on educational merit also rather directly than indirectly (in both models, 21 % mediated). A more substantial mediation only occurs for the positive effect of the belief in the importance of one's own hard work for admission on the preference for grade-based admission (.13). 50 % of this total effect is mediated by the variance in perceiving the admission procedure as just, and the direct effect misses the threshold of statistical significance. Of the total negative effects of luck belief on the preference for grade-based admission, 20 % are mediated by the perception of the admission procedure as just, and 37 % of the total negative effect of social background belief on this preference.

Overall, *HIII.4a* on mediations of belief effects on preference for equal distribution cannot clearly be supported, except for a small mediation of the effect of the nonmeritocratic belief in the importance of social background on the preference for equal income distribution. *HIII.4b* on mediations of belief effects on preference for distribution based on educational merit can partly be supported for the effect of hard work belief, luck belief, and social background beliefs on the preference for school grade-based distribution of places in the program, and for effects of abilities beliefs on the preference for distribution of places in the program and income based on educational merit, even though only parts of the effects can be explained by differences in perceptions of justice.

Consequences of abilities beliefs: Differences by growth and fixed mindsets

A central finding of the previously presented SEMs is that the belief in the importance of abilities for success is crucial for the legitimation of inequality. The belief that one's own admission depends on abilities is positively associated with the perception of the admission procedure as just and the preferences for grade-based admission of hypothetical remaining places in the program, and tentatively negatively associated with the preferences for equal admission of paces in the program through a lottery. The belief that success in society generally depends on abilities is positively associated with the perception of social inequalities as just and the preference for income distribution based on educational merit and negatively associated with the preferences for equal income distribution.

At the end of Chapter 3.1, I discussed that one key feature of meritocratic ideology that makes it inequality-legitimizing is viewing inequality as the result of natural differences in individual abilities. This belief entails that people are born with innate and unalterable abilities, and thus inequality in outcomes is inevitable (Friedman et al., 2023; Solga, 2015). However, Dweck's (2006) social psychological mindset theory suggests that not everyone views abilities (here: talent and intelligence) as unalterable. While some people view abilities as stable (i.e., 'fixed mindset'), others may view them as alterable by the individual (i.e., 'growth mindset').

According to the argument that the perceived natural foundation of abilities legitimizes inequality, the effect of the belief that success depends on abilities on justice perceptions may be particularly strong among those with a fixed mindset. The argument stands in contrast to considerations of Rawlsian ethic of luck egalitarianism, whereby only differences based on choices that individuals can control are just (Rawls, 1999 [1971]). To investigate these considerations empirically, I conducted subgroup analyses separately for respondents who stated that they believe abilities are alterable and for those who believe they are unalterable. The majority of respondents (78 %) believed that abilities are rather unalterable.

Table 6.6 shows the results of the subgroup SEMs. A test for group invariance of parameters revealed that none of the group differences in effects of the abilities belief on the outcomes between respondents with a fixed mindset and a growth mindset are statistically significant. However, it needs to be considered that this lack of significance may also be influenced by the small sample size of the group with a growth mindset ($N = 352$).

Overall, the findings of this additional analysis further stressed the importance of the belief that success depends on abilities for the legitimation of educational inequality. It has inequality-legitimizing consequences among people who believe that these abilities are alterable and among the majority who believe that abilities are unalterable.

Table 6.6: Subgroup models: Direct and total effects of abilities beliefs on perceptions of justice and distributive preferences, separated by the belief that abilities are alterable vs. unalterable

	Domain-specific model: University admission					
	Abilities are alterable (N = 352)			Abilities are unalterable (N = 1,373)		
	Direct effect	Total effect	% of total effect via mediation	Direct effect	Total effect	% of total effect via mediation
Abilities beliefs → Perception of justice						
DV: Perception of admission as just						
Abilities Belief	.16 (.14)	No ind. path	-	.30** (.08)	No ind. path	-
Abilities beliefs → Distributive preferences (incl. mediation via perception of justice)						
DV: Equality preference - Admission through lottery						
Abilities belief	-.16 (.23)	-.18 (.23)	11	-.06 (.12)	-.06 (.12)	8
DV: Educational meritocracy preference - Admission based on grades						
Abilities belief	.26 (.16)	.31 (.16)	15	.30** (.09)	.39** (.09)	9
Goodness-of-fit-statistics						
SRMR		.053			.039	
	Societal model: Societal inequalities					
	Abilities are alterable (N = 352)			Abilities are unalterable (N = 1,373)		
	Direct effect	Total effect	% of total effect via mediation	Direct effect	Total effect	% of total effect via mediation
Abilities beliefs → Perception of justice						
DV: Perception of inequalities as just						
Abilities belief	.14 (.20)	No ind. path	-	.39** (.12)	No ind. path	-
Abilities beliefs → Distributive preferences (incl. Mediation via perception of justice)						
DV: Equality preference – Equal distribution of income						
Abilities belief	-.17 (.25)	-.22 (.26)	21	-.09 (.12)	-.16 (.12)	45
DV: Educational meritocracy preference – Income distribution based on degrees						
Abilities belief	.40 (.22)	.44 (.23)	9	.24 (.13)	.32* (.13)	27
Goodness-of-fit-statistics						
SRMR		.068			.046	

Note. Standardized coefficients. Full models conducted but only abilities beliefs displayed. None of the group differences in effects are statistically significant (p < .05). Source: Medical applicant data, author's calculations.

Tentatively, in line with expectations of the inequality-legitimizing effect of abilities belief due to the belief in the natural foundation of abilities, the results suggest that the effect of this belief on perceptions of justice may be stronger among those with a fixed mindset than among those with a growth mindset (.30 vs. .16 in the domain-specific model and .39 vs. .14 in the societal model). Regarding the consequences for distributive preferences, there were no systematical differences in the effects of abilities belief between respondents who adhere to the fixed or growth mindset.

6.4.2 Social differences in inequality beliefs contribute to different distributive preferences

In this chapter, I will answer my research question of whether social differences in inequality beliefs, and the resulting perception of justice, partly explain the association between parental education and distributive preferences.

Paths 2.1 (Parental education → Distributive preferences)

HII.5 that applicants from privileged backgrounds have a weaker preference for equal distribution and a stronger preference for distribution based on educational meritocracy than their less privileged peers is supported by the results for domain-specific distributive preferences for distribution of places in the program and for preferences for income distribution. Having two college-educated parents in comparison to none, has a negative effect on the preference for equal admission through a lottery (-.27) and the preference for equal income distribution (-.18). Furthermore, it has a positive effect on the preference for admission based on school grades (.20) and the preference on income distribution based on educational degrees (.23). The effects of having one college-educated parent (in comparison to none) are not statistically significant but coefficients point in the expected direction for preferences regarding income distribution (but not for preferences regarding distribution of places in the program).

Path 2.2 (Parental education → Inequality beliefs)

In Chapter 5, I already partly confirmed *HI.2* that applicants from privileged backgrounds hold stronger meritocratic and weaker nonmeritocratic beliefs than their less privileged peers. Even though inequality beliefs are in this chapter measured as distinct types derived from the extended belief scale included in wave 3, similar social differences in inequality beliefs can be observed in the SEMs (see bottom of Table 6.5). Having two college-educated parents (in comparison to none) has a positive effect on the belief that one's own admission depends on hard work (.17), and the effect on the belief that societal success depends on hard work (.06) points in the expected direction but misses the common threshold of statistical significance ($p < .05$). In wave 3, structural beliefs about success in one's own admission were also collected, and it becomes visible that having one or two college-educated parents (in comparison to none) has negative effects on the belief that admission depends on social background (-.21 and -.30). Furthermore, it also (tentatively) has negative effects on the belief that societal success depends on social background (-.15 and -.11).[38]

Mediation of path 2.1 (Parental education → Inequality beliefs → Perceptions of justice → Distributive preferences)

Now, I will discuss the results regarding *HII.6* that social differences in inequality beliefs, and the resulting perception of justice, partly mediate the relationship between parental education and distributive preferences for equality and educational meritocracy. For that purpose, I will report how much of the total effect of parental education on distributive preferences can be explained by differences in beliefs and distributive preferences (see top of Table 6.5). Only mediation of statistically significant effects of parental education will be reported.

Regarding preference for distribution of places in the program, of the total negative effect of having two college-educated parents on preference for equal admission through a lottery, 12 % are mediated by social differences in inequality beliefs and perceptions of justice. Of the total positive effect on the preference for grade-based admission, 45 % can be explained by differences in beliefs and the perception of the admission procedure as just, and this direct effect is not statistically significant. Regarding preferences for income distribution, of the total negative effect of having two college-educated parents on preference for equal distribution, 24 % can be explained by beliefs and justice perception, and 16 % of the total positive effect of it on the preference for income distribution based on educational degrees can be explained by it.

Overall, these findings support *HII.6* and suggest that differences in inequality beliefs, particularly stronger beliefs that their own admission depends on hard work and weaker beliefs that their own admission and societal success in general depends on social background among applicants from privileged backgrounds can partly explain social differences in distributive preferences.

Furthermore, when referring to university admission, social differences in the perception of the admission procedure as just may mediate part of the effect of parental education on the preferences for grade-based admission. Having two college-educated parents has a total positive effect on the perception of the admission procedure as just (.18) and this perception has a positive effect on the preference for grade-based admission (.29). However, 45 % of the effect of having two college-educated parents on the perception of justice is mediated by differences in inequality beliefs and the direct effect on perceiving the admission procedure as just is statistically insignificant, supporting the idea that indeed consequences of different beliefs can explain why those from privileged

---

[38] The effect of having two college-educated parents on this belief misses with $p = .07$ the common threshold of statistical significance only slightly.

background have stronger inequality-reproducing distributive preferences than their less privileged peers.

6.4.3 The role of the admission outcome in the relationship between the concepts

In Chapter 5, I already showed that success and failure in admission shape inequality beliefs and can (partly) explain the relationship between parental education and inequality beliefs. I will now reexamine these findings looking at the distinct types of inequality beliefs. Furthermore, in an exploratory manner, I will examine the role of admission outcomes (measured as admitted at the first attempt, admitted at the further attempt, and not admitted) for perceptions of justice and distributive preferences.

For that, I included admission status in the SEMs. Theoretically, one could expect that parental education influences admission chances, that the experience of being admitted influences inequality beliefs in a self-serving way, and (consequently) perceptions of justice and distributive preferences. As nominal categorical variables cannot be included as mediators in SEMs, I included admission outcomes at the same level as parental education and will examine their mediating effect by comparing the coefficients in this additional analysis to the base model results (Table 6.5). The results are displayed in Table 6.7. For the domain-specific model, the inclusion of this variable reduced the model fit (see GoF statistics), so this model should be interpreted with caution.

Admission outcome → Inequality beliefs

Self-serving mechanisms in inequality beliefs following success or failure in admission that were already confirmed in Chapter 5 are reflected in the findings of the SEMs. Compared with not being admitted, being admitted at the first and further attempts have (strong) positive effects on the domain-specific belief that one's own admission depends on hard work (1.12 and .59). Being admitted at the first attempt has a positive effect on the belief that admission depends on abilities (.49) and a negative effect on the belief that it depends on school grades (-.14) and luck (-.47). Being admitted at the first and further attempt have negative effects on the belief that admission depends social background (-.59 and -.39). Similar effects can be found for societal beliefs, even though—in line with my theoretical expectations and findings from Chapter 5—those effects are weaker. Being admitted at the first and further attempt have positive effects on the belief that societal success depends on hard work (.25 and .18), and being admitted at the first attempt has a positive effect on the belief that societal success depends on abilities (.14) and a negative effect on the belief that it depends on social background (-.15).

Unlike effects in the longitudinal analysis in Chapter 5, these cross-sectional effects reflect all of the differences between individuals such as pre-admission differences in beliefs, belief changes after admission and rejection, and potential effects of studying medicine and being surrounded by those who were successful in the admission. These results confirm that the winners have stronger beliefs that the admission procedure and societal success generally are meritocratic than those who were not successful. The effect of being admitted at the first attempt (in comparison to not being admitted) on the belief that one's own admission depends on effort is large in size, suggesting that—when considering the medium-sized effects in analyses presented in Chapter 5—differences in this belief between winners and losers may grow even further apart over time.

Table 6.7: Direct and total effects of parental education, admission outcome, inequality beliefs, and perceptions of justice on distributive preferences, and mediation mechanisms

	Domain-specific model: University admission			Societal model: Social inequalities		
	Direct effect	Total effect	% of total effect via mediation			
Path 1.1: Inequality beliefs → Distributive preference (incl. mediation via perception of justice) & Path 1.3: Perception of justice → Distributive preference & Path 2.1: Parental education → Distributive preference (incl. mediation via inequality beliefs and perception of justice)						
DV: Equality preference - Admission through lottery				*Equal distribution of income*		
Inequality beliefs:						
Hard work	.00 (.10)	-.00 (.10)	200	-.15 (.10)	-.15 (.10)	0
Abilities	-.11 (.12)	-.11 (.12)	3	-.11 (.11)	-.17 (.11)	23
Educational merit	-.04 (.06)	-.04 (.06)	0	.04 (.03)	.03 (.03)	-12
Luck	.10** (.03)	.10** (.03)	0	-.01 (.02)	-.02 (.02)	60
Social background	-.00 (.05)	.00 (.05)	33	.08* (.03)	.12 (.03)	33
Perception of justice	-.01 (.04)	No ind. path	-	-.21** (.03)	No ind. path	-
1 col.-ed. parent	.00 (.09)	.01 (.10)	50	-.06 (.06)	-.09 (.06)	30
2 col.-ed. parents	-.21* (.09)	-.21* (.09)	-0	-.12* (.06)	-.16** (.06)	22
Admitted at first attempt	-.33** (.12)	-.43** (.09)	24	-.11 (.06)	-.18** (.07)	35
Admitted at further attempt	-.06 (.10)	-.07 (.08)	21	-.10 (.06)	-.12 (.06)	18
DV: Educational meritocracy preference— Admission through grades				*Income distribution based on degrees*		
Inequality beliefs:						
Hard work	-.03 (.07)	.01 (.07)	273	.04 (.10)	.04 (.10)	0
Abilities	.36** (.09)	.43** (.09)	16	.29** (.11)	.37** (.11)	20
Educational merit	.02 (.04)	.03 (.04)	37	.01 (.03)	.02 (.02)	31
Luck	-.06** (.02)	-.07** (.02)	17	.06** (.03)	.07** (.02)	15
Social background	-.04 (.03)	-.07* (.03)	39	-.02 (.03)	-.06 (.04)	70
Perception of justice	.24** (.03)	No ind. path	-	.24** (.03)	No ind. path	-
1 col.-ed. parent	-.04 (.06)	-.02 (.07)	-56	.08 (.06)	.11 (.06)	28
2 col.-ed. parents	.06 (.06)	.06 (.06)	-0	.17** (.06)	.20** (.06)	15

	Domain-specific model: University admission			Societal model: Social inequalities		
	Direct effect	Total effect	% of total effect via mediation			
Admitted at first attempt	.59** (.08)	1.00** (.07)	41	.19** (.06)	.23** (.06)	19
Admitted at further attempt	.14* (.07)	.19** (.06)	30	.16** (.05)	.16** (.05)	3

Path 1.2: Inequality beliefs → Perception of justice & Parental education → Perception of justice (incl. mediation via inequality beliefs)

DV: Perception of admission as just   Perception of inequalities as just

Inequality beliefs:

Hard work	.17** (.06)	No ind. path	-	.00 (.09)	No ind. path	-
Abilities	.29** (.08)	No ind. path	-	.31** (.10)	No ind. path	-
Educational merit	.04 (.04)	No ind. path	-	.02 (.02)	No ind. path	-
Luck	-.05** (.02)	No ind. path	-	.04* (.02)	No ind. path	-
Social background	-.12** (.03)	No ind. path	-	-.18** (.03)	No ind. path	-
1 col.-ed. parent	.07 (.06)	.08 (.06)	15	.01 (.06)	.05 (.06)	86
2 col.-ed. parents	.06 (.05)	.07 (.06)	13	.06 (.05)	.08 (.05)	29
Admitted at first attempt	.44** (.07)	.86** (.06)	49	-.09 (.06)	-.03 (.06)	-262
Admitted at further attempt	-.01 (.06)	.15** (.05)	109	-.10* (.05)	-.08 (.05)	-36

Path 2.2: Parental education → Inequality beliefs

DV: Hard work

1 col.-ed. parent	.01 (.07)	No ind. Path	-	-.04 (.05)	No ind. path	-
2 col.-ed. parents	.01 (.07)	No ind. path	-	.03 (.04)	No ind. path	-
Admitted at first attempt	1.12** (.08)	No ind. Path	-	.25** (.05)	No ind. path	-
Admitted at further attempt	.59** (.06)	No ind. path	-	.18** (.04)	No ind. path	-

DV: Abilities

1 col.-ed. parent	-.04 (.07)	No ind. path	-	.07 (.05)	No ind. path	-
2 col.-ed. parents	-.09 (.06)	No ind. path	-	.03 (.04)	No ind. path	-
Admitted at first attempt	.49** (.07)	No ind. Path	-	.14** (.05)	No ind. path	-
Admitted at further attempt	.04 (.06)	No ind. path	-	.05 (.04)	No ind. path	-

DV: Educational merit

1 col.-ed. parent	-.04 (.04)	No ind. path	-	-.06 (.06)	No ind. path	-
2 col.-ed. parents	.01 (.04)	No ind. Path	-	-.05 (.06)	No ind. path	-
Admitted at first attempt	-.14** (.04)	No ind. Path	-	-.06 (.06)	No ind. path	-
Admitted at further attempt	.01 (.03)	No ind. Path	-	-.01 (.05)	No ind. path	-

DV: Luck

1 col.-ed. parent	-.01 (.08)	No ind. path	-	-.08 (.07)	No ind. path	-
2 col.-ed. parents	-.07 (.07)	No ind. Path	-	-.02 (.07)	No ind. path	-
Admitted at first attempt	-.47** (.08)	No ind. Path	-	-.02 (.07)	No ind. path	-
Admitted at further attempt	-.07 (.07)	No ind. path	-	-.00 (.06)	No ind. path	-

	Domain-specific model: University admission			Societal model: Social inequalities		
	Direct effect	Total effect	% of total effect via mediation			
DV: Social background						
1 col.-ed. parent	-.18** (.07)	No ind. path	-	-.14* (.06)	No ind. path	-
2 col.-ed. parents	-.22** (.06)	No ind. path	-	-.09 (.06)	No ind. path	-
Admitted at first attempt	-.59** (.07)	No ind. Path	-	-.15* (.07)	No ind. path	-
Admitted at further attempt	-.39** (.06)	No ind. path	-	-.06 (.06)	No ind. path	-
Goodness-of-fit-statistics						
CFI		.898			.912	
RMSEA		.068			.063	
SRMR		.038			.036	

Note. Standardized coefficients. All path models controlled for participation in experiment dummy. Reference for admitted at first / further attempt: not admitted. Reference for 1 / 2 coll.-ed. parent(s): No college-educated parent. Hard work, abilities, and social background are latent constructs. Percentage of total effect via mediation calculated based on nonrounded coefficients. N = 1,725; ** p < .01 * p < .05. Source: Medical applicant data, author's calculations.

Path 2.2 (Parental education → Inequality beliefs), when controlled for admission outcome

The base model results displayed in Table 6.5 suggested that there are substantial differences in the domain-specific hard work belief and domain-specific and societal social background beliefs by parental education. When including respondents' admission status (Table 6.7), the effect of having two college-educated parents on the domain-specific hard work belief becomes substantially smaller and statistically insignificant (.01, p = .85), while the effects of parental education on the domain-specific and societal social background beliefs become slightly smaller compared to the base model but remained substantial. Having one and having two college-educated parents compared to none have negative effects on the belief that social background is important for one's own admission, beyond social differences in the admission outcomes (-.18 and -.22). Furthermore, having one college-educated parent has a negative effect on the belief that social background is important for societal success in general (-.15), while the effect of having two college-educated parents on it points in the expected direction but is not statistically significant (-.11, p = .14). While social differences in the domain-specific hard work belief seem to be mainly driven by social differences in experiences of success and failure in admission[39], privileged parental education seems to have an independent neg-

---

39 In this model, the admission outcome is likely also a proxy for other educational experiences (such as GPA or, for admitted applicants, experiences in medical

ative effect on the belief that social background is important for one's own admission as well as for societal success in general.

Admission outcome → Perceptions of justice and distributive preferences

Being admitted at first and further attempt (in comparison to not being admitted) have total positive effects on perceiving the admission as just (.86 and .15) and on the preference for grade-based admission (1.00 and .19), and being admitted at the first attempt (but not at the further attempt) has a negative effect on the preference for equal admission through a lottery (-.43). The effect of being admitted at the first attempt is stronger than the effects of being admitted at the further attempt. These findings are in line with previous experimental research suggesting that winners tend to perceive the game as just (Molina et al., 2019). Furthermore, respondents who were admitted (especially at the first attempt) may have a certain self-interest to not support equal admission through a lottery and support grade-based admission, as they want to see the way through which they were admitted as just and legitimized, which can explain the findings.

Importantly, the SEMs suggest that part of the total effect of respondents' experience of success and failure in admission on these domain-specific outcomes is mediated by differences in inequality beliefs and distributive preferences by differences in inequality beliefs and perception of justice. Accordingly, 49 % of the total positive effect of being admitted at the first attempt on the perception of the admission procedure as just is mediated by differences in inequality beliefs, 24 % of the total negative effect on preference for equal admission through a lottery is mediated by differences in inequality belief and perceptions of justice, and 41 % of the total positive effect on the preference for admission based on school grades is mediated by differences in inequality beliefs and perceptions of justice. While there is a direct effect of the admission outcome on the variables of interest, part of the effect can be explained by differences in beliefs, which are shaped in a self-serving way by experiences in admission.

While being admitted at first or further attempt increases the perception of the admission procedure as just, being admitted does not increase the perception of societal inequalities as just. Indeed, it even seems to (tentatively) have direct negative effects on this perception (-.09 and -.10), which is suppressed by differences in inequality beliefs. Winners in admission are more likely to

---

school), as it measures whether applicants were admitted at the first attempt, further attempt or not admitted at least 2.5 years after they first applied. Thus, these findings do not contradict the findings in Chapter 5 that one admission decision itself can only to a small extent explain social differences in effort beliefs.

view the admission procedure as just than losers but may not necessarily view societal inequality in society in general as just. However, being admitted at the first attempt reduces the preference for equal income distribution (-.18), and being admitted at first and further attempts increases the preference for income distribution based on educational merit (.23 and .16). However, these effects are rather small in size compared to the strong effects on distributive preferences regarding admission. 35 % of the total negative effect of being admitted at the first attempt on equal income distribution is meditated by differences in inequality beliefs and perception of justice, and 19 % (3 %) of the total positive effect of being admitted at first (further) attempt on the preference for income distribution based on educational merit are mediated by these differences.

Change in associations between concepts, when controlled for admission outcome

When including admission outcomes, the effect of having two college-educated parents on perceiving the admission procedure as just (.07) and on the preference for distribution of places in the program based on school grades (.06) become smaller compared to the base model and are no longer statistically significant but still point in the expected direction. Part of the effect of having two college-educated parents on perceiving the admission procedure as just (.07) is mediated by differences in inequality beliefs (13 %). The negative effect of having two college-educated parents on the preference for equal admission through a lottery (-.21) remains statistically significant. Social differences in perceiving the admission procedure as just and in preference for grade-based admission seem to be mainly driven by differences in experiences of success and failure in admission, while there seems to be an independent effect of parental background on the preferences for equal admission through a lottery. The effects of parental education on distributive income preferences that were found in the main analysis (Table 6.5) remain when including the admission outcome, suggesting an effect of parental education on these preferences beyond the individual experience of success or failure in admission.

Most effects of inequality beliefs on perceptions of justice and distributive preferences, and of perceptions of justice on distributive preferences did not change substantially when including respondents' admission outcome. Only the effect of the domain-specific hard work belief on preference for grade-based admission became substantially smaller and statistically insignificant (.01, $p = .84$). Hence, this effect might be spurious: More applicants who were ultimately admitted to medical school (at either their first or subsequent attempt) were represented among those who have strong beliefs that admission depends on hard work, which is associated with a stronger preference for the allocation of remaining medical school places based on school grades.

6.5 Summary: How inequality beliefs (de)legitimize educational inequality

I will now briefly summarize and discuss the main findings presented in this chapter. A systematic summary of the results regarding the hypotheses can be found in Table 6.8 at the end of this chapter.

Before testing my hypotheses for this chapter's research objective, I identified distinct types of inequality beliefs using factor analyses. Subsequently, I examined how these distinct types of inequality beliefs influence perceptions of justice, and distributive preferences, and how the effects of inequality beliefs on the latter are mediated by perceptions of justice using SEM. Finally, I examined whether respondents' distributive preferences differ by parental education, and how social differences in inequality beliefs and justice perception contribute to these differences in distributive preferences.

Empirical research has explored the effects of meritocratic beliefs in the importance of hard work for success on perceptions of justice (e.g., Batruch et al., 2022; Mijs, 2021; Sachweh & Sthamer, 2019) and distributive preferences (e.g., Alesina & Giuliano, 2011; García-Sánchez et al., 2020; Kluegel & Miyano, 1995; Marquis & Rosset, 2021), but the effect of the belief in the importance of abilities for success as well as the effects on the preference for distribution based on educational inequality remain understudied.

Furthermore, instead of combining perceptions of justice and distributive preferences to investigate the relationship between them, most studies have only focused on one of these outcomes, even though some studies on distributive preferences imply that the effect of meritocratic belief is mediated by perception of justice in their theoretical arguments (Alesina & Giuliano, 2011). Empirical studies focus on the effect of the meritocratic belief that success depends on hard work, even though theoretical arguments suggest that the belief that it depends on abilities is also crucial for the legitimation of inequality (Solga, 2015). Finally, social background is not considered in these studies, even though previous research shows that it is associated with distributive preferences (e.g., Alesina & Giuliano, 2011; Lee, 2023; O'Grady, 2019).

This study contributes in several ways to research on the inequality-legitimizing effect of meritocratic beliefs. First, it explores the relationship between parental education, inequality beliefs, perception of justice, and distributive preferences—concepts that have not yet been combined in one study—and it considers potential mediation mechanisms. Second, it sheds light on the different consequences that distinct types of meritocratic and nonmeritocratic beliefs have for perceptions of justice and distributive preferences. Third, it allows comparing the effect of domain-specific inequality beliefs, referring to admission to highly selective medical programs, to the effect of societal inequality beliefs, referring to societal inequality generally.

The results of the factor analysis are in line with expectations of attributional theory and suggest that there are 3 distinct meritocratic beliefs and 2 distinct nonmeritocratic beliefs: meritocratic hard work beliefs, abilities beliefs and educational merit belief, and nonmeritocratic luck beliefs and social background beliefs.

The findings reinforce the notion that beliefs about inequality are crucial in (de)legitimizing (educational) inequality but reveal different consequences of distinct types of inequality beliefs for perceptions of justice and distributive preferences and differences in the evaluation of one's own admission and of societal inequalities in general. While the meritocratic belief that one's own admission depends on hard work is positively associated with perceiving the admission procedure as just and with the preference for admission based on school grades[40], the belief that societal success depends on hard work is not substantially associated with the perception of societal inequalities or with preferences for income distribution. The meritocratic belief that one's own admission depends on abilities has stronger effects on these outcomes, and seems to be more crucial for the legitimation of (educational) inequality than hard work beliefs: Referring to admission as well as societal inequalities, abilities beliefs are positively associated with perceptions of justice and the preference for distribution (of places in the program and income) based on educational merit. The belief that success in admission or society in general depends on educational merit has no inequality-legitimizing consequences.

When referring to admission, luck and background beliefs are negatively associated with the perception of justice and the preferences for distribution based on educational merit, and luck belief is positively associated with the preferences for equal distribution. By contrast, when referring to societal inequalities, the belief that success depends on luck has no inequality-delegitimizing consequences but the belief that it depends on social background is negatively associated with the perception of justice and positively with the preference for equal distribution.

While meritocratic beliefs—particularly abilities belief—increase the perception of justice of admission and societal inequalities and the preference distribution based on educational merit, they only tentatively reduce the preference for equal distribution. This preference is rather influenced by nonmeritocratic beliefs: the luck belief for admission, and the social background belief for income distribution.

Overall, inequality beliefs influence perceptions of justice and distributive preferences, but can the effect on distributive preference be explained by their effect on perceptions of justice? The findings show that the relationship between inequality beliefs, perception of justice, and distributive preferences is

---

40 As suggested by the additional analyses in Chapter 6.4.3 including applicants' admission outcome (Table 6.7) the effect of hard work belief on preference for grade-based admission may be spurious.

more complex than this assumption (e.g., Alesina & Giuliano, 2011). Although the proposed mediation paths are partly supported by the findings, perceptions of justice only mediate part of the belief effects on distributive preferences and direct effects of inequality beliefs remain. No clear pattern in which distinct meritocratic or nonmeritocratic beliefs influence distributive preferences rather directly or indirectly could be observed. As I decided that it is only feasible to discuss mediation of substantial effects, I can also not draw any clear conclusion as to whether perceptions of justice play a more important role in the effect of inequality beliefs on the preference for equal distribution or on the preference for distribution based on educational meritocracy.

In line with my expectations, the findings show that applicants from privileged backgrounds have stronger domain-specific hard work beliefs and weaker domain-specific and societal hard work beliefs, a weaker preference for equal distribution, and a stronger preference for distribution based on educational merit. They support the proposed arguments that differences in inequality beliefs (particularly differences in social background beliefs), and resulting perception of justice, partly mediate the effect of privileged social origin on inequality-reproducing distributive preferences. However, a substantial direct effect of parental education on distributive preferences remains, even when controlling for inequality beliefs and perception of justice. Previous research suggests that self-interest (Fong, 2001; Langsaether & Evans, 2020), early socialization (O'Grady, 2019), and group identity affect distributive preferences (Ku & Salmon, 2013)—a line of research that deserves further scholarly attention.

The additional analyses including admission outcomes stress the importance of inequality beliefs for the (de)legitimation of inequality by showing that the effects of the admission outcome on perceptions of justice and distributive preferences—effects that are particularly strong in the domain-specific model—can to a large extent be explained by self-serving mechanism in inequality beliefs related to success or failure in admission. Furthermore, the findings confirm and complement the longitudinal analyses in Chapter 5, and suggest that differences in inequality beliefs between winners and losers (particularly in the belief in the importance of effort for one's own admission) may even widen over time.

Table 6.8: Systematic illustration of results of hypotheses testing II

Hypotheses	Domain-specific model		Societal model	
	Meritocratic Beliefs	Nonmeritocratic Beliefs	Meritocratic Beliefs	Nonmeritocratic Beliefs
HII.1 (path 1.1): Meritocratic beliefs are negatively associated with the preference for equal distribution and positively with the preference for distribution based on educational meritocracy, while the opposite is true for nonmeritocratic beliefs.	(+) Not supported for equality preferences For educational meritocracy preference: Supported for hard work and abilities belief	(+) For equality preferences: Supported for luck belief For educational meritocracy preference: Supported for luck and social background belief	(+) Not supported for equality preferences For educational meritocracy preference: Supported for abilities belief	(+) For equality preferences: Supported for social background belief Not supported for educational meritocracy preference (positive effect of luck belief)
HII.2 (path 1.2): Meritocratic beliefs lead to the perception of higher justice, while nonmeritocratic beliefs lead to a perception of lower justice.	+ Supported for hard work and abilities beliefs	+ Supported for luck and social background beliefs	+ Supported for abilities belief	(+) Supported for social background belief (luck belief has a positive effect)
HII.3 (path 1.3): The more people perceive inequality as just, the more opposed they will be to equal distribution and the more they will support educational meritocracy.	(+) Supported for educational meritocracy preference		+ Supported for equality preferences and educational meritocracy preference	
HII.4a: Perception of justice mediates the negative relationship between meritocratic beliefs and the preference for equal distribution, and mediates the positive relationship between nonmeritocratic beliefs and this preference.	− (No effect of meritocratic beliefs)	(+) (Only 2 % of total positive effect of luck belief mediated by perception of justice)	− (No statistically significant effect of meritocratic beliefs)	(+) 33 % of total positive effect of social background mediated by perception of justice
HII.4b: Perception of justice mediates the positive relationship between meritocratic beliefs and the preference for distribution based on educational meritocracy, and mediates the negative relationship between nonmeritocratic beliefs and this preference.	(+) 50 % of total positive effects of hard work belief and 21 % of total positive effect of abilities belief are mediated by perception of justice	(+) 20 % of total negative effect of luck belief 37 % of total negative of social background belief mediated by perception of justice	(+) 21 % of total positive effects of abilities belief is mediated by perception of justice	− (Positive effect of luck belief and no statistically significant effect of social background belief)

Hypotheses	Domain-specific model	Societal model
HII.5 (path 2.1): Applicants from privileged backgrounds have a weaker preference for equal distribution and a stronger preference for distribution based on educational meritocracy than their less privileged peers.	+ Supported for equality preference and educational meritocracy preference	+ Supported for equality preference and educational meritocracy preference
HII.6: Social differences in inequality beliefs, and the resulting perception of justice, partly mediate the relationship between parental education and distributive preferences for equality and educational meritocracy.	+ For equality preference: 12 % of total negative effect of having two college-educated parents mediated by inequality beliefs and perception of justice For educational meritocracy preference: 45 % of total positive effect of having two college-educated parents mediated by inequality beliefs and perception of justice	+ For equality preference: 24 % of total negative effect of having two college-educated parents mediated by inequality beliefs and perception of justice For educational meritocracy preference: 26 % of total positive effect of having two college-educated parents mediated by inequality beliefs and perception of justice

Note. [a] Effect of hard work belief on preferences for grade-based admission may be spurious (driven by its association with admission status). Meritocratic beliefs = hard work belief, abilities belief, and educational merit belief. Nonmeritocratic beliefs = luck belief and social background beliefs. Hypotheses only supported for mentioned beliefs. Grey areas are not divided into meritocratic and nonmeritocratic beliefs. Author's illustration

7 The experience of rejection and the association between beliefs in meritocratic admission and persistence in goal pursuit

Findings from Chapter 5 supported my theoretical expectations that experiencing failure in admission (tentatively) reduces the meritocratic belief that one's own admission depends on effort and increases the belief that one's own admission depends on luck. Beyond these direct effects of the admission outcome, findings in Chapters 5 and 6 showed that the groups of admitted applicants hold stronger meritocratic and weaker nonmeritocratic beliefs about the admission than rejected applicants, which is partly caused by pre-admission differences in experiences of success and failure related to their GPA. However, even among rejected applicants, within-group differences in inequality beliefs remain and may be socially stratified.

In this chapter, I explore how beliefs in meritocratic admission after a first rejection affect applicants' persistence in goal pursuit. This chapter addresses the research questions a) whether there are differences in the persistence in goal pursuit after a first rejection of medical applicants by parental education; b) how beliefs in meritocratic admission affect persistence in goal pursuit; c) whether social differences in beliefs in meritocratic admission mediate part of the effect of parental education on persistence in goal pursuit, and; d) whether the effect of beliefs in meritocratic admission on persistence in goal pursuit differs by parental education.

7.1 Descriptive statistics: Persistence and beliefs in meritocratic admission

In this chapter, I examine a specific group of applicants to medical school, namely first-time applicants who were rejected when applying for the winter semester of 2018. As described in Chapter 4.1, wave 2 was conducted in November 2018 (immediately after applicants received their first rejection), and wave 3 was conducted in February 2021. Since admissions take place every semester, between waves 2 and 3, rejected applicants had potentially four times the chance to reapply and be admitted (or rejected). The longitudinal data allows observing applicants' self-predicted persistence in goal pursuit in wave 2 and their actual reapplication behavior between the summer semester of 2018 and the winter semester of 2020/21.

As argued in Chapter 4.3, I decided to include only first-time applicants in the main analyses, as I expect previous experiences of rejection to affect persistence in goal pursuit and inequality beliefs. For the group of repeatedly rejected applicants in 2018, it is unclear when and how many times they previously applied,[41] and therefore it would not be possible to properly account for previous experiences in admission.

The sample of first-time rejected applicants is furthermore restricted to only those who did still indicate medicine as their preferred field of study (in wave 2 or wave 3, depending on the outcome variable). The main reason for that is that the variables goal engagement, goal disengagement, reapplication intention, and number of reapplication attempts were only collected for this group. It did not seem feasible to ask these questions to applicants who changed their preferred field of study. In wave 2, 27 % no longer reported medicine as their preferred field of study, while in wave 3, 36 % did. However, a change in the preferred field of study may also be a sign of a weak persistence in goal pursuit, an issue that will be discussed in the limitations and robustness checks section (Chapter 7.5).

Table 7.1 shows the main variables of interest[42] and their distributions in the sample included in the analyses with self-predicted persistence in goal pursuit (sample IIIa), and the sample included in the analyses with applicants' reapplication behavior (sample IIIb). Sample IIIa comprises 594 respondents (first-time rejected applicants who participated in waves 1 and 2 and did not change their preferred field of study), and sample IIIb comprises 190 respondents (those of sample IIIa who participated in wave 3 and did not change their preferred field of study). Descriptive statistics on gender, age, GPA, and parental education were provided in Chapter 4.5 (Table 4.2).

Inequality beliefs, goal engagement, goal disengagement, and reapplication intention were measured in all waves; retrospective reapplication behavior between waves 2 and 3 was measured in wave 3. For inequality beliefs, goal engagement, goal disengagement, and reapplication intention, I use the measures in wave 2 because I am interested in how the beliefs in meritocratic admission after receiving a rejection affects the self-predicted persistence in goal pursuit at that point, and how it affects the actual behavior following afterward between waves 2 and 3.

Table 7.1 shows that applicants have very high levels of goal engagement (4.50 on a 5-point scale), and rather low levels of goal disengagement (1.78 on a 5-point scale). 93 % of the respondents chose 5, the highest possible value on the scale, for reapplication intention. I therefore decided to dichotomize the

---

41 In waves 1 and 2, repeat applicants were not asked how many times they previously applied, and in wave 3 only the subgroup of those who reapplied at least once between wave 2 and 3 were asked this question.
42 The concepts and questionnaire item design were more thoroughly described in Chapter 4.2.

initial variable (5-point scale) into a dummy variable called high reapplication behavior.

Table 7.1: Description and distributions of persistence and inequality beliefs

Concept	Description	Scale	% or mean (sd)	
			Sample IIIa	Sample IIIb
N			594	190
			Mean (sd) / distributions	
Persistence in goal pursuit				
Goal engagement (W2)	Index out of 3 items: Commitment to pursue the goal of studying at medical school	1-5	4.50 (.64)	-
Goal disengagement (W2)	Index out of 2 items: Willingness to change the field of study/career goal	1-5	1.78 (.82)	-
High reapplication intention (W2)	Plan to reapply	Original 1-5, due to skewed distribution recoded: 1-4 = 0; 5 = 1	7 % low reapplication intention; 93 % high reapplication intention	-
Number of reapplication attempts (W3)	Number of times applicants reapplied between waves 2 and 3	0-4 (analyses controlled for admitted in semester x)	-	2.29 (1.33) 12 % 0 attempts 15 % 1 attempt 33 % 2 attempts 13 % 3 attempts 27 % 4 attempts
Inequality beliefs (W2) Own admission depends on:				
Effort			3.32 (1.24)	3.48 (1.18)
Talent			3.09 (1.22)	3.08 (1.17)
Luck			3.88 (1.15)	4.01 (1.10)

Note. Sampling and panel weights applied. Variables are more thoroughly described in Chapter 4.2 and Table A4.1. Source: Medical applicant data, author's illustration.

First-time rejected applicants are most in agreement that their own admission depends on luck but also believe that it depends on effort and talent. All item scores are relatively close to each other suggesting that they believe that their own admission depends on a combination of these meritocratic and nonmeritocratic factors. Due to sample attrition from wave 2 to wave 3, there are slight differences in inequality beliefs (measured in W2) between the samples. Applicants who remained in the survey have slightly stronger beliefs that their own admission depends on effort but also stronger beliefs that it depends on luck compared to the whole W2 sample.

7.2 Methodological approach

To test *HIII.1*, I examine whether persistence in goal pursuit after a first rejection differs by parental education. First, I compare applicants' self-predicted persistence in goal pursuit (i.e., goal (dis)engagement, reapplication intention) and reapplication attempts and outcomes for each application time point (e.g., winter 2018, summer 2019, winter 2019, summer 2020, winter 2020) between applicants with no, one, and two college-educated parents. Subsequently, I conduct bivariate discrete-time hazard models[43] of reapplication behavior and present the so-called survival probability of an individual from a given social background—the conditional likelihood that an event will not occur and that an individual will remain in the risk set at a certain point of time if the event has not occurred yet (Singer & Willett, 2003). The method of discrete-time hazard models allows the temporal dimension of events and the resulting censoring to be considered. Censoring occurs when the event of interest has not taken place yet after the observed period (Singer & Willett, 2003), here from the summer semester of 2019 to the winter semester of 2020. In my figures, the survival probabilities show the conditional likelihood of an individual (from a given social background) of not reapplying for a given semester (if they have not yet reapplied).

To reexamine *HIII.1* and test *HIII.2—HIII.4*, I conduct step-wise (linear and logistic) regression models to examine how parental education and beliefs in meritocratic admission affect self-predicted persistence in goal pursuit (i.e., goal engagement, goal disengagement, reapplication intention) immediately after being rejected, and how they affect reapplication behavior (i.e., number of reapplication attempts) between waves 2 and 3. The first model contains only parental education and the control variables (age and gender), in the second model beliefs in meritocratic admission were added, and in the third model interaction terms between beliefs in meritocratic admission and parental education were added. The models with the numbers of reapplication attempts also include a control variable whether and when applicants were admitted (as the

---

43 To conduct the models, the Stata command 'prsnperd' was used to construct person-period data, and the 'dthaz' command was used to estimate the discrete-time hazard models, and illustrate the bivariate relationship between parental education and applicants' conditional likelihood to reapply for each time point.

highest possible number of reapplication attempts depends on this variable) and a dummy variable whether respondents participated in the experimental survey (see control variables, Chapter 4.2).

7.3 Social differences in persistence and beliefs in meritocratic admission

As a first descriptive step to access social differences in self-predicted persistence, reapplication behavior, and beliefs in meritocratic admission, I will examine the bivariate relationship between parental education and these outcomes.

Social differences in self-predicted persistence

Table 7.2 shows the average measurements of first-time rejected applicants' persistence in goal pursuit by parental education.

Table 7.2: Persistence in goal pursuit after a first rejection by parental education

Parental education	No college-educated parent	One college-educated parent	Two college-educated parents
N	190	165	239
	Mean (sd) / distributions		
Goal engagement	4.45 (0.68)	4.47 (0.67)	4.54 (0.59)
Goal disengagement	1.80 (0.94)	1.77 (0.76)	1.76 (0.77)
High reapplication intention	95 %	91 %	92 %

Note. None of the means statistically significant ($p < .05$) different from each other. Sampling and panel weights applied. Source: Medical applicant data, author's calculations.

While the differences in group means of goal engagement point in the expected direction, none of the social differences in persistence is statistically significant ($p < .05$). Tentatively, applicants with two college-educated parents have a slightly stronger goal engagement (.09, one-seventh of a standard deviation), but other group differences are even smaller in size (less than one-eighth of a standard deviation) and should thus not be considered substantial. The number of reapplication attempts is not included in the table, as the maximum number of reapplication attempts is conditional on when and whether applicants were admitted, and hence a group mean comparison would be misleading.

Social differences in reapplication behavior and outcomes

Table 7.3 shows the application and admission shares of first-time applicants by parental education for the winter semester 2018, and the reapplication behavior and reapplication outcomes for the consecutive semesters. The applicants who have been rejected at one point in time are those who could potentially reapply at the next point in time, and thus the sample size decreases in each row.[44]

Among first-time applicants for the winter semester of 2018, the group of applicants with two college-educated parents is the largest. Furthermore, applicants with two college-educated parents are also substantially more likely to be admitted (admission rate: 42 %) than those with no college-educated parent (admission rate: 30 %). The admission rate of those with one college-educated parent (38 %) falls in the middle of these two poles. This descriptive finding reconfirms *HI.1* already tested in Chapter 5.

What happens after these initial differences in admission chances? The descriptive statistics show tentatively that there are differences in reapplication behavior by applicants' parental education. The share of applicants who decided not to apply is the highest among applicants with no college-educated parent for all time points of possible application (except for the summer semester of 2019) compared to applicants with one or two college-educated parents.

Social differences in the reapplication behavior for the summer semester of 2020 are particularly pronounced. While 53 % of applicants with no college-educated parent and 49 % of applicants with one college-educated parent decided not to reapply, this was only the case for 31 % of those with two college-educated parents. This difference of 22 percentage points in reapplication behavior between applicants with no and two college-educated parents corresponds to almost one-half of a standard deviation, reflecting a medium effect size (J. Cohen, 1992). However, all social differences in reapplication behavior are statically insignificant (based on Bonferroni post-hoc tests)—a finding that—considering the effects sizes—is most likely caused by the small case numbers.

---

44 Note that percentages of admission / reapplication shares are weighted but case numbers (N) are not. The N of potential applicants does not change from summer 2019 to winter 2019, as none of the applicants included in the sample was admitted in the summer semester of 2019. Considerably fewer universities offer admission in the summer semesters than in the winter semester, which is reflected in the admission and application shares.

Table 7.3: Reapplication behavior and outcomes for each semester by parental education

Semester of Application	No college-educated parent			One college-educated parent			Two college-educated parents			N
	Applied	Not re-applied	N	Applied	Not re-applied	N	Applied	Not re-applied	N	
	Admitted / Rejected			Admitted / Rejected			Admitted / Rejected			
Winter 18	30 % / 70 %	-	387	38 % / 62 %	-	415	42 % ** / 58 % **	-	709	1511
Summer 19[1]	0 % / 59 %	41 %	61	0 % / 64 %	36 %	49	0 % / 57 %	43 %	80	190
Winter 19	21 % / 59 %	20 %	61	28 % / 57 %	15 %	49	47 % ** / 38 % **	15 %	80	190
Summer 20	6 % / 41 %	53 %	46	9 % / 42 %	49 %	35	10 % / 59 %	31 %	40	121
Winter 20	15 % / 51 %	34 %	43	21 % / 48 %	31 %	34	24 % / 44 %	32 %	32	106

Note. Sample includes only first-time applicants (in winter 2018) who stated that they applied to their preferred field of medicine. Cases with missing values on any of the variables included in the models are excluded. 1 Those who stated in the third wave (February 2021), that their preferences had changed in the meantime were not asked about the reapplication behavior between summer 19 and winter 20; all cases with missing values on the reapplication behavior variable were excluded. Significance of group differences in admission rate (Asterix placed at share of admitted & rejected) and reapplication behavior (Asterix placed at share of not applied) in comparison to applicants with no college-educated parent: ** $p < .01$ * $p < .05$. Sampling weight applied for admission in winter semester 2018, panel weight applied for subsequent semesters (see weighting strategy in Chapter 4.4). Absolute numbers (N) not weighted. Source: Medical applicant data, author's calculations.

Beyond the reapplication behavior, there are furthermore differences in the admission likelihood in these further attempts by parental education. For all time points, the share of admitted is the highest among applicants with two college-educated parents and the lowest among applicants with no college-educated parent. For the winter semester of 2019, differences are the largest in size (one-half of a standard deviation) and statistically significant. While only 21 % of applicants with no college-educated parent and 28 % of applicants with one college-educated parents are admitted, 47 % of applicants with two college-educated parents are admitted. This difference in admission likelihood can to a large extent be explained by social differences in applicants' GPA. In sample IIIb, applicants with no college-educated parent have an average GPA of 1.99 and applicants with one college-educated parent of 2.02, while applicants with two college-educated parents have an average GPA of 1.81.

Overall, these findings support *HI.1* beyond initial differences in admission chances by parental education. Even at further attempts of admission, applicants from privileged backgrounds are more likely to be admitted. Social differences in reapplication behavior may contribute to these differences in admission likelihood to a minor extent, although this cannot clearly be supported by the findings, as social differences in reapplication behavior point in the expected direction but are statistically insignificant.

Figure 7.1: Survival probabilities for reapplication behavior by parental education (discrete-time hazard models)

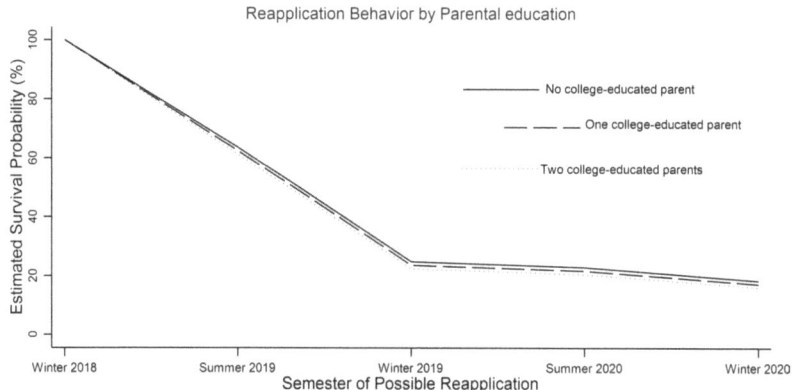

Note. Retrospective data on reapplication behavior after first-time rejection from the 3rd survey wave. N: 0 coll.-ed. parent: 131 (32 censored); 1 coll.-ed. parent: 111 (20 censored); 2 coll.-ed. parents: 174 (40 censored). Censored = Never applied. Only those included whose preference to study a specific field of medicine did not change. Group differences not statistically significant $p > .05$. Panel weight applied. Source: Medical applicant data, author's calculations.

To investigate the relationship between parental education and reapplication behavior further; I conducted discrete-time hazard models.

Figure 7.1 shows the result of these models and the likelihood of each individual from a certain social background of not applying at a certain time point (here: semester), conditionally on not having applied yet (survival probabilities). Hence, it investigates social differences in reapplying at least once in the two years after receiving the first rejection.

The results suggest that there are no substantial differences, whereby differences are neither substantial in size nor statistically significant. The conditional likelihood of not having reapplied at the latest observed time point (winter semester 2020) for applicants with no college-educated parent is 18 %, compared with 17 % for those with one or two college-educated parents.

Overall, the findings presented in this chapter, suggest that there are no substantial differences in applicants' persistence by parental education and that *HIII.1*—that applicants from privileged backgrounds show a stronger persistence in goal pursuit than their less privileged peers—cannot be supported.

However, while differences in self-predicted persistence (goal engagement, goal disengagement, and high reapplication intention) are small in size and not substantial, the lack of statistical significance of group differences in reapplication behavior may be caused by the small case numbers of sample IIIb. Although the likelihood to reapply at least once seems to be very high (less than one-fifth did not reapply within the observed two-year period) and does not seem to differ by parental education, the descriptive statistics reveal that the share of applicants who decided to not to apply is the highest among applicants with no college-educated parent for winter semester 2019, summer semester 2020, and winter semester 2020 compared to applicants with one or two college-educated parents. Thus, in the regression models, I will examine the association between parental education and the number of reapplication attempts (controlled for when and whether applicants were admitted).

Social differences in beliefs in meritocratic admission

In Chapter 5.3, the analyses confirmed that applicants with two college-educated parents hold a stronger meritocratic belief that their own admission depends on effort than those with no college-educated parent—a difference that is shaped by differences in educational experiences (experiences in school measured through GPA as a proxy and experiences in admission).[45]

Table 7.4: Average domain-specific inequality beliefs by parental education

	Sample IIIa			Sample IIIb		
	No college-educated parent (N = 190)	One college-educated parent (N = 165)	Two college-educated parents (N = 239)	No college-educated parent (N = 87)	One college-educated parent (N = 82)	Two college-educated parents (N = 113)
	mean (sd)			mean (sd)		
Domain-specific inequality beliefs: Admission depends on one's own:						
Effort	3.19	3.37	3.37	3.36	3.39	3.43
	(1.23)	(1.16)	(1.29)	(1.27)	(1.20)	(1.27)
Talent	3.10	3.06	3.11	2.97	3.07	3.18
	(1.22)	(1.15)	(1.27)	(1.27)	(1.14)	(1.28)
Luck	3.88	3.87	3.89	3.99	3.84	3.92
	(1.23)	(1.12)	(1.11)	(1.22)	(1.15)	(1.06)

Note. Scale of Beliefs in the Importance of Different Factors for Success: 1 – 5. None of the means statistically significant ($p < .05$) different from each other. Sampling weight applied. Source: Medical applicant data, author's calculations.

---

45 Analyses in Chapter 6.4.3 suggested that the effect of parental education on the domain-specific effort belief can be entirely explained by differences in applicants' admission outcome (measured as admitted at first and further attempt, and not admitted). However, here the application outcome after at least 2 years (respondents applied latest in 2018 for the first time) is considered, which is likely to reduce the variance in GPA even further: Those with a GPA close to the threshold may eventually be admitted after several attempts.

While only looking at the group of first-time rejected applicants removes the variance in experiences in admission, applicants may still vary in their broader educational experiences. Additional analyses provided in Chapter 5 suggest that (previous) experiences in admission only explain part of social differences in the beliefs that one's own admission depends on effort, while differences in GPA within the group of admitted and rejected applicants explain the other part.

Table 7.4 shows social differences in domain-specific beliefs about one's own admission for sample IIIa and sample IIIb. Tentatively, applicants with one and two college-educated parents have slightly stronger beliefs that their own admission depends on effort than applicants with no college-educated parent but these differences fail to reach statistical significance ($p < .05$). Social differences in this belief in sample IIIa are small but may be considered substantial (effect size: one-sixth of a standard deviation), and the lack of significance may be mostly caused by small case numbers. Differences in sample IIIb are not substantial in size (effect size: one-seventeenth of a standard deviation): Those who participated in wave 3 have slightly stronger beliefs that their own admission depends on effort than the whole sample of first-time rejected applicants that participated in wave 2 and may be more homogenous in this belief.

7.4 Influence of parental education and beliefs in meritocratic admission on persistence in goal pursuit

Table 7.5 shows the results from the step-wise regression models on three measurements of self-predicted persistence in goal pursuit: goal engagement, goal disengagement, and the binary-coded variable high reapplication intention. Furthermore, it shows the models on the number of reapplication attempts between waves 2 and 3.[46] The discrete-time hazard models (Figure 7.1) examined differences in the likelihood to reapply at least once, considering the temporal dimension of the potential application time points, under the condition, that applicants have not reapplied yet. The outcome observed here—the num-

---

[46] The number of possible reapplication attempts is restricted by whether and when applicants were admitted between waves 2 and 3. If an applicant was admitted for the winter semester 2019, their maximum possible number of reapplication attempts is two, while if they were only admitted for the winter semester 2020 or were not admitted at all in the observed period, their maximum possible number of reapplication attempts is four. Therefore, I included an 'admitted in semester X' dummy variable to only examine variation within the group of applicants with the same possible number of reapplication attempts.

ber of reapplication attempts—complements these findings. The question here is not only whether they reapply at all but how often they reapply.

Consistently across all models, applicants' parental education is not significantly associated with their persistence in goal pursuit, including the number of application attempts—although the coefficients of this variable point in the expected directions[47]. Eventually, *HIII.1* cannot be supported based on the analyses. However, tentatively, applicants with one and two college-educated parents have a slightly higher number of reapplication attempts than those with no college-educated parent (M1: .14 / .18).

The belief that one's own admission depends on effort is positively associated with applicants' goal engagement (M2: .07). For the other outcome variables and beliefs that admission depends on talent or luck, there seem to be no statistically significant associations. However, the coefficient for the effect of the belief that admission depends on talent on the number of reapplication attempts is somewhat larger (M2: -.11), which tentatively suggests that this belief may be negatively associated with the number of reapplication attempts. However, the effect fails to reach statistical significance (see Footnote 47). Overall, *HIII.2*—that beliefs in meritocratic admission are positively associated with persistence in goal pursuit, while the opposite is true for beliefs in nonmeritocratic admission—can only be partly confirmed.

Since I neither find the expected association of parental education with persistence in goal pursuit, nor a substantial association of parental education with belief in meritocratic admission, it is not appropriate to expect that (non-substantial) social differences in beliefs about meritocratic admission mediate part of the (not-confirmed) effect of parental education on persistence in goal pursuit as expected in *HIII.3*. Hence, for the group of first-time rejected applicants to medical school, this hypothesis must be rejected.

Regarding heterogeneity of belief effects, findings from model 3 suggest some interaction between the belief effect and parental education. Compared with applicants with no college-educated parent, the belief that one's own admission depends on effort has a more negative effect on goal disengagement for applicants with one college-educated parent than for those with no college-educated parent (-.18). The interaction effect with having two college-educated parents points in the same direction (-.08) but is statistically insignificant. Furthermore, for applicants with one college-educated parent, the belief that one's own admission depends on effort has (tentatively) a more positive effect on the number of reapplication attempts (.46, $p < .10$), and the belief that it depends on talent has tentatively a more negative effect on the number of reapplication attempts (-.44, $p < .10$) than for applicants with no college-educated parent.

---

[47] The models on the number of reapplication attempts indicate large standard errors that are likely caused by a small sample size. Hence, some effects may miss the threshold of statistical significance due to the small number of cases included in the models.

Table 7.5: Effects of parental education and beliefs in meritocratic admission on persistence in goal pursuit

	Goal Engagement (1-5)			Goal Disengagement (1-5)			High Reapplication Intention (0-1)			Number of Reapplication Attempts (0-4)		
	b (std. err.)			b (std. err.)			margins (std. err.)			b (std. err.)		
	M1	M2	M3	M1	M2	M3	M1	M2	M3	M1	M2	M3
Parental education (ref. no college-educated parent)												
1 college-educated parent	-.00 (.08)	-.01 (.08)	-.39 (.46)	-.05 (.10)	-.05 (.08)	.91 (.50)	-.04 (.03)	-.04 (.03)	-.08 (.24)	.14 (.27)	.13 (.26)	-.52 (1.43)
2 college-educated parents	.05 (.07)	.04 (.07)	.43 (.34)	-.07 (.10)	-.07 (.10)	.12 (.45)	-.03 (.03)	-.02 (.03)	.01 (.13)	.18 (.27)	.19 (.27)	-.92 (1.33)
Belief that one's own admission depends on …												
Effort		.07 ** (.03)	.07 (.05)		-.01 (.03)	.04 (.05)		-.00 (.01)	.01 (.02)		.03 (.09)	-.14 (.20)
Talent		-.01 (.02)	-.01 (.04)		.01 (.03)	-.00 (.05)		.02 (.01)	-.01 (.01)		-.11 (.09)	.04 (.08)
Luck		.03 (.03)	.05 (.05)		.01 (.04)	.07 (.04)		-.01 (.01)	-.00 (.02)		-.06 (.08)	-.18 (.14)
Interaction: Beliefs * Parental education												
Effort#1-col			.08 (.07)			-.18 * (.09)			-.03 (.03)			.46 ° (.25)
Effort#2-col			-.04 (.06)			-.08 (.08)			-.01 (.02)			.14 (.20)

	Goal Engagement (1-5)			Goal Disengagement (1-5)			High Reapplication Intention (0-1)			Number of Reapplication Attempts (0-4)		
	b (std. err.)			b (std. err.)			margins (std. err.)			b (std. err.)		
	M1	M2	M3	M1	M2	M3	M1	M2	M3	M1	M2	M3
Talent#1-col			.06 (.07)			-.03 (.09)			.03 (.02)			-.44° (.23)
Talent#2-col			-.02 (.06)			.09 (.08)			.03 (.02)			-.10 (.19)
Luck#1-col			-.02 (.07)			-.07 (.09)			.01 (.02)			.09 (.22)
Luck#2-col			-.05 (.06)			-.05 (.09)			-.02 (.02)			.22 (.18)
Control variables												
Female	-.07 (.06)	-.08 (.06)	-.08 (.06)	.08 (.07)	.10 (.08)	.07 (.09)	.03 (.03)	.03 (.03)	.03 (.02)	-.18 (.21)	-.21 (.21)	-.24 (.21)
Age (z-standardized)	-.05 (.03)	-.04 (.03)	-.05 (.03)	-.09** (.03)	-.10** (.03)	-.09** (.03)	.01 (.01)	.01 (.01)	.01 (.01)	-.11 (.10)	-.11 (.10)	-.10 (.11)
Admitted in semester X dummy applied										Yes	Yes	Yes
Participated in experiment dummy applied										Yes	Yes	Yes
Constant	4.52** (.07)	4.21** (.17)	4.12** (.28)	1.76* (.12)	1.72** (.22)	1.44** (.36)	-	-	-	2.72** (.40)	3.19** (.72)	3.86** (1.12)
(Pseudo) R2	.01	.03	.05	.01	.01	.03	.02	.03	.04	.18	.19	.22
N	594	594	594	594	594	594	594	594	594	190	190	190

Note. First-time rejected applicants. ** p < .01 * p < .05 ° p < .10. Source: Medical applicant data, author's calculations.

Overall, these findings partly support HIII.4 that beliefs in meritocratic admission have a more positive effect on persistence in goal pursuit for applicants from privileged backgrounds than for their less privileged peers. However, only the belief that one's own admission depends on effort may be more advantageous for applicants with one college-educated parent (in comparison to none), while the belief that it depends on talent may even be more disadvantageous for this group. Furthermore, effect differences are not substantial between applicants with two and no college-educated parent(s).

As an additional analysis, I also conducted logistic regression models with success in admission between waves 2 and 3 as the dependent variable (see Table A7.1) to determine whether applicants' self-predicted persistence after a first rejection indeed matters for eventual success. The results from these models show that having a high intention to reapply is indeed associated with a higher likelihood of eventual success, while goal engagement and goal disengagement have no substantial effect on it. Beliefs in meritocratic admission are not substantially associated with the likelihood of eventual success. The findings further suggest that there are social differences in eventual success among first-time rejected applicants. These differences do not seem to be driven by the (non-substantial) social differences in self-predicted persistence after a first rejection[48] but are likely mostly driven by social differences in applicants' GPAs as discussed in Chapter 7.3.

7.5 Limitations due to sample selectivity and sample sizes

The two main limitations of the analyses presented in this chapter are that a) the sample is a rather selective group of first-time rejected applicants: those who after receiving a rejection still participated in the second (or even third) survey way, and who still stated that medicine is their preferred field of study, and b) there is a rather small number of cases, particularly in the analyses on applicants' reapplication behavior.

Although I can partly reduce bias due to survey participation and attrition by applying sampling and panel weights (see discussion in Chapter 4.4), the sample is limited to only those who still indicated medicine as their preferred field of study. However, changing the preferred field of study may also be a sign of weak persistence in goal pursuit. Therefore, the results may underestimate differences in persistence in goal pursuit, as those with the lowest persis-

---

48 Of course, applicants can only be admitted if they apply, but the number of reapplication attempts is dependent on when and whether applicants were admitted which is why it was not feasible to include it as an independent variable in the model.

tence may be excluded from the sample. However, an additional sensitivity analysis is reassuring: Whether applicants changed their preferred field of study is not substantially associated with applicants' parental education or their inequality beliefs. Indeed, the model including parental education, inequality beliefs, and the control variables gender and age only explains 1 % of the variance in the outcome variable change in the preferred field of study (see appendix, Table A7.2). Based on this sensitivity analysis, it seems that the group that did not change their preferred field of study does not substantially differ from the whole sample of first-time rejected applicants in terms of their social background or inequality beliefs.

The second limitation is the rather small number of cases. Despite the discussed problem that variance in previous experiences in admission among repeat applicants cannot properly be accounted for, as a robustness check to increase case numbers, I conducted models including the whole sample of rejected applicants (first-time and repeat applicants) in the appendix (see Table A73). The W2 sample then includes 1,578 rejected applicants, and the W3 sample includes 603 rejected applicants.

The results of the regression models on persistence in goal pursuit (Table A7.3) are quite similar to the results of the models only including first-time applicants. For most outcomes, parental education is not substantially associated with persistence in goal pursuit. However, the findings suggest that having one college-educated parent (in comparison to none) has a positive effect on the number of reapplication attempts (M1: .37, $p < .01$) and the coefficient of having two college-educated parents points in the same direction (M1: .21) but misses the common threshold of statistical significance ($p = .15$). These social differences in the number of reapplication attempts cannot substantially be explained by differences in inequality beliefs. However, similarly to the main analysis, the belief that one's own admission is positively associated with goal engagement (M2: .05, $p < .01$).

7.6 Summary: Parental education does not affect persistence but beliefs do

In this empirical chapter, I examined whether applicants' persistence in goal pursuit after receiving a first rejection differs by parental education, and what role beliefs in meritocratic admission play for (differences in) the persistence in goal pursuit. Table 7.6 summarizes the main results of the hypotheses testing systematically.

This is the first study to examine measurements of persistence in goal pursuit of applicants to medical schools in Germany after they received a first rejection, and how it may differ by parental education. Furthermore, it contributes to research on meritocratic beliefs by exploring how these beliefs may affect different concepts related to persistence in goal pursuit, like self-predicted persistence and reapplication behavior.

Overall, the findings suggest that there are no substantial differences in applicants' persistence in goal pursuit by parental education, consistently for several concepts like goal engagement, goal disengagement, reapplication intention, and reapplication behavior (conditional likelihood to reapply at least once, and number of reapplication attempts). However, tentatively, having one or two college-educated parents may be positively associated with the number of reapplication attempts, and when adding repeat rejected applicants to the sample, these effects become even larger, suggesting that after several failed attempts there may be social differences in reapplication behavior.

The non-substantial differences in reapplication behavior in the first years after a failed application attempt stand in contrast to findings from studies conducted in other contexts such as on applicants to Finish universities by Heiskala et al. (2023): They found that applicants with at least one college-educated parent more often reapply after one or more rejections than those without college-educated parents (conditional likelihood to reapply). In the context of selective admission to German medical schools, self-selection into the initial application and social differences in the admission likelihood may be more important drivers behind the social selectivity among medical applicants and students than differences in persistence after rejections. Most applicants have above-average school grades compared to adolescents in Germany generally, and a very high commitment to pursue their goal. For this highly positively selective group, no differences in persistence in goal pursuit by parental education remain. Educational inequality between applicants from different social backgrounds may already play out before the initial selection into application takes place, while the group of applicants to Finish universities may be more heterogeneous in their goal persistence.

Examining the role of belief in meritocratic admission for applicants' goal persistence, I find, in line with theoretical expectations, that the belief that one's own admission depends on effort is positively associated with goal engagement. Furthermore, supporting ideas of attributional theory (Weiner, 1985), the results tentatively suggest that the belief that it depends on talent is negatively associated with applicants' number of reapplication attempts (even though the effect misses the threshold of statistical significance.) One possible explanation could be that applicants who strongly believe that talent is important may, after (several) rejections, believe that they do not possess the necessary talent to succeed in the admission[49], and thus might give up on their goal

---

49 This may be particularly the case for rejected applicants who adhere to a fixed mindset that innate abilities are unalterable. However, due to the very low case numbers of those with a growth mindset in sample IIIb, it was not feasible to test this expectation empirically.

(Skinner et al., 1998; Smith & Skrbiš, 2017; Weiner, 1985). However, all effects are rather small in size, which may be caused by a very high overall persistence among first-time rejected applicants to medical school, not allowing for considerable interpersonal variance in persistence.

As I did not find substantial social differences in persistence and in beliefs in meritocratic admission for the group of first-time rejected applicants (the effort belief was only tentatively stronger among the privileged than the less privileged in sample IIIa), it was not feasible to test for the expected mediation of the effect of parental education on persistence through beliefs in meritocratic admission. However, as in the whole applicant population, there are indeed social differences in beliefs in meritocratic admission (see Chapter 5.3), for a more heterogenous group social differences in beliefs in meritocratic admission may still contribute to unequal persistence in goal pursuit and educational attainment between adolescent from different social backgrounds.

Table 7.6: Systematic illustration of results of hypotheses testing III

Hypotheses	Confirmed?	Description of findings
HIII.1: Applicants from privileged backgrounds show a stronger persistence in goal pursuit than their less privileged peers.	-	• Not clearly supported for any measurement of persistence in goal pursuit (goal engagement, goal disengagement, reapplication intention, likelihood to reapply at least once, and number of reapplication attempts) • Tentatively supported for the number of reapplication attempts
HIII.2: Beliefs in meritocratic admission are positively associated with persistence in goal pursuit, while the opposite is true for the belief in nonmeritocratic admission.	(+)	• Meritocratic belief that admission depends on effort is positively associated with goal engagement • Tentatively: Meritocratic belief that admission depends on talent is negatively associated with the number of reapplication attempts • Not supported for other beliefs or measurements of persistence in goal pursuit
HII.3: Social differences in inequality beliefs about admission mediate part of the effect of parental education on persistence in goal pursuit.	-	• No substantial differences in beliefs in meritocratic admission (tentatively: stronger effort belief in sample IIIa among privileged) or persistence in goal pursuit by applicants' parental education (tentatively: more reapplication attempts among the privileged) • Not feasible to test for mediation
HIII.4: Beliefs in meritocratic admission have a more positive effect on persistence in goal pursuit for applicants from privileged backgrounds than for their less privileged peers.	(+)	• Tentatively partly supported: Effort belief is more strongly negatively associated with goal disengagement and more strongly positively associated with the number of reapplication attempts for applicants with one than with no college-educated parent • But: Talent belief is more strongly positively associated with the number of reapplication attempts for applicants with one than with no college-educated parent • Effect differences between applicants with two and no college-educated parent not substantial

Note. Author's illustration.

Finally, the result partly supported my hypothesis that beliefs in meritocratic admission have a more positive effect on persistence in goal pursuit for applicants from privileged backgrounds than for their less privileged peers. For applicants with one college-educated parent, the effort belief is more advantageous in preventing them from giving up on their goal (i.e., goal disengagement) and (tentatively) increasing their number of reapplication attempts than for applicants with no college-educated parent.

8 Summary, discussion, and conclusion

Social position is largely determined by educational attainment, although there is no level playing field for success in the educational game. Children from privileged backgrounds can draw on parental capital that gives them an advantage in school and makes it more likely for them to attain higher levels of educational attainment and better school grades. The persistent link between social background and educational attainment is a consistent finding in sociological and educational research (Autorengruppe Bildungsberichterstattung, 2022; Heisig et al., 2020).

However, despite the persistence of (educational) inequality, growing concern about this inequality and a demand for a more equal distribution of resources fails to materialize (Mijs, 2021). One reason for this lack of concern suggested in the literature is the inequality-legitimizing ideology of meritocracy (Bills, 2019; Mijs, 2016; Solga, 2015). Inequality is seen primarily as a result of individual merit, while the influence of luck and social background on success is underestimated.

This dissertation contributes to this debate by investigating how parental education and educational experiences shape inequality beliefs, as well as the consequences of these beliefs for the legitimation and reproduction of educational inequality. To answer this research question, I have focused on a specific and highly selective educational experience: success or failure in admission to medical school in Germany.

I will now first briefly summarize my theoretical arguments and the key findings of this study, before discussing its contributions to the theoretical debate and empirical research. Subsequently, I will discuss the limitations of this study, and conclude this dissertation by discussing the implications of the findings for understanding and reducing educational inequality.

8.1 Theoretical arguments

While meritocratic beliefs are widespread in modern societies such as Germany, individuals differ in the extent to which they attribute success to meritocratic or nonmeritocratic factors. Drawing on reproduction theory (Bourdieu, 1977; Bourdieu & Passeron, 1990) and Mijs' (2017) framework of socially stratified educational institutions as 'inferential spaces,' I argue that applicants from privileged backgrounds form stronger meritocratic and weaker nonmeritocratic beliefs than their less privileged peers due to the transmission of parental beliefs and the social homogeneity in educational institutions. Educational institutions play a crucial role in shaping inequality beliefs at a time point where these beliefs are likely not yet consolidated (Mijs, 2017; Warikoo, 2018). Thus, I propose that another important reason behind social differences in inequality beliefs may be the higher likelihood of experiencing success in school and the higher admission chances of applicants from privileged backgrounds resulting from mechanisms behind vertical and horizontal educational inequality (Boudon, 1974; Bourdieu, 1977; Lucas, 2001).

System-justification theory (Jost & Banaji, 1994) suggests that under certain conditions, individuals are motivated to justify the existing system; for example, by attributing failure to their own or their group's lack of merit. However, in the case of success or failure in admission, I expect self-serving belief mechanisms to outweigh system-justification mechanisms, as applicants may not have a strong motivation to justify the admission procedure. The legitimacy of the procedure has been publicly debated in recent years and applicants are not locked in the system but have the option of choosing other career paths. Self-serving beliefs theory (Bénabou & Tirole, 2016) proposes that experiences of success and failure bias inequality beliefs in a way that serves one's self-image by attributing success to meritocratic factors, such as hard work, and failure to external factors, such as luck. These expectations are in line with findings from experimental game studies showing that winners are more likely to attribute their success to effort and talent, while losers are more likely to attribute their losses to external factors—regardless of their initial condition in the game (Fehr & Vollmann, 2020; Molina et al., 2019). Thus, I expect that success strengthens meritocratic beliefs and weakens nonmeritocratic beliefs, whereas failure weakens meritocratic beliefs and strengthens nonmeritocratic beliefs.

These changes in beliefs through success and failure may contribute to differences in beliefs between applicants from different social backgrounds and between winners and losers. Drawing on arguments of cumulative inequality theory (DiPrete & Eirich, 2006; Schafer et al., 2011), previous experiences may even increase the effects of (yet another) experience of failure in admission for applicants from less privileged backgrounds and those who previously applied unsuccessfully, as this new experience confirms prior doubts that merit-based success is possible. On the other hand, an eventual experience of success for this group—albeit which is less likely to occur—may outweigh these prior doubts and may particularly strengthen beliefs that merit-based success against the odds is possible.

Meritocratic beliefs may legitimize educational inequality through a perception of unequal outcomes as a result of natural differences in individual merit that can be objectively assessed by educational institutions. As success is framed as a reward for individual merit, some degree of inequality in outcomes may be regarded as necessary for motivation (Mijs, 2016; Solga, 2015). Recent empirical research supports the theoretical arguments of inequality-

(de)legitimizing consequences of inequality beliefs but comes with certain research gaps. Studies have examined the effects of inequality beliefs on either the perception of justice (e.g., Batruch et al., 2022; Mijs, 2021; Sachweh & Sthamer, 2019) or the preference for equal distribution (e.g., Alesina & Giuliano, 2011; García-Sánchez et al., 2020; Marquis & Rosset, 2021), but the effect of inequality beliefs on the preference for distribution based on educational meritocracy has so far been understudied. Furthermore, these studies focus on the consequences of the meritocratic belief that success depends on hard work, and do not explore the effect that success depends on abilities. Finally, the effects of inequality beliefs on perceptions of justice and distributive preferences are examined in different studies. Studies on the latter assume that inequality beliefs affect distributive preferences through the perception of inequality as just (Alesina & Giuliano, 2011; Marquis & Rosset, 2021), although this theoretical assumption has yet to be empirically tested.

Research on distributive preferences suggests that people from similar backgrounds tend to have similar preferences due to their socialization and experiences (Liebig & Sauer, 2016). Drawing on the previously made arguments on social differences in inequality beliefs, I propose that these differences in beliefs mediate the effects of parental education on distributive preferences.

Beyond legitimizing educational inequality, (social) differences in meritocratic beliefs may also be a mechanism behind education inequality. Skinner argues that there is a "beliefs-performance cycle" (Skinner et al. 1998:v) in which meritocratic effort beliefs increase goal engagement, which increases academic performance and the likelihood of success, and success further reinforces meritocratic beliefs. While Skinner (1998) examined beliefs and performance in school among the heterogeneous group of children from third to seventh grade, even among the group of rejected medical school applicants, there may still be (smaller) social differences in persistence that can be explained by differences in beliefs. Drawing on Boudon's (1974) secondary effects and Breen and Goldhorpe's (1997) rational choice model for educational decisions, applicants from privileged social backgrounds may show a stronger persistence in goal pursuit after experiencing failure than their less privileged peers—for instance, due mechanisms such as motivation for status maintenance and differences in resources and constraints.

While social differences in reapplication behavior have been found in the context of university admission in Finland (Heiskala et al., 2023), it has not yet been tested empirically whether there are indeed social differences in persistence after rejections among medical applicants in Germany. As motivational theory (Heckhausen et al., 2010) suggests that meritocratic beliefs—particularly beliefs in success through effort—increase adolescents' persistence, I argue that social differences in inequality beliefs may reproduce educational inequality by leading to a higher persistence in goal pursuit among applicants from privileged backgrounds compared to applicants from less privileged backgrounds. Attributional theory (Weiner, 1985), suggests that while the belief that success depends on effort has a motivational effect, after experiencing failure the belief that it depends on abilities may have a demotivational effect, as abilities are perceived as stable and uncontrollable. Moreover, the positive effect of the belief that success depends on effort may be more beneficial for the persistence of privileged applicants because they have to face fewer structural barriers and effort-based success may indeed be more attainable for them than for their less privileged peers (Darnon et al., 2017; García-Sierra, 2023).

Overall, I propose that inequality beliefs are shaped by educational experiences and that differences in beliefs may amplify their consequences for educational inequality even further: Strong meritocratic and weak nonmeritocratic beliefs legitimize inequality especially among those from privileged backgrounds and the winners of the educational game—those who are likely to be the future decision-makers—and contribute to a stronger persistence in goal pursuit among this group.

8.2 Key findings

To address the research question of this dissertation of how parental education and educational experiences shape inequality beliefs, and what consequences these beliefs have for the legitimation and reproduction of educational inequality, I used medical applicant data (Finger et al., 2023). I examined social differences in inequality beliefs and changes in inequality beliefs through the real-life experience of success or failure in admission to medical schools in Germany, and the consequences of (differences in) these inequality beliefs for perceptions of justice, distributive preferences, and applicants' persistence in goal pursuit after a first rejection. To consider the theoretical debate on ways in which distinct meritocratic beliefs contribute to education inequality and close empirical research gaps, I examined changes and consequences of distinct types of meritocratic and nonmeritocratic beliefs about one's own admission (i.e., domain-specific beliefs) and societal success in general (i.e., societal beliefs). I also explored heterogeneity in the effect of success and failure on inequality beliefs (by parental education and between first-time and repeat applicants) and social differences in the effect of inequality beliefs on applicants' persistence.

I will now briefly recapitulate the key findings for the three main research objectives of this study (see Figure 1.1). More comprehensive summaries of these findings were provided at the end of the respective empirical chapters (Chapters 5.6, 6.5, and 7.6).

Research objective I: Do success in admission and inequality beliefs differ by parental education? How do experiences of success and failure shape inequality beliefs, and do differences in experiences explain social differences in beliefs? Do the effects of success and failure differ depending on applicants' previous experiences?

Consistent with expectations of (horizontal) educational inequality, applicants with two college-educated parents are more than 6 percentage points more likely to be admitted than applicants with no college-educated parent—an effect that seems to be largely driven by differences in GPA. This highlights that applicants from different social backgrounds already differ from each other before receiving their admission outcome in their experiences of success and failure in school. The findings of this study suggest that these experiences shape applicants' inequality beliefs in a self-serving way. Applicants with two college-educated parents have stronger meritocratic beliefs that their own admission as well as societal success generally depends on effort and have weaker nonmeritocratic beliefs that societal success depends on family background and money. These social differences in inequality beliefs (particularly in effort beliefs) can partly be explained by differences in previous experiences such as by the likelihood of previous failure in admission and differences in GPA.

Findings from the longitudinal analyses (pre and post mean comparison and individual fixed-effects models) indeed confirm that success or failure in admission influences inequality beliefs in a mostly self-serving way. Being admitted strengthens applicants' domain-specific belief in how important one's own effort is for the admission outcome and weakens their societal belief in how important family background and money are for societal success. Being rejected weakens domain-specific and societal beliefs in the importance of effort and strengthens the domain-specific belief in the importance of luck and societal beliefs in the importance of family background and money. Beyond these changes in beliefs, already before applicants learned about their admission outcome, those who will be admitted have stronger meritocratic and weaker nonmeritocratic beliefs than applicants who will be rejected. Overall, these findings suggest diverging paths in inequality beliefs for winners and losers that are amplified by the (new) experiences in admission. Additionally, the higher admission likelihood of applicants from privileged backgrounds contributes to a widening gap in effort beliefs between applicants from different social backgrounds.

Beyond increasing differences in inequality beliefs through differences in the admission likelihood between winners and losers, and between applicants from different social backgrounds, findings tentatively suggest that meritocratic effort beliefs are the most stable and resistant to failure among applicants with two college-educated parents. For repeat applicants, eventual success has a greater positive effect on the belief in the importance of effort in admission than it does for first-time applicants, partly outweighing differences in prior beliefs. On the other hand, tentatively, results suggest that the negative effect that yet another rejection—the more likely event due to the on average worse GPA of repeat applicants—has on the belief in the importance of effort for admission is larger for repeat applicants than the effect of a rejection for first-time applicants.

Research objective II: How do inequality beliefs influence distributive preferences through perceptions of justice? Do social differences in inequality beliefs, and the resulting perception of justice, partly explain the association between parental education and distributive preferences?

Using SEM, this study has examined the complex relationship between applicants' parental education, their inequality beliefs, perceptions of justice, and distributive preferences for equality and educational meritocracy—one domain-specific model refers to admission to medical school and one societal model refers to societal inequality in general.

The findings reinforce the notion that beliefs about inequality are crucial in (de)legitimizing (educational) inequality but reveal different consequences of distinct inequality beliefs for perceptions of justice and distributive preferences, as well as differences in the evaluation of one's own admission and societal inequalities in general. While meritocratic beliefs—particularly the belief that success depends on abilities—increase the perception of justice of admission and societal inequalities and the preference for distribution based on educational merit, they only tentatively reduce the preference for equal distribution. This preference is rather influenced by nonmeritocratic beliefs. The belief that admission depends on luck increases the preference for equal distribution of vacant places in the program, and the belief that societal success depends on social background increases the preference for equal income distribution.

Contrary to the argument proposed by previous research that the effect of meritocratic beliefs on the preference for equal distribution can be primarily explained by their effects on the perception of justice (e.g., Alesina & Giuliano, 2011), findings show that the relationship between inequality beliefs, perception of justice, and distributive preferences is more complex. Although the proposed mediation paths are partly supported by the findings, perceptions of justice only mediate part of the belief effects on distributive preferences and direct effects of inequality beliefs remain.

The findings support the expectations that applicants from privileged backgrounds have a weaker preference for equal distribution and a stronger preference for distribution based on educational merit—regarding both the distribution of vacant places in the program and income distribution. They further support my proposed argument that social differences in inequality beliefs, and the resulting perception of justice, partly explain the positive associations between privileged social background and inequality-reproducing distributive preferences. However, a substantial direct effect of parental education on distributive preferences remains, even when controlling for inequality beliefs and perception of justice.

Research objective III: Are there social differences in the persistence in goal pursuit after a first rejection? Do beliefs in meritocratic admission increase applicants' persistence? Do social differences in beliefs in meritocratic admission explain part of the effect of parental education on persistence? Do the effects of belief in meritocratic admission differ by parental education?

Contrary to expectations of persistence in goal pursuit as a secondary effect of parental education on eventual admission, the findings reveal no substantial differences in applicants' persistence in goal pursuit by parental education, consistently for several concepts like goal engagement, goal disengagement, reapplication intention, and reapplication behavior. However, tentatively, having one or two college-educated parents is positively associated with the number of reapplication attempts, and when adding repeat rejected applicants to the sample, these effects become even larger.

The findings from regression analyses show that the belief that one's own admission depends on effort is positively associated with goal engagement. Furthermore, the results tentatively suggest that the belief that it depends on talent is negatively associated with applicants' number of reapplication attempts. The effect of believing in effort-based admission on goal disengagement is (tentatively) more negative for applicants with one college-educated parent than for applicants with no college-educated parent, and its effect on the number of reapplication attempts is (tentatively) more positive for applicants with one college-educated parent than for applicants with no college-educated parent, suggesting that for this group the belief is more advantageous for their goal persistence. However, the belief that admission depends on one's own talent has (tentatively) a more negative effect on the number of reapplication attempts for applicants with one college-educated parent than for applicants with no college-educated parent.

8.3 Discussion and contributions to theoretical debate and empirical research

This study contributes to the theoretical debate on meritocracy as an inequality-legitimizing ideology by developing a theoretical framework for the formation of inequality beliefs and their consequences for educational inequality by combining sociological and social psychological theories. The academic debate on meritocracy as an inequality-legitimizing ideology (Bills, 2019; Mijs, 2016; Solga, 2015) has focused on the consequences of this generally widespread notion. However, interpersonal differences in inequality beliefs and mechanisms of how these beliefs are formed—suggested by self-serving beliefs theory (Bénabou & Tirole, 2016)—can amplify the consequences of inequality beliefs for educational inequality. Social differences in inequality beliefs may explain social differences in distributive preferences and persistence.

Furthermore, the study contributes empirically to questions raised in the theoretical debate and research gaps in previous empirical studies. This is the first study to longitudinally examine changes in adolescents' meritocratic and nonmeritocratic inequality beliefs after a crucial real-life experience for applicants' future social positioning: success or failure in admission to medical school in Germany. Findings show that this experience not only shapes beliefs about one's own admission but—albeit to a smaller extent—also beliefs about societal inequality in general. In line with theoretical expectations (Mijs, 2017; Warikoo, 2018), educational experiences are crucial for the formation of inequality beliefs—beliefs that have consequences for applicants' perceptions of justice, distributive preferences, and persistence in goal pursuit.

The findings of diverging paths in inequality beliefs between winners and losers and between applicants from different social backgrounds help improve the understanding of the persistence of educational inequality. The observed self-serving bias in beliefs may make success feel more deserved, and failure may not be perceived as self-imposed but rather blamed on external and uncontrollable factors (Jost & Hunyady, 2003). Whereas this mechanism may temporarily benefit the individual's self-perception and well-being, on a societal level, it reinforces structural inequality.

Applicants from privileged backgrounds and successful applicants have stronger beliefs that success depends on effort and weaker structural beliefs that it depends on social background than their less privileged or unsuccessful peers. Social differences in effort beliefs seem to be mostly driven by differences in educational experiences, while social differences in social background beliefs may also be driven by the transmission of parental beliefs or by being surrounded by peers with a similarly privileged background.

This study contributes theoretically and empirically to research on meritocracy by showing that stronger effort beliefs and weaker social background beliefs among the privileged and successful are crucial for the legitimation of inequality. These beliefs partly explain why this group has stronger inequality-reproducing distributive preferences (i.e., opposition towards equal distribution and preference for educational meritocracy) compared to their less privileged or unsuccessful peers. In addition, eventual experience of success outweighs prior doubt that success through effort is possible for those who previously experienced failure or are from a less privileged social background, suggesting that successful people seem to forget their past difficulties and perceive success as primarily effort-based. Self-serving bias is especially strong in domain-specific beliefs, and thus strong domain-specific meritocratic and weak nonmeritocratic beliefs may influence distributive preferences, particularly for the domain in which the winners are most involved and could potentially reduce inequality.

My expectation that there are social differences in first-time rejected applicants' persistence in goal pursuit—differences that can be explained by social differences in inequality beliefs—could not be clearly confirmed by my analysis. These findings stand in contrast to findings from studies conducted in other contexts, such as a study by Heiskala et al. (2023) on applicants to Finish universities that showed that applicants with at least one college-educated parent reapplied more often after one or more rejections than those without college-educated parents. This is the first study to examine social differences in persistence after a first rejection in the context of selective admission to German medical schools. The null findings suggest that self-selection in the initial application and social differences in the admission likelihood may be more important drivers behind the social selectivity among medical applicants and medical students than differences in persistence after rejection. Most applicants have a very high commitment to pursue their goal and no differences in applicants' persistence in goal pursuit by parental education remain. Educational inequality between applicants from different social backgrounds seems to already play out before the initial selection into application takes place, while in other contexts, applicants may be more heterogeneous in their goal persistence. However, tentatively, having one or two college-educated parents may be positively associated with one outcome of persistence: the number of reapplication attempts. As suggested by stronger effects in the pooled sample including repeat applicants, after several failed attempts there may be social differences in reapplication behavior—differences in line with expectations of social differences in educational decisions (Boudon, 1974; Breen & Goldthorpe, 1997). Rejected applicants from different social backgrounds may state and believe that they have a high commitment to pursue their goal to study medicine further, but particularly after several failed attempts, those from less privileged backgrounds may have fewer resources and are less motivated by status maintenance than their more privileged peers, eventually preventing them from reapplying.

Furthermore, my expectations that the belief that one's own admission depends on effort is positively associated with goal engagement were confirmed, even among the homogenous group of first-time rejected applicants. This belief is tentatively less beneficial for applicants from less privileged backgrounds than for their more privileged peers—possibly because effort-based success is more difficult to attain for this group. As I did not find substantial social differences in persistence after a first rejection, it was not feasible to test whether social differences in the belief in effort-based admission contribute to them. However, social differences in this belief may have already affected students' persistence and performance in school, and hence, their admission likelihood—a mechanism that could not be tested with the medical applicant data, as inequality beliefs were only measured after applicants received their final GPA score. Furthermore, repeat experiences of failure reduce the belief that one's own admission depends on effort, and since this belief is important for persistence in goal pursuit, this mechanism may contribute to cumulative inequality over the life course (DiPrete & Eirich, 2006; Skinner et al., 1988).

Overall, these findings stress that not only meritocratic beliefs themselves but also interpersonal differences in these beliefs contribute to the persistence of educational inequality. Those who are more likely to end up in positions of power (winners and those from privileged backgrounds) hold stronger meritocratic beliefs and weaker nonmeritocratic beliefs and may be less inclined to counteract structural barriers, while those who end up being less successful are more aware of structural barriers but have fewer opportunities to change these structures, and may additionally be more likely to give up on their goals due to these beliefs. The findings of this study apply to differences between the winners and losers among the highly educated—a limitation of this study that will be discussed in Chapter 8.4. Nevertheless, differences within this group may amplify the consequences of inequality beliefs for educational inequality, as mostly the winners among this group will end up in positions of power.

Despite the focus of this dissertation on the consequences of differences in inequality beliefs, theoretically and empirically this study does not contradict the notion that meritocratic beliefs are widespread and contribute to the legitimation of inequality among all groups. Overall, applicants believe that success in one's own admission and in society generally depends on meritocratic and nonmeritocratic factors, while meritocratic beliefs are slightly stronger and nonmeritocratic beliefs are slightly weaker regarding success in society than regarding one's own admission.

This study contributes to the research on the inequality-legitimizing consequences of meritocratic beliefs by exploring not only the effect of meritocratic hard work belief on perceptions of justice or the preference for equal income distribution empirically, but by also examining the effects of the meritocratic abilities belief and distinct nonmeritocratic beliefs on these preferences, and by examining how inequality beliefs affect the preference for distribution based on educational meritocracy.

The findings highlight that not only the belief that success depends on hard work but even more the belief that it depends on abilities contribute to the legitimation of educational inequality. This belief may legitimize inequality of outcomes, especially in the German context, due to the crucial role of early ability sorting in the educational system that is legitimized by the idea that children have either practical talents or theoretical abilities (Kurtz-Costes et al., 2005; Powell & Solga, 2011) and due to the strong link between perceived academic ability and placement in the labor market (Shavit et al., 2007). In line with Warikoo's (2018) argument that students adopt the values and beliefs of educational institutions, young adults may adopt the belief embedded in the German educational system that success depends on differences in abilities, and hence unequal educational outcomes are natural and inevitable (Friedman et al., 2023; Solga, 2015). Norms of educational systems can shape adolescents' inequality beliefs and contribute to the legitimation and persistence of inequality.

This study combines meritocratic and nonmeritocratic beliefs in one study and shows that both play an important role in the (de)legitimation of inequality. Especially since I find social differences in beliefs that success depends on social background, underestimating structural barriers seems to be a crucial reason for the legitimation and persistence of inequality. The findings also confirm theoretical expectations that inequality beliefs not only influence the preference for equal distribution but also the preference for distribution based on educational merit.

The findings could also show that inequality beliefs not only influence distributive preferences through perceptions of justice but to an even larger extent directly affect them, suggesting that there are other mechanisms at play. One explanation could be that, even if applicants may perceive the admission procedure or societal inequality as not very just (e.g., due to unequal opportunities to achieve merit or due to the extent of inequality in outcomes), perceiving success as merit-based may still increase their inequality-reproducing preferences because it makes distribution based on educational merit appear to be the most just among the available options. In addition, they may believe that a certain degree of inequality in outcomes is necessary for motivation (Davis & Moore, 1945). The finding of these direct effects further stresses the important role of inequality beliefs for distributive preferences.

The findings support attributional theory (Weiner, 1985) suggesting that there are distinct meritocratic and nonmeritocratic beliefs that are differently influenced by experiences and have different consequences for perceptions of justice, distributive preferences, and persistence in goal pursuit. Experiences in admission only affect beliefs about the importance of effort for success in a self-serving effect—a factor that lies within the individual's control—but not beliefs about the importance of talent. There are no social differences in abilities beliefs but these beliefs seem to have even stronger inequality-legitimizing consequences than hard work beliefs, while for applicants' persistence after a first rejection effort beliefs may be advantageous but not talent beliefs. The belief that success depends on abilities seems to be a universal belief that applicants hold regardless of their own experiences, and the stronger this belief is, the more people seem to perceive merit-based educational inequality as legitimate. After (repeatedly) experiencing failure this belief also contributes to giving up on one's goal, as one may believe that one simply does not have the required abilities to achieve this goal. By contrast, beliefs that success depends on hard work differ more between groups and are shaped by educational experiences, and while the effects of these beliefs on distributive preferences are weaker than the effects of abilities beliefs, effort beliefs may especially contribute to the persistence of inequality by the inequality-legitimizing consequences of such beliefs among the winners and privileged, as well as by increasing their persistence in goal pursuit.

Furthermore, both nonmeritocratic luck and social background beliefs delegitimize inequality. In the context of the supposedly strongly merit-based context of selective university admission, believing that luck is involved in the admission delegitimizes the current procedure. In the broader societal context, differences due to luck seem to be accepted by young adults—likely because luck is equally distributed between individuals—while differences based on social background are not. While there are no social differences in luck beliefs, there are differences in background beliefs, which may additionally contribute to the persistence of inequality beliefs.

In contrast to studies by Shane and Heckhausen (2013; 2016), I do not find any substantial (negative) association between the luck belief and persistence.[50] It is possible that in the case of selective admission to medical school in Germany, attributing the event of rejection to an unstable factor like luck might keep up motivation or at least have no effect. When a group of applicants with above-average school grades competes against each other, believing that a certain level of luck is required to succeed may not be understood as nonmeritocratic—and thus have no demotivational consequences.

Overall, the findings suggest that rather than summarizing distinct meritocratic beliefs (hard work, abilities, and educational merit beliefs) or distinct nonmeritocratic beliefs (luck and social background beliefs) in one index as undertaken in previous research (e.g., Shane and Heckhausen 2013; 2016; Hu et al. 2020), future research should investigate these beliefs separately.

8.4 Limitations of study and avenues for future research

In studying the formation and consequences of inequality beliefs of applicants to medical programs—the most selective university programs in Germany—I focused on a rather specific educational experience and group of adolescents. Due to mechanisms of self-selection in application, applicants to medical school are a positively selected group in terms of academic performance and

---

50 I could not examine the effect of social background beliefs on persistence, as domain-specific background beliefs were only measured in Wave 3.

motivation. Even those who are rejected will typically not be those who one would refer to as the losers of society, but rather they are the losers among the winners. Especially applicants from less privileged backgrounds have already overcome structural barriers to a large extent by the time they apply for entry to highly selective medical programs, which may also explain why I do not find social differences in persistence after a first rejection.

One cannot unhesitatingly transfer the findings of diverging paths in inequality beliefs between winners and losers and applicants from different social backgrounds to other groups (e.g., applicants for all university programs, applicants to vocational training or job positions) or experiences (e.g., less selective admissions or hiring decisions). Drawing on arguments of cumulative inequality (DiPrete & Eirich, 2006), I would argue that belief differences between winners and losers and between adolescents from different social backgrounds may even be larger in the whole society than among the selective group of applicants to medical school. In a less positively selected group of adolescents, disadvantaged groups are likely to have accumulated more experiences of failure, which should widen the gap in inequality beliefs between winners and losers and potentially amplify the decrease in meritocratic beliefs following yet another experience of failure.

However, arguments of system-justification theory (Jost & Banaji, 1994; Jost & Hunyady, 2003), suggest that if it is hard for individuals to escape the existing system (e.g., the whole educational system or structures of the labor market), they may be motivated to justify the system to reduce ideological dissonance, even if this goes against their self- or group-interest. Furthermore, previous empirical research showed that a higher educational level is associated with more awareness of structural inequality (Wodtke, 2012, 2018).

To at least give an insight into differences in inequality beliefs between different groups of adolescents in Germany, I used NEPS data to compare average inequality beliefs among those with and without Abitur, and those who did and those who did not aspire to become doctors (see Chapter 4.6). Overall, differences in group means are rather small in size. Adolescents who have an Abitur and those who aspire to become doctors have slightly stronger meritocratic beliefs than those who do not. Interestingly, adolescents with Abitur have stronger social background beliefs than those without Abitur, but those who aspire to become doctors have weaker social background beliefs than the whole sample with Abitur. These descriptive findings suggest that a lower educational level and system-justification mechanisms may lead to weaker structural beliefs among adolescents without Abitur than among those with Abitur. Among those with Abitur, experiences of success that make adolescents more likely to aspire to become doctors may reduce structural beliefs due to self-serving mechanisms, similar to the self-serving effects of success and failure in admission on inequality beliefs that I showed in this dissertation. However, these are only speculations based on average inequality beliefs of different groups in the NEPS data, partly comprising very few cases (e.g., 166 adolescents who aspire to become doctors).

To properly test how universal the mechanism of diverging paths in inequality beliefs is, studying less selective groups and situations for the effects that individual experiences have on inequality beliefs seems to be an important avenue for future research. These studies could further explore whether in less selective procedures social differences in persistence occur, and the extent to which these differences can be explained by social differences in inequality beliefs.

Another restriction of this study is that research objective II could only be examined cross-sectionally. Hence, reversed causality about the effect of inequality beliefs on the perception of justice and distributive preferences cannot be ruled out. To explore causality, it would be desirable to conduct research with longitudinal data on these different concepts.

To explore the effect of parental education and beliefs in meritocratic admission on reapplication behavior (research objective III), a crucial limitation is small case numbers (N = 190). While the findings consistently show that there are no social differences in self-predicted persistence, they tentatively suggest that there may be social differences in the actual reapplication behavior: the number of reapplication attempts. The lack of statistical significance may be driven by the small sample size. Thus, it would be desirable to replicate the analysis with a larger sample to determine whether there are indeed social differences in reapplication behavior among medical applicants. In addition, it would contribute to studying the role of inequality beliefs for social differences in persistence to already measure adolescents' inequality beliefs before they receive their GPA: Persistence in achieving a very good GPA will critically affect applicants' chances of entering medical school or other selective fields of study.

8.5 Implications of findings

Overall, the findings of this study contribute to the understanding of the persistence of educational inequality by a) showing self-serving mechanisms leading to stronger meritocratic and weaker nonmeritocratic beliefs among successful medical applicants and applicants from privileged social backgrounds, b) showing the inequality (de)legitimizing consequences of distinct inequality beliefs for perceptions of justice and distributive preferences, and c) showing that inequality-reproducing distributive preferences of the privileged and successful can partly be explained by their strong meritocratic and weak nonmeritocratic beliefs. Furthermore, while the findings did not support expectations of social differences in persistence after a first rejection among medical applicants, they contribute to the research on applicants' persistence by d) showing that the belief in effort-based admission has a positive effect on this persistence.

These findings have implications beyond the context of application to medical school. I showed that meritocratic beliefs (particularly the belief that success depends on abilities) legitimize educational inequality by increasing the preferences for distribution based on educational meritocracy—a system in favor of the privileged—and by reducing the preference for equal distribution. On the other hand, nonmeritocratic beliefs delegitimize merit-based educational inequality. Understanding the consequences of inequality beliefs is crucial for increasing support for equal distribution—a first step in reducing inequality in opportunities and outcomes.

Furthermore, interpersonal differences in inequality beliefs may amplify the consequences of these beliefs for the legitimation and persistence of inequality. The successful and the privileged—those who are more likely to be in charge of decisions that could potentially alter structural barriers—may not be inclined to do so because they interpret processes of status attainment as merit-based, and underestimate structural barriers. These beliefs increase their support of the status quo—distribution based on educational meritocracy—and reduce their support of equal distribution. Even those who previously experienced failure or possibly structural barriers interpret processes of status attainment as more merit-based than they used to once they have reached positions of power. However, even among the winners, those from less privileged backgrounds have slightly stronger structural beliefs that social background is important for success than those from privileged backgrounds. Those who are less successful are even more aware of structural inequality and hold weaker meritocratic beliefs that success depends (solely) on effort, but may have fewer opportunities to change exciting structures and promote more equality in opportunities and outcomes. Furthermore, weaker beliefs that success depends on effort among the less successful may make them eventually give up on their goals, contributing to cumulative inequality over the life course.

With these considerations in mind, it seems important to think about ways to counteract changes in belief that exacerbate inequality. How can those from privileged backgrounds become more aware of the role of structural factors for success, and how can winners remain aware of these structural barriers? How can those from less privileged backgrounds and the less successful continue to believe enough in effort-based success to remain motivated?

Skepticism about the possibility of effort-based upward mobility—particularly among adolescents from less privileged backgrounds—should be counteracted because it could be detrimental to motivation. On the other hand, awareness of structural barriers—particularly among adolescents from privileged backgrounds—should be promoted, considering its consequences for distributive preferences. Furthermore, the belief that success depends on abilities plays an important role in the legitimation and support of merit-based educational inequality and further contributes to adolescents giving up on their goals after (repeat) experiences of failure. Promoting a growth mindset that abilities are alterable by the individual rather than a fixed mindset that these beliefs are natural and unalterable (Dweck, 2006) may be helpful not only for increasing individual motivation but also for reducing inequality-reproducing preferences.

The findings of this study stress the important role of educational institutions in shaping adolescents' inequality beliefs. Educational experiences of success and failure shape beliefs, and students seem to have adopted the ideology embedded in the highly stratified German educational system that success in education and society depends on innate abilities, legitimizing inequalities. Previous studies have shown that brief interventions using information priming young adults' meritocratic or structural beliefs can indeed affect their beliefs in school meritocracy or a meritocratic society, at least in the short term, and increase awareness of structural barriers (Becker, 2020; Darnon et al., 2017; Mijs & Hoy, 2022). Mijs's (2017) study suggests that structural beliefs increase through diversity in the social environment and exchange with people from different social backgrounds in school. Educational institutions could aim at promoting a balanced understanding that structural factors and merit (especially hard work) alike shape success in society through information and clear communication on structural inequality, and by enhancing diversity in the student body.

Overall, this study showed that inequality beliefs, and interpersonal differences in these beliefs, play a crucial role in the legitimation and persistence of educational inequality. Promoting balanced inequality beliefs among adolescents could be a crucial tool to increase future support for inequality-reducing policies. It could pave the way for societal change and a more equal educational system and society in terms of outcomes and opportunities.

References

Acock, A. C. (2013). *Discovering structural equation modeling using Stata* (Rev. ed.). *A Stata Press publication*. Stata Press.

Alesina, A., & Giuliano, P. (2011). Preferences for redistribution. In J. Benhabib, A. Bisin, & M. Jackson (Eds.), *Handbook of Social Economics* (Vol. 1, pp. 93–131). Elsevier.

Allerbeck, K., Allmendinger, J., Müller, W., Opp, K., Pappi, F., Erwin K., & Ziegler, R. (2017). *Allgemeine Bevölkerungsumfrage der Sozialwissenschaften ALLBUS 1994.* https://doi.org/10.4232/1.12823

Allport, G. (1954). *The nature of prejudice*. Basic Books.

Alwin, D. F., & Krosnick, J. A. (1991). Aging, cohorts, and the stability of sociopolitical orientations over the life span. *American Journal of Sociology, 97*(1), 169–195.

Angrist, J. D., & Pischke, J.-S. (2015). *Mastering 'metrics: The path from cause to effect.* Princeton University Press.

Aronson, P. (2017). Contradictions in the American dream: High educational aspirations and perceptions of deteriorating institutional support. *International Journal of Psychology, 52*(1), 49–57.

Autorengruppe Bildungsberichterstattung (2016). *Bildung in Deutschland 2016.* wbv Media.

Autorengruppe Bildungsberichterstattung. (2020). *Bildung in Deutschland 2020.* wbv Media.

Autorengruppe Bildungsberichterstattung. (2022). *Bildung in Deutschland 2022.* wbv Media.

Baetschmann, G., Ballantyne, A., Staub, K., & Winkelmann, R. (2020). feologit: A new command for fitting fixed-effects ordered logit models. *The Stata Journal: Promoting Communications on Statistics and Stata, 20*(2), 253–275.

Barone, C. (2006). Cultural capital, ambition and the explanation of inequalities in learning Outcomes: A Comparative Analysis. *Sociology, 40*(6), 1039–1058.

Batruch, A., Jetten, J., van de Werfhorst, H., Darnon, C., & Butera, F. (2022). Belief in school meritocracy and the legitimization of social and income inequality. *Social Psychological and Personality Science, 14*(5), 621–635.

Bauer, D., & Sterba, S. (2011). Fitting multilevel models with ordinal outcomes: Performance of alternative specifications and methods of estimation. *Psychological Methods, 16*(4), 373–390.

Becker, B. (2020). Mind the income gaps? Experimental evidence of information's lasting effect on redistributive preferences. *Social Justice Research, 33*(2), 137–194.

Becker, K., Baillet, F., & Weber, A. (2019). *21. Sozialerhebung: Daten- und Methodenbericht.* FDZ-DZHW.

Becker, R., Haunberger, S., & Schubert, F. (2010). Studienfachwahl als Spezialfall der Ausbildungsentscheidung und Berufswahl. *Zeitschrift Für ArbeitsmarktForschung, 42*(4), 292–310.

Bénabou, R., & Tirole, J. (2016). Mindful economics: The production, consumption, and value of beliefs. *Journal of Economic Perspectives, 30*(3), 141–164.

Bernardi, F., & Triventi, M. (2020). Compensatory advantage in educational transitions. *Acta Sociologica, 63*(1), 40–62.

Bills, D. (2019). The problem of meritocracy: the belief in achievement, credentials and justice. In R. Becker (Ed.), *Research handbook on the sociology of education* (pp. 88–105). Edward Elgar Publishing.
Boudon, R. (1974). *Education, opportunity, and social inequality: Changing prospects in Western society*. Wiley.
Bourdieu, P. (1977). Cultural reproduction and social reproduction. In Jerome Karabel & A.H. Halsey (Eds.), *Power and Ideology in Education* (pp. 487–511). Oxford University Press.
Bourdieu, P. (1984). *Distinction: A social critique of the judgement of taste* (Repr). Harvard University Press.
Bourdieu, P. (1986). The forms of capital. In John G. Richardson (Ed.), *Handbook of Theory and Research in the Sociology of Education* (pp. 241–258). Greenwood Press.
Bourdieu, P. (1994). *In other words: Essays towards a reflexive sociology* (Rev. ed.). Stanford University Press.
Bourdieu, P., & Passeron, J.-C. (1971). *Die Illusion der Chancengleichheit: Untersuchungen zur Soziologie des Bildungswesens am Beispiel Frankreichs*. Klett.
Bourdieu, P., & Passeron, J.-C. (1990). *Reproduction in education, society and culture* (Rev. ed.). Sage Publications.
Bourdieu, P., & Passeron, J.-C. (2007). *Die Erben: Studenten, Bildung und Kultur*. UVK-Verlag-Gesellschaft.
Breen, R., & Goldthorpe, J. H. (1997). Explaining educational differentials. *Rationality and Society, 9*(3), 275–305.
Brunello, G., & Checchi, D. (2007). Does school tracking affect equality of opportunity? New international evidence. *Economic Policy, 22*(52), 782–861.
Carifio, J., & Perla, R. J. (2007). Ten common misunderstandings, misconceptions, persistent myths and urban legends about Likert scales and Likert response formats and their antidotes. *Journal of Social Sciences, 3*(3), 106–116.
Cech, E., & Blair-Loy, M. (2010). Perceiving glass ceilings? Meritocratic versus structural explanations of gender inequality among women in science and technology. *Social Problems, 57*(3), 371–397.
Choi, G. (2021). Individuals' socioeconomic position, inequality perceptions, and redistributive preferences in OECD countries. *The Journal of Economic Inequality, 19*(2), 239–264.
Cohen, D., & Blanc-Goldhammer, D. (2011). Numerical bias in bounded and unbounded number line tasks. *Psychonomic Bulletin & Review, 18*(2), 331–338.
Cohen, J. (1992). A power primer. *Psychological Bulletin, 112*(1), 155–159.
Coleman, A., Norris, C., & Preston, C. (1997). Comparing rating scales of different lengths: Equivalence of scores from 5-point and 7-point scales. *Psychological Reports, 80*(2).
Darnon, C., Smeding, A., & Redersdorff, S. (2017). Belief in school meritocracy as an ideological barrier to the promotion of equality. *European Journal of Social Psychology, 48*(4), 523–534.
Darnon, C., Wiederkehr, V., Dompnier, B., & Martinot, D. (2018). Where there is a will, there is a way: Belief in school meritocracy and the social-class achievement gap. *British Journal of Social Psychology, 57*(1), 250–262.
Davis, K., & Moore, W. (1945). Some principles of stratification. *American Sociological Review, 10*(2), 242–249.

Destin, M. (2020). The double-edged consequences of beliefs about opportunity and economic mobility. *The Future of Children, 30*(1), 153–164.

Deutsch, M. (1975). Equity, equality, and need: What determines which value will be used as the basis of distributive justice? *Journal of Social Issues, 31*(3), 137–149.

DiPrete, T., & Eirich, G. (2006). Cumulative advantage as a mechanism for inequality. *Annual Review of Sociology, 32*(1), 271–297.

Douglas, M. (1973). *Natural symbols: Explorations in cosmology* (2nd ed.). Barrie and Rockliff.

Du, H., & King, R. B. (2022). What predicts perceived economic inequality? The roles of actual inequality, system justification, and fairness considerations. *British Journal of Social Psychology, 61*(1), 19–36.

Dumont, H., Klinge, D., & Maaz, K. (2019). The many (subtle) ways parents game the system: Mixed-method evidence on the transition into secondary-school tracks in Germany. *Sociology of Education, 92*(2), 199–228.

Dumont, H., Maaz, K., Neumann, M., & Becker, M. (2014). Soziale Ungleichheiten beim Übergang von der Grundschule in die Sekundarstufe I: Theorie, Forschungsstand, Interventions- und Fördermöglichkeiten. *Zeitschrift Für Erziehungswissenschaft, 17*(24), 141–165.

Dupraz, Y. (2013). *Using weights in Stata.* http://www.parisschoolofeconomics.eu/docs/dupraz-yannick/using-weights-in-stata(1).pdf

Duru-Bellat, M., & Tenret, E. (2012). Who's for meritocracy? Individual and contextual variations in the faith. *Comparative Education Review, 56*(2), 223–247.

Dweck, C. (2006). *Mindset: The new psychology of success.* Random House.

Fehr, D., & Vollmann, M. (2020). Misperceiving economic success: Experimental evidence on meritocratic beliefs and inequality acceptance. *AWI Discussion Paper Series*, Article 695.

Finger, C. (2022). *Soziale Herkunft und die Umsetzung von Studienaspirationen.* Budrich Academic Press.

Finger, C., & Solga, H. (2023). Test participation or test performance: Why do men benefit from test-based admission to higher education? *Sociology of Education, 96*(4), 344–366.

Finger, C., Solga, H., & Elbers, B. (2024). Social inequality in admission chances for prestigious higher education programs in Germany: do application patterns matter? *European Sociological Review*. Advance online publication.

Finger, C., Wetter, R., & Solga, H. (2023). *Zugang zu medizinischen und pharmazeutischen Studiengängen in Deutschland: Bewerber*innenbefragung (Wintersemester 2018/19).* https://doi.org/10.7802/2515

Försterling, F. (1985). Attributional retraining: A review. *Psychological Bulletin, 98*(3), 495–512.

Frank, R. (2016). *Success and luck: Good fortune and the myth of meritocracy.* Princeton University Press.

Friedman, S., Ellersgaard, C., Reeves, A., & Larsen, A. G. (2023). The meaning of merit: Talent versus hard work legitimacy. *Social Forces*. Advance online publication.

García-Sánchez, E., Osborne, D., Willis, G., & Rodríguez-Bailón, R. (2020). Attitudes towards redistribution and the interplay between perceptions and beliefs about inequality. *British Journal of Social Psychology, 59*(1), 111–136.

García-Sierra, A. (2023). The dark side of meritocratic beliefs: Is believing in meritocracy detrimental to individuals from low socioeconomic backgrounds? *Social Justice Research, 36*(1), 385–409.

Gogescu, F. (2024). Mapping the distinct patterns of educational and social stratification in European countries. *Journal of European Social Policy*. Advance online publication.

Graaf, D, Graaf, M., & Kraaykamp, G. (2000). Parental cultural capital and educational attainment in the Netherlands: A refinement of the cultural capital perspective. *Sociology of Education, 73*(2), 92–111.

Hällsten, M., & Thaning, M. (2018). Multiple dimensions of social background and horizontal educational attainment in Sweden. *Research in Social Stratification and Mobility, 56*(1), 40–52.

Harpe, S. E. (2015). How to analyze Likert and other rating scale data. *Currents in Pharmacy Teaching and Learning, 7*(6), 836–850.

Heckhausen, J., & Schulz, R. (1995). A life-span theory of control. *Psychological Review, 102*(2), 284–304.

Heckhausen, J., Wrosch, C. & Schulz, R. (2010). A motivational theory of life-span development. *Psychological Review, 117*(1), 32–60.

Heisig, J. P., Elbers, B., & Solga, H. (2020). Cross-national differences in social background effects on educational attainment and achievement: absolute vs. relative inequalities and the role of education systems. *Compare: A Journal of Comparative and International Education, 50*(2), 165–184.

Heiskala, L., Kilpi-Jakonen, E., Sirniö, O., & Erola, J. (2023). Persistent university intentions: Social origin differences in stopping applying to university after educational rejection(s). *Research in Social Stratification and Mobility, 85*(1), Article 100801.

Herbaut, E. (2021). Overcoming failure in higher education: Social inequalities and compensatory advantage in dropout patterns. *Acta Sociologica, 64*(4), 383–402.

Hoyt, C., Burnette, J., Forsyth, R., Parry, M., & DeShields, B. (2021). Believing in the American dream sustains negative attitudes toward those in poverty. *Social Psychology Quarterly, 84*(3), 203–215.

Hu, S., Shen, X., Creed, P., & Hood, M. (2020). The relationship between meritocratic beliefs and career outcomes: The moderating role of socioeconomic status. *Journal of Vocational Behavior, 116*(2), 1–11.

Hülle, S., Liebig, S., & May, M. J. (2018). Measuring attitudes toward distributive justice: The basic social justice orientations scale. *Social Indicators Research, 136*(2), 663–692.

Jackson, M. (2013). *Determined to succeed?* Stanford University Press.

Jolliffe, I. (1986). *Principal component analysis*. Springer Science+Business Media.

Jost, J., & Banaji, M. (1994). The role of stereotyping in system-justification and the production of false consciousness. *British Journal of Social Psychology, 33*(1), 1–27.

Jost, J., & Hunyady, O. (2003). The psychology of system justification and the palliative function of ideology. *European Review of Social Psychology, 13*(1), 111–153.

Jost, J., Pelham, B., Sheldon, O., & Ni Sullivan, B. (2003). Social inequality and the reduction of ideological dissonance on behalf of the system: evidence of enhanced system justification among the disadvantaged. *European Journal of Social Psychology, 33*(1), 13–36.

Karabel, J. (1984). Status group struggle, organizational interests, and the limits of institutional autonomy: The transformation of Harvard, Yale, and Princeton, 1918-1940. *Theory and Society, 13*(1), 1–40.
Karabel, J. (2005). *The chosen: the hidden history of admission and exclusion at Harvard, Yale, and Princeton.* Houghton Mifflin.
Kim, H., & Lee, Y. (2018). Socioeconomic status, perceived inequality of opportunity, and attitudes toward redistribution. *The Social Science Journal, 55*(3), 300–312.
Kluegel, J., & Miyano, M. (1995). Justice beliefs and support for the welfare state in advanced capitalism. In J. Kluegel, D. Mason, & B. Wegener (Eds.), *Social Justice and Political Change: Public Opinion in Capitalist and Post-communist States* (pp. 81–105). Walter Gruyter.
Kluegel, J., & Smith, E. (1986). *Beliefs about inequality: Americans' views of what is and what ought to be.* Taylor and Francis; Aldine de Gruyter.
Kreidl, M. (2000). Perceptions of poverty and wealth in Western and Post-Communist countries. *Social Justice Research, 13*(2), 151–176.
Kurtz-Costes, B., McCall, R., Kinlaw, R., Wiesen, C., & Joyner, H. (2005). What does it mean to be smart? The development of children's beliefs about intelligence in Germany and the United States. *Journal of Applied Developmental Psychology, 26*(2), 217–233.
Lareau, A. (2003). *Unequal Childhoods: Class, Race, and Family Life.* University of California Press.
Laurin, K. (2012). Social disadvantage and the self-regulatory function of justice beliefs. *Journal of Personality and Social Psychology, 100*(1), 149–171.
Lee, J. (2023). Consider your origins: Parental social class and preferences for redistribution in the United States from 1977 to 2018. *Social Science Research, 110(1),* Article 102840.
Lerner, M. (1980). *The belief in a just world: A fundamental delusion* (1st ed.). Perspectives in Social Psychology. Springer.
Liebig, S., & Lengfeld, H. (2002). Arbeit, Organisation und moralische Überzeugungen. Eine Grid-Group-Theorie der Gerechtigkeit in Unternehmen. *Soziale Welt, 53*(2), 115–140.
Liebig, S., & Mau, S. (2005). Wann ist ein Steuersystem gerecht? *Zeitschrift Für Soziologie, 34*(6), 468–491.
Liebig, S., & Sauer, C. (2016). Sociology of Justice. In C. Sabbagh & M. Schmitt (Eds.), *Handbook of Social Justice Theory and Research* (pp. 37–59). Springer New York.
Liebig, S., & Schupp, J. (2008). Leistungs- oder Bedarfsgerechtigkeit? Über einen normativen Zielkonflikt des Wohlfahrtsstaats und seiner Bedeutung für die Bewertung des eigenen Erwerbseinkommens. *Soziale Welt, 59*(1), 7–30.
Likert, R. (1932). A technique for the measurement of attitudes. *Archives of Psychology, 22*(140), 5–55.
Limesurvey GmbH. (2006-2020). *LimeSurvey: An open source survey tool* [Computer software]. http://www.limesurvey.org
Lohbeck, A., Grube, D., & Moschner, B. (2017). Academic self-concept and causal attributions for success and failure amongst elementary school children. *International Journal of Early Years Education, 25*(2), 190–203.
Lörz, M. (2012). Mechanismen sozialer Ungleichheit beim Übergang ins Studium: Prozesse der Status- und Kulturreproduktion. In R. Becker & H. Solga (Eds.), *Kölner*

Zeitschrift für Soziologie und Sozialpsychologie. Soziologische Bildungsforschung (Vol. 52, pp. 302–324). Springer Fachmedien Wiesbaden.

Loveday, V. (2016). Embodying deficiency through affective practice: Shame, relationality, and the lived experience of social class and gender in higher education. *Sociology, 50*(6), 1140–1155.

Lübker, M. (2007). Inequality and the demand for redistribution: are the assumptions of the new growth theory valid? *Socio-Economic Review, 5*(1), 117–148.

Lucas, S. R. (2001). Effectively maintained inequality: Education transitions, track mobility, and social background effects. *American Journal of Sociology, 106*(6), 1642–1690.

Marquis, L., & Rosset, J. (2021). When explanations for poverty help explain social policy preferences: The case of European public opinion amidst the economic recession (2009–2014). *Social Justice Research, 34*(4), 428–459.

Marx, K., & Engels, F. (2004 [1845/46]). Die deutsche Ideologie. In S. Landshut & K. Marx (Eds.), *Kröners Taschenausgabe: Vol. 209. Die Frühschriften* (7th ed., pp. 405–594). Kröner.

Mayer, K. U., Müller, W., & Pollak, R. (2007). Germany: Institutional change and inequalities of access in higher education. In Y. Shavit, R. Arum, & A. Gamoran (Eds.), *Stratification in Higher Education* (pp. 240–265). Stanford University Press.

Mijs, J. (2016). The unfulfillable promise of meritocracy: Three lessons and their implications for justice in education. *Social Justice Research, 29*(1), 14–34.

Mijs, J. (2017). *Institutions as inferential spaces: How people learn about inequality* [Doctoral dissertation]. Harvard University, Graduate School of Arts & Sciences.

Mijs, J. (2020). Earning rent with your talent: Modern-day inequality rests on the power to define, transfer and institutionalize talent. *Educational Philosophy and Theory, 53*(8), 810–818.

Mijs, J. (2021). The paradox of inequality: income inequality and belief in meritocracy go hand in hand. *Socio-Economic Review, 19*(1), 7–35.

Mijs, J., Daenekindt, S., Koster, W. de, & van der Waal, J. (2022). Belief in meritocracy reexamined: Scrutinizing the role of subjective social mobility. *Social Psychology Quarterly, 85*(2), 131–141.

Mijs, J., & Hoy, C. (2022). How information about inequality impacts belief in meritocracy: Evidence from a randomized survey experiment in Australia, Indonesia and Mexico. *Social Problems, 69*(1), 91–122.

Miller, D. (1979). *Social Justice*. OUP Oxford.

Mkumbo, K., & Amani, J. (2012). Perceived university students' attributions of their academic success and failure. *Asian Social Science, 8*(7), 247–255.

Molina, M., Bucca, M., & Macy, M. (2019). It's not just how the game is played, it's whether you win or lose. *Science Advances, 5*(7), 1–7.

Mulligan, T. (2018). *Justice and the meritocratic state. Political philosophy for the real world: Vol. 2*. Routledge.

NEPS Network (2021). *National Educational Panel Study, scientific use file of starting cohort grade 5*. doi:10.5157/NEPS:SC3:11.0.1

Newman, B., Johnston, C., & Lown, P. (2014). False consciousness or class awareness? Local income inequality, personal economic position, and belief in American meritocracy. *American Journal of Political Science, 59*(2), 326–340.

Nießen, D., Adriaans, J., Liebig, S., & Lechner, C. M. (2023). Justice evaluation of the income distribution (JEID): Development and validation of a short scale for the subjective assessment of objective differences in earnings. *PloS One, 18*(1), 1–23.

O'Grady, T. (2019). How do economic circumstances determine preferences? Evidence from long-run panel data. *British Journal of Political Science, 49*(4), 1381–1406.

Olivos, F. (2021). Motivation, legitimation, or both? Reciprocal effects of parental meritocratic beliefs and children's educational performance in China. *Social Psychology Quarterly, 84*(2), 110–131.

Palacios-Abad, A. (2021). Strive to succeed? The role of persistence in the process of educational attainment. *American Behavioral Scientist, 65*(11), 1555–1576.

Powell, J., & Solga, H. (2011). Why are higher education participation rates in Germany so low? Institutional barriers to higher education expansion. *Journal of Education and Work, 24*(1/2), 49–68.

Rawls, J. (1999 [1971]). *A theory of justice* (Rev. ed.). Belknap.

Roksa, J., & Potter, D. (2011). Parenting and academic achievement. *Sociology of Education, 84*(4), 299–321.

Sachweh, P., & Sthamer, E. (2019). Why do the affluent find inequality increasingly unjust? Changing inequality and justice perceptions in Germany, 1994–2014. *European Sociological Review, 35*(5), 651–668.

Sampson, R., & Bartusch, D. (1998). Legal cynicism and (subcultural?) tolerance of deviance: The neighborhood context of racial differences. *Law & Society Review, 32*(4), 777–804.

Sandel, M. (2021). *The tyranny of merit: What's become of the common good?* Penguin Books.

Schafer, M., Ferraro, K., & Mustillo, S. (2011). Children of misfortune: Early adversity and cumulative inequality in perceived life trajectories. *American Journal of Sociology, 116*(4), 1053–1091.

Schindler, S., & Lörz, M. (2012). Mechanisms of social inequality development: Primary and secondary effects in the transition to tertiary education between 1976 and 2005. *European Sociological Review, 28*(5), 647–660.

Schnapp, T. (2021). *Samples, weights, and nonresponse: the sample of starting cohort 3 of the National Educational Panel Study (Wave 11)*. Leibniz Institute for Educational Trajectories, National Educational Panel Study.

Sears, D. O., & Funk, C. L. (1999). Evidence of the long-term persistence of adults' political predispositions. *The Journal of Politics, 61*(1), 1–28.

Shane, J., & Heckhausen, J. (2013). University students' causal conceptions about social mobility: Diverging pathways for believers in personal merit and luck. *Journal of Vocational Behavior, 82*(1), 10–19.

Shane, J., & Heckhausen, J. (2016). For better or worse: Young adults' opportunity beliefs and motivational self-regulation during career entry. *International Journal of Behavioral Development, 40*(2), 107–116.

Shane, J., & Heckhausen, J. (2017). It's only a dream if you wake up: Young adults' achievement expectations, opportunities, and meritocratic beliefs. *International Journal of Psychology, 52*(1), 40–48.

Shavit, Y., Arum, R., & Gamoran, A. (2007). *Stratification in higher education*. Stanford University Press.

Singer, J., & Willett, J. (2003). *Applied longitudinal data analysis*. Oxford University Press.

Skinner, E., Chapman, M., & Baltes, P. (1988). Children's beliefs about control, means-ends, and agency: Developmental differences during middle childhood. *International Journal of Behavioral Development, 11*(3), 369–388.

Skinner, E., Zimmer-Gembeck, M., Connell, J., Eccles, J., & Wellborn, J. (1998). Individual differences and the development of perceived control. *Monographs of the Society for Research in Child Development, 63*(2/3), i–231.

Smith, J., & Skrbiš, Z. (2017). A social inequality of motivation? The relationship between beliefs about academic success and young people's educational attainment. *British Educational Research Journal, 43*(3), 441–465.

Solga, H. (2015). The social investment state and the myth of meritocracy. In A. Gallas, H. Herr, F. Hoffer, & C. Scherrer (Eds.), *Combating inequality: The global north and south* (pp. 199–211). Routledge, Taylor & Francis.

Spangenberg, H., Beuße, M., & Heine, C. (2011). *Nachschulische Werdegänge des Studienberechtigtenjahrgangs 2006*. HIS Hochschul-Informations-System.

Thaning, M. (2021). Resource specificity in intergenerational inequality: The case of education, occupation, and income. *Research in Social Stratification and Mobility, 75(1)*, Article 100644.

Thomas, W., & Thomas, D. (1928). *The child in America: Behavior problems and programs*. Knopf.

Traini, C., Kleinert, C., & Bittmann, F. (2021). How does exposure to a different school track influence learning progress? Explaining scissor effects by track in Germany. *Research in Social Stratification and Mobility, 76(1)*, Article 100625.

Valero, V. (2022). Redistribution and beliefs about the source of income inequality. *Experimental Economics, 25*(3), 876–901.

van Hootegem, A., Abts, K., & Meuleman, B. (2020). Differentiated distributive justice preferences? Configurations of preferences for equality, equity and need in three welfare domains. *Social Justice Research, 33*(3), 257–283.

Warikoo, N. (2016). *The diversity bargain: And other dilemmas of race, admissions, and meritocracy at elite universities*. The University of Chicago Press.

Warikoo, N. (2018). What meritocracy means to its winners: Admissions, race, and inequality at elite universities in the United States and Britain. *Social Sciences, 7*(1), Article 131.

Weber, M. (1991 [1921]). *From Max Weber: Essays in sociology*. Routledge (First published in German in 1921: Wirtschaft und Gesellschaft, Mohr.).

Wegener, B. (1992). Gerechtigkeitsforschung und Legitimationsnormen. *Zeitschrift Für Soziologie, 21*(4), 269–283.

Wegener, B. (2006). *International Social Justice Project 1996 und 2000 (ISJP 1996 und 2000) - Deutschland*. https://doi.org/10.4232/1.4409

Wetter, R., & Finger, C. (2023). Do experiences of success and failure influence beliefs about inequality? Evidence from selective university admission. *Social Psychology Quarterly, 86*(2), 170–194.

Weiner, B. (1985). An attributional theory of achievement motivation and emotion. *Psychological Review, 92*(4), 548–573.

Wiederkehr, V., Bonnot, V., Krauth-Gruber, S., & Darnon, C. (2015). Belief in school meritocracy as a system-justifying tool for low status students. *Frontiers in Psychology, 6*(1), Article 1053.

Wodtke, G. (2012). The impact of education on inter-group attitudes: A Multiracial Analysis. *Social Psychology Quarterly, 75*(1), 80–106.

Wodtke, G. (2018). The effects of education on beliefs about racial inequality. *Social Psychology Quarterly*, *81*(4), 273–294.
Wrosch, C., Heckhausen, J., & Lachman, M. E. (2000). Primary and secondary control strategies for managing health and financial stress across adulthood. *Psychology and Aging*, *15*(3), 387–399.
Wysmułek, I., & Wysmułek, J. (2024). Generational differences in attitudes to meritocracy: Sources of change in valuing education, innate abilities, and hard work in Poland. *Acta Sociologica*, *67*(2), 131–148.
Young, M. (1994 [1958]). *The rise of the meritocracy*. Routledge.

Appendix

Table A3.1: List of hypotheses

Theoretical Chapter	Hypotheses
3.1: Educational inequality	HI.1: Applicants from privileged backgrounds are more likely to be admitted to medical school than their less privileged peers.
3.2: How parental education and educational experiences shape inequality beliefs	HI.2: Applicants from privileged backgrounds hold stronger meritocratic and weaker nonmeritocratic beliefs than their less privileged peers.
	HI.3: Success strengthens meritocratic beliefs and weakens nonmeritocratic beliefs, whereas failure weakens meritocratic beliefs and strengthens nonmeritocratic beliefs.
	HI.4a: Success strengthens meritocratic beliefs and weakens nonmeritocratic beliefs more strongly for less privileged applicants than for their more privileged peers.
	HI.4b: Failure weakens meritocratic beliefs and strengthens nonmeritocratic beliefs more strongly for less privileged applicants than for their more privileged peers.
	HI.5a: Success strengthens meritocratic beliefs and weakens nonmeritocratic beliefs more strongly for repeat applicants than for first-time applicants.
	HI.5b: Failure weakens meritocratic beliefs and strengthens nonmeritocratic beliefs more strongly for repeat applicants than for first-time applicants.
3.3: Consequences of inequality beliefs for perceptions of justice and distributive preferences	HII.1: Meritocratic beliefs are negatively associated with the preference for equal distribution and positively with the preference for distribution based on educational meritocracy, while the opposite is true for nonmeritocratic beliefs.
	HII.2: Meritocratic beliefs lead to a perception of higher justice, while nonmeritocratic beliefs lead to a perception of lower justice.
	HII.3: The more people perceive inequality as just, the more opposed they will be to equal distribution and the more they will support educational meritocracy.
	HII.4a: Perception of justice mediates the negative relationship between meritocratic beliefs and the preference for equal distribution, and mediates the positive relationship between nonmeritocratic beliefs and this preference.
	HII.4b: Perception of justice mediates the positive relationship between meritocratic beliefs and the preference for distribution based on educational meritocracy, and mediates the negative relationship between nonmeritocratic beliefs and this preference.
	HII.5: Applicants from privileged backgrounds have a weaker preference for equal distribution and a stronger preference for distribution based on educational meritocracy than their less privileged peers.
	HII.6: Social differences in inequality beliefs, and the resulting perception of justice, partly mediate the relationship between parental education and distributive preferences for equality and educational meritocracy.
3.4: Inequality beliefs, persistence in goal pursuit, and educational inequality	HIII.1: Applicants from privileged backgrounds show a stronger persistence in goal pursuit than their less privileged peers.
	HIII.2: Beliefs in meritocratic admission are positively associated with persistence in goal pursuit, while the opposite is true for the belief in nonmeritocratic admission.
	HIII.3: Social differences in inequality beliefs about admission mediate part of the effect of parental education on persistence in goal pursuit.
	HIII.4: Beliefs in meritocratic admission have a more positive effect on persistence in goal pursuit for applicants from privileged backgrounds than for their less privileged peers.

Note. Author's illustration.

Table A4.1: Translated questionnaire items (from German) of main variables

Items referring to university admission to medical programs	Items referring to inequalities in society generally
Success in admission 0 (no) | 1 (yes) In the last survey, you told us that you applied for medicine at hochschulstart [central clearinghouse]. Did you receive admission for this?	-
First vs. repeat applicant 0 (no) | 1 (yes) Have you previously applied for a human medicine at hochschulstart or the former central allocation office for places in the program?	-
Inequality beliefs 1 (totally disagree) – 5 (totally agree) Two years ago, you reported that you applied for human medicine. Now, we want to ask for your opinion about the admission procedure. An admission can depend on several factors. How much do you agree to the following statements: An admission depends on … a) **how much effort I put in and how hard-working I am.** b) **how talented and intelligent I am.** c) how good my subject-specific skills are. d) how good my school grades are. e) how strong my endurance is. f) **how lucky I am.** How much do you agree to the following statements: An admission depends on … a) how much initiative I show. b) from which family I am. c) how much money and assets I have. d) whether I have connections to the right people. e) which gender I have.	*Inequality beliefs* 1 (totally disagree) – 5 (totally agree) Now, we ask for your opinion. On what does it actually depend on in Germany whether someone is successful and climbs up the social ladder? a) **One must put in effort and be hard-working.** b) **One must be talented and intelligent.** c) One must have good subject-specific skills in one's area. d) One must have a good educational degree. e) One must be dynamic and show initiative. f) One must possess endurance. g) **One must be from the right family.** h) **One must possess money and assets.** i) One must have connections to the right people. j) One must have the right gender; men have better opportunities for upward mobility. On what does it, furthermore, depend on whether someone is successful and climbs up the social ladder in Germany? k) One must be lucky. l) One must be born in Germany. People who were born in Germany have better opportunities.
Perception of justice 1 (very unjust) – 5 (very just) As how just do you evaluate the admission procedure for human medicine that has been applied until the winter semester of 2019/20?	*Perception of justice* 1 (totally disagree) – 5 (totally agree) How much do you agree with the following statement? a) I think social inequalities in Germany are, overall, just. b) In Germany today, people all have the same opportunities to get ahead. c) In Germany today, people all have the same opportunities to achieve a good educational qualification.
Distributive preferences 1 (very unjust) – 5 (very just) Imagine, after the current procedure took place, there are still 100 places in the program available. These places should be distributed among the remaining applicants. How should the selection take place, according to your opinion? Please tell us how just you evaluate the following procedures. a) A lottery decides so that everyone has the same chances. b) Those people get the places who got the best school grades. c) If the admission requirements are the same, places are given to those who do not come from an academic household.	*Distributive preferences* 1 (totally disagree) – 5 (totally agree) How much do you agree with the following statements? a) The most just way to distribute income and wealth would be to give everyone the same share. b) As long as there are equal opportunities for all, it is just for some to have more money and wealth than others. c) It is just that people keep what they have earned through work, even if this means that some are richer than others. d) It is just that people who work hard earn more than others.

Items referring to university admission to medical programs	Items referring to inequalities in society generally
d) If the admission requirements are the same, the places go to people whose parents are doctors, as they have already gained insight into the professional field. e) The places go to people who have already gained relevant professional experience. f) If the admission requirements are the same, the places go to those whose gender is underrepresented in the group of previously admitted students. g) Places in the progam are awarded to those who are prepared to work where they are most urgently needed after completing their studies.	e) It is just that parents pass on their wealth to their children, even if this means that the children of rich parents have better opportunities in life. f) The most important thing is that people get what they need to live, even if the higher earners have to give up some of their income. g) It is just a coincidence that some people are more talented and intelligent than others, so they should not be entitled to a high income. h) It is just if people who come from prestigious families have advantages in life as a result. i) It is just if disadvantaged groups are helped so that they have the same opportunities in life. j) It is just that people with high educational degrees earn more than others.

Persistence in goal pursuit
  1 (totally disagree) – 5 (totally agree)
Goal engagement
To what extent do the following statements apply to you?
a) I am prepared to do everything necessary to get a place in my preferred subject
b) If it proves difficult to get a place in my preferred subject, I will try even harder.
c) When it comes to getting a place in my preferred subject, I make sure that nothing distracts me from my goal.
d) When it comes to getting a place in my preferred subject, I keep telling myself that I will definitely be successful.

Goal disengagement
  1 (totally disagree) – 5 (totally agree)
And how willing are you to do so…
a) move to a place that is not your first choice in order to study your preferred subject?
b) take up another subject that is easier to study?
c) take a different career path?

Reapplication intention
  1 (totally disagree) – 5 (totally agree)
To what extent do the following statements match your plans?
I will probably apply for medicine at hochschulstart.

Reapplication behavior
For which semesters have you applied for your favorite subject since the winter semester of 2018/19?
Please select all that apply.
Not at all, for the summer semester of 2019, for the winter semester of 2019/20, for the summer semester of 2020, for the winter semester of 2020/21.

General items

Parental education
Please indicate your mother's / father's highest professional qualification.
Coded as college-educated parent: Doctorate, university degree, degree from a university of applied sciences
Coded as not college-educated parents: Vocational training or no professional qualification

Grade-point-average (GPA)
Please enter the average grade of your university entrance qualification: 1.0 – 4.0

(Non)meritocratic factor innate or alterable?
  0 (rather innate) | 1 (rather alterable)
In your opinion, which of the following characteristics are more innate and fixed at birth, and which can be changed by your own actions?

Items referring to university admission to medical programs	Items referring to inequalities in society generally
a) Effort and hard work b) Talent and intelligence c) School performance d) Perseverance e) Family of origin f) Social environment and relationships e) Financial situation in childhood	

Note. Original question wording in German can be found in published questionnaires: https://doi.org/10.7802/2515. For inequality beliefs, only bold items included in analyses for research objective I and III. Grey items not included in analyses—only included in table to display whole scale. Author's translation.

Table A4.2: Question wording and scales of inequality beliefs in NEPS data and medical applicant data

	NEPS data	Medical applicant data
Domain-specific beliefs	1 (disagree) – 5 (agree) Success at work can depend on a variety of things. How much do you agree with the following very general statements? Whether I am successful at work depends on … a) how hard I work and how diligent I am. b) how talented and intelligent I am. […] d) how lucky I am.	1 (total disagree) – 5 (strongly agree) Admission to medical school can depend on various factors. How much do you agree with the following statements regarding admission for your applications via hochschulstart? Whether I receive admission to medical school depends on… a) how hard I work and how diligent I am. b) how talented and intelligent I am. […] f) how lucky I am.
Societal beliefs	1 (total disagree) – 4 (strongly agree) In your opinion, what does it really depend on in Germany whether someone is successful and rises socially? Please indicate to what extent you agree with each of the following statements. a) You have to work hard and be diligent. […] c) You have to be talented and intelligent. d) You have to come from the right family. […] f) You have to have money and assets.	1 (total disagree) – 5 (strongly agree) In your opinion, what does it really depend on in Germany whether someone is successful and rises socially? a) You have to work hard and be diligent. b) You have to be talented and intelligent. […] g) You have to come from the right family. h) You have to have money and assets.

Note. Source: NEPS data (11th wave of 3rd cohort) and medical applicant data, author's calculations. Author's translation.

Table A5.1: Correlation matrix of inequality beliefs (W1 beliefs)

		Domain-specific beliefs: University admission depends on one's own			Societal beliefs: Societal success depends on			
		Effort	Talent	Luck	Effort	Talent	Family	Money
		Person's Correlation Coefficient						
Domain-specific beliefs: University admission depends on one's own	Effort	1.00						
	Talent	.51 **	1.00					
	Luck	-.12 **	-.06 **	1.00				
Societal beliefs: Societal success depends on	Effort	.26 **	.21 **	-.05 **	1.00			
	Talent	.12 **	.29 **	.02	.33 **	1.00		
	Family	-.14 **	-.09 **	.08 **	-.35 **	-.07 **	1.00	
	Money	-.17 **	-.11 **	.11 **	-.37 **	-.09 **	.78 **	1.00

Note. ** $p < .01$ * $p < .05$. N = 4,138. Sampling weight applied. Source: Medical applicant data, author's calculations.

Table A5.2: Logistic regression model results: Effect of parental education on admission chances (marginal effects)

Dependent variable: Admission chances	Model 1: Including age and gender	Model 2: Including age, gender, and GPA
	margins (se)	
Parental education (reference: no college-educated parent):		
One college-educated parent	.03	.01
	(.02)	(.01)
Two college-educated parents	.08 **	.03 *
	(.01)	(.01)
Age (z-standardized)	.35 **	2.37 **
	(.10)	(.12)
Gender	.01	-.03
	(.01)	(.01)
GPA (1.0 – 4.0)	-	-.51 **
		(.01)
Pseudo R^2	.01	.31

Note. ** $p < .01$ * $p < .05$. N = 4,138. Sampling weight applied. Source: Medical applicant data, author's calculations.

Table A5.3: Robustness check with different weighting strategies: Admission rates by parental education

Parental education	No college-educated parent (N = 1,150)	One college-educated parent (N = 1,203)	Two college-educated parents (N = 1,785)
Sampling weight:			
Admission rate	22 %	24 %	28 % **
No weight:			
Admission rate	37 %	41 %	48 % **
Panel weight:			
Admission rate	21 %	23 %	28 % **

Note. Statistically significant difference to the reference category (no college-educated parent): ** p < .01. Source: Medical applicant data, author's calculations.

Table A5.4: Robustness check with different weighting strategies: Average inequality beliefs by parental education (W1 beliefs)

	Domain-specific beliefs: University admission depends on my own ...			Societal beliefs: Societal success depends on ...		
	No college-educated parent (N = 1,150)	One college-educated parent (N = 1,203)	Two college-educated parents (N = 1,785)	No college-educated parent (N = 1,150)	One college-educated parent (N = 1,203)	Two college-educated parents (N = 1,785)
Sampling weight:						
Meritocratic Beliefs						
Effort	3.09 (1.40)	3.12 (1.33)	3.26 ** (1.33)	3.97 (0.97)	4.10 ** (0.92)	4.08 ** (0.91)
Talent	2.76 (1.26)	2.73 (1.25)	2.86 (1.23)	3.42 (0.90)	3.48 (0.92)	3.49 (0.90)
Nonmeritocratic Beliefs						
Luck	3.43 (1.31)	3.47 (1.28)	3.42 (1.24)	-	-	-
Family	-	-	-	3.46 (1.34)	3.34 (1.24)	3.29** (1.21)
Money	-	-	-	3.35 (1.32)	3.15 ** (1.22)	3.02 ** (1.18)
No weight:						
Meritocratic Beliefs						
Effort	3.19 (1.38)	3.22 (1.38)	3.37 ** (1.33)	4.00 (0.95)	4.12 ** (0.90)	4.12 ** (0.88)
Talent	2.85 (1.24)	2.84 (1.23)	2.95 (1.22)	3.46 (0.88)	3.50 (0.90)	3.54 (0.89)
Nonmeritocratic Beliefs						
Luck	3.41 (1.30)	3.42 (1.28)	3.38 (1.24)	-	-	-
Family	-	-	-	3.47 (1.31)	3.36 (1.20)	3.30 ** (1.19)
Money	-	-	-	3.34 (1.28)	3.15 ** (1.18)	3.00 ** (1.14)
Panel weight:						
Meritocratic Beliefs						
Effort	3.11 (1.39)	3.14 (1.39)	3.28 ** (1.33)	3.98 (0.97)	4.11 ** (0.92)	4.08 * (0.92)
Talent	2.76 (1.26)	2.75 (1.24)	2.88 * (1.23)	3.43 (0.90)	3.48 (0.92)	3.49 (0.90)
Nonmeritocratic Beliefs						
Luck	3.42 (1.32)	3.47 (1.29)	3.42 (1.24)	-	-	-
Family	-	-	-	3.45 (1.35)	3.33 * (1.25)	3.28 ** (1.22)
Money	-	-	-	3.34 (1.32)	3.13 ** (1.22)	3.01 ** (1.18)

Note. Statistically significant difference to the reference category (no college-educated parent): ** $p < .01$ * $p < .05$. Source: Medical applicant data, author's calculations.

Table A5.5: Linear fixed-effects models with alternative weighting strategies

	No weights applied		Panel weight applied		Cross-sectional sampling weight applied	
N	4,167		4,125		4,138	
	Belief change of rejected applicants (reference group)	Belief change* admission (ref. rejection)	Belief change of rejected applicants (reference group)	Belief change* admission (ref. rejection)	Belief change of rejected applicants (reference group)	Belief change* admission (ref. rejection)
			b (se)			
Domain-specific agency beliefs:						
University admission depends on one's own						
Effort	-.07 *	.30 **	-.07 *	.33 **	-.07 *	.31 **
	(.03)	(.04)	(.03)	(.05)	(.03)	(.05)
Talent	-.12 **	-.04	.10 **	-.00	.09 **	-.00
	(.03)	(.04)	(.03)	(.04)	(.03)	(.04)
Luck	.33 **	-.28 **	.34 **	-.27 **	.33 **	-.29 **
	(.03)	(.04)	(.03)	(.04)	(.03)	(.04)
Societal beliefs:						
Societal success depends on						
Effort	-.09 **	.08 **	-.09 **	.07 *	-.09 **	.09 **
	(.02)	(.03)	(.02)	(.03)	(.02)	(.03)
Talent	-.06 **	-.11 **	-.06 **	-.10 **	-.06 **	-.10 **
	(.02)	(.03)	(.02)	(.03)	(.02)	(.03)
Family	.10 **	-.21 **	.12 **	-.22 **	.16 **	-.23 **
	(.02)	(.04)	(.03)	(.04)	(.03)	(.04)
Money	.12 **	-.19 **	.14 **	-.22 **	.13 **	-.21 **
	(.02)	(.04)	(.03)	(.04)	(.03)	(.04)

Note. ** $p < .01$ * $p < .05$. Source: Medical applicant data, author's calculations.

Table A5.6: Fixed-effects ordered logit models (margins)

	Linear fixed-effects models (xtreg, fe)		Fixed-effects ordered logit models (feologit)	
N	4,138		2,593	
	Belief change of rejected applicants (reference group)	Belief change* admission (ref. rejection)	Belief change of rejected applicants (reference group)	Belief change* admission (ref. rejection)
	b (se)		margins (se)	
Domain-specific beliefs:				
University admission depends on one's own				
Effort	-.07 * (.03)	.31 ** (.05)	-.07 * (.03)	.33 ** (.05)
Talent	.09 ** (.03)	-.00 (.04)	.09 ** (.03)	.01 (.05)
Luck	.33 ** (.03)	-.29 ** (.04)	.35 ** (.03)	-.31 ** (.05)
Societal beliefs:				
Societal success depends on				
Effort	-.09 ** (.02)	.09 ** (.03)	-.13 ** (.03)	.14 ** (.05)
Talent	-.06 ** (.02)	-.10 ** (.03)	-.08 ** (.03)	-.15 ** (.05)
Family	.12 ** (.03)	-.23 ** (.04)	.14 ** (.03)	-.28 ** (.05)
Money	.13 ** (.03)	-.21 ** (.04)	.16 ** (.03)	-.26 ** (.05)

Note. Sampling weight applied. ** $p < .01$ * $p < .05$. Source: Medical applicant data, author's calculations.

Table A5.7: Fixed-effects fuzzy RDD models with interaction term: Belief change*admission

	Belief change of rejected applicants (reference group)	Belief change*admission (ref. rejection)
	b (se)	
Domain-specific beliefs:		
University admission depends on one's own		
Effort	-.05 (.08)	.38 ** (.11)
Talent	.05 ** (.08)	.09 (.09)
Luck	.22* (.09)	-.14 (.11)
Societal beliefs:		
Societal success depends on		
Effort	-.03 (.06)	.12 (.08)
Talent	-.04 (.06)	-.06 (.08)
Family	-.06 (.07)	-.02 (.09)
Money	-.09 (.07)	-.05 (.09)

Note. Restricted to applicants with a high school GPA of 1.3 and 1.4. Authors' calculations. ** $p < .01$ * $p < .05$. N = 608; sampling weight applied. Source: Medical applicant data, author's calculations.

Table A5.8: Heterogeneity in effect of admission on beliefs by admission quota: Linear fixed-effects models with interaction terms (belief change*admission quota)

	Belief change after admission through waiting-period quota (ref. group)	Belief change after admission through GPA quota (ref.: waiting-period quota)	Belief change after admission through university-specific quota (ref.: waiting-period quota)
	b (se)		
Domain-specific beliefs:			
University admission depends on one's own			
Effort	.58 ** (.11)	-.53 ** (.13)	-.39 ** (.12)
Talent	.44 ** (.09)	-.50 ** (.12)	-.41 ** (.10)
Luck	.10 (.09)	-.14 (.13)	-.08 (.10)
Societal beliefs:			
Societal success depends on			
Effort	.06 (.07)	-.12 (.09)	-.05 (.08)
Talent	-.03 (.07)	-.15 (.10)	-.16 * (.08)
Family	-.15 (.08)	-.11 (.11)	.08 (.09)
Money	-.08 (.08)	-.03 (.11)	.00 (.09)

Note. ** $p < .01$ * $p < .05$. N = 1,663. Sampling weight applied. Source: Medical applicant data, author's calculations.

Table A5.9: Linear fixed-effects models with interaction terms: Belief change*parental education

	Admitted applicants (N = 1,764)			Rejected applicants (N = 2,374)		
	Belief change after admission of applicants with two college-educated parents (ref. group)	Belief change after admission* no college-educated parent (ref. two college-educated parents)	Belief change after admission* one college-educated parent (ref. two college-educated parents)	Belief change after rejection of applicants with two college-educated parents (ref. group)	Belief change after rejection* no college-educated parent (ref. two college-educated parents)	Belief change after rejection* one college-educated parent (ref. two college-educated parents)
	b (se)					
Domain-specific beliefs:						
University admission depends on one's own						
Effort	.26 ** (.05)	-.04 (.08)	-.03 (.08)	-.02 (.05)	-.08 (.08)	-.09 (.08)
Talent	.08 (.04)	.05 (.08)	-.02 (.07)	.04 (.05)	.08 (.08)	.10 (.08)
Luck	-.03 (.05)	.05 (.09)	.20 ** (.07)	.38 ** (.05)	-.07 (.08)	-.07 (.07)
Societal beliefs:						
Societal success depends on						
Effort	-.01 (.03)	.05 (.06)	.02 (.06)	-.04 (.03)	-.07 (.06)	-.10 (.06)
Talent	-.22 ** (.03)	.12 (.06)	.10 (.06)	-.01 (.04)	-.10 (.06)	-.08 (.06)
Family	-.08 (.04)	-.03 (.07)	-.09 (.07)	.08 (.04)	.05 (.07)	.06 (.06)
Money	-.02 (.04)	-.12 (.07)	-.10 (.07)	.11 ** (.04)	.02 (.06)	.05 (.06)

Note. ** $p < .01$ * $p < .05$. Sampling weight applied. Source: Medical applicant data, author's calculations.

Table A5.10: Linear fixed-effects models with interaction terms: Belief change*repeat applicant

	Admitted applicants (N = 1,764)		Rejected applicants (N = 2,374)	
	Belief change after admission of first-time applicants (ref. group)	Belief change after admission*repeat applicant (ref. first-time applicants)	Belief change after rejection of first-time applicants (ref. group)	Belief change after rejection*repeat applicant (ref. first-time applicants)
	b (se)			
Domain-specific beliefs:				
University admission depends on one's own				
Effort	.15 ** (.04)	.19 ** (.07)	-.04 (.05)	-.06 (.07)
Talent	-.05 (.04)	.31 ** (.06)	.05 (.05)	.08 (.06)
Luck	-.06 (.04)	.22 ** (.07)	.31 ** (.05)	.05 (.06)
Societal beliefs:				
Societal success depends on				
Effort	-.00 (.03)	.02 (.05)	-.10 ** (.04)	.02 (.05)
Talent	-.21 ** (.03)	.10 * (.05)	-.07 (.04)	.02 (.04)
Family	-.09 * (.04)	-.05 (.06)	.10 * (.04)	.03 (.05)
Money	-.06 (.04)	-.04 (.06)	.16 ** (.04)	.03 (.05)

Note. ** $p < .01$ * $p < .05$. Sampling weight applied. Source: Medical applicant data, author's calculations.

Table A6.1: Weighted models: Direct and total effects of parental education and inequality beliefs on distributive preferences and mediation mechanisms

	Domain-specific model: University admission			Societal model: Social inequalities		
	Direct effect	Total effect	% of total effect via mediation	Direct effect	Total effect	% of total effect via mediation

Path 1.1: Inequality beliefs → Distributive preference (incl. mediation via perception of justice) & Path 1.3: Perception of justice → Distributive preference & Path 2.1: Parental education → Distributive preference (incl. mediation via inequality beliefs and perception of justice)

DV: Equality preference - Admission through lottery				Equal distribution of income		
Beliefs:						
Hard work	-.08 (.10)	-.09 (.10)	6	-.11 (.12)	-.10 (.12)	-13
Abilities	-.06 (.12)	-.06 (.12)	8	-.13 (.15)	-.22 (.15)	40
Educational merit	-.11 (.07)	-.11 (.07)	-0	.05 (.03)	.05 (.03)	-9
Luck	.06 (.04)	.09 (.03)	2	-.02 (.03)	-.03 (.03)	33
Social background	.04 (.05)	.04 (.05)	5	.07* (.04)	.11** (.04)	32
Perception of justice	-.02 (.05)	No ind. path	-	-.21** (.03)	No ind. path	
1 col.-ed. parent	-.03 (.10)	-.04 (.10)	39	-.09 (.08)	-.15 (.08)	39
2 col.-ed. parents	-.32** (.10)	-.35** (.09)	9	-.18** (.07)	-.24** (.07)	24

DV: Educational meritocracy preference - Admission through grades				Income distribution based on degrees		
Beliefs:						
Hard work	.07 (.06)	.13* (.07)	49	.01 (.12)	-.00 (.13)	140
Abilities	.26** (.08)	.33** (.08)	22	.33* (.15)	.43** (.15)	23
Educational merit	.05 (.06)	.06 (.06)	11	.01 (.03)	.01 (.03)	38
Luck	-.07** (.02)	-.08* (.02)	15	.06* (.03)	.07* (.03)	15
Social background	-.05 (.03)	-.08* (.03)	38	-.00 (.04)	-.04 (.04)	100
Perception of justice	.29** (.03)	No ind. path	-	.23** (.03)	No ind. path	-
1 col.-ed. parent	.05 (.07)	.09 (.07)	44	.11 (.07)	.16* (.08)	30
2 col.-ed. parents	.09 (.06)	.16* (.07)	43	.21** (.07)	.26** (.07)	17

Path 1.2: Inequality beliefs → Perception of justice & Parental education → Perception of justice (incl. mediation via inequality beliefs)

DV: Perception of admission as just				Perception of inequalities as just		
Beliefs:						
Hard work	.22** (.06)	No ind. path	-	-.06 (.11)	No ind. path	-
Abilities	.25** (.08)	No ind. path	-	.43** (.13)	No ind. path	-
Educational merit	.02 (.05)	No ind. path		.02 (.03)	No ind. path	
Luck	-.04* (.02)	No ind. path	-	.05* (.02)	No ind. path	-
Social background	-.10** (.03)	No ind. path	-	-.17** (.03)	No ind. path	-
1 col.-ed. parent	.07 (.07)	.11** (.07)	31	.07 (.07)	.13* (.06)	47
2 col.-ed. parents	.12* (.06)	.17** (.06)	30	.07 (.06)	.12* (.06)	44

	Domain-specific model: University admission			Societal model: Social inequalities		
	Direct effect	Total effect	% of total effect via mediation	Direct effect	Total effect	% of total effect via mediation
Path 2.2: Parental education → Inequality beliefs						
DV: Hard work						
1 col.-ed. parent	.04 (.09)	No ind. path	-	.02 (.05)	No ind. path	-
2 col.-ed. parents	.10 (.08)	No ind. path	-	.06 (.05)	No ind. path	-
DV: Abilities						
1 col.-ed. parent	-.04 (.08)	No ind. path	-	.07 (.05)	No ind. path	-
2 col.-ed. parents	-.05 (.07)	No ind. path	-	.04 (.05)	No ind. path	-
DV: Educational merit						
1 col.-ed. parent	-.02 (.05)	No ind. path	-	-.09 (.07)	No ind. path	-
2 col.-ed. parents	-.00 (.05)	No ind. path	-	-.09 (.07)	No ind. path	-
DV: Luck						
1 col.-ed. parent	-.05 (.09)	No ind. path	-	-.09 (.09)	No ind. path	-
2 col.-ed. parents	-.14 (.08)	No ind. path	-	.01 (.08)	No ind. path	-
DV: Social background						
1 col.-ed. parent	-.29** (.08)	No ind. path	-	-.24** (.08)	No ind. path	-
2 col.-ed. parents	-.35** (.08)	No ind. path	-	-.22** (.08)	No ind. path	-
Goodness-of-fit-statistics						
SRMR	.036			.042		

Note. Standardized coefficients. All path models controlled for participation in experiment dummy. Reference for 1 / 2 coll.-ed. parent(s): No college-educated parent. Hard work, abilities, and social background are latent constructs. Panel weight applied. Percentage of total effect via mediation calculated based on nonrounded coefficients. ** $p < .01$ * $p < .05$. N = 1,725. Source: Medical applicant data, author's calculations.

Table A7.1: Effect of parental education, beliefs in meritocratic admission, and self-predicted persistence on eventual success in admission

	Eventual success in admission (between wave 2 and 3)		
	margins (std err.)		
	M1	M2	M3
Parental education (ref.: no college-educated parent)			
1 college-educated parent	.13 (.10)	.13 (.10)	.15 (.09)
2 college-educated parents	.26 ** (.09)	.26 ** (.09)	.28 ** (.09)
Belief that one's own admission depends on …			
Effort		.04 (.04)	.04 (.03)
Talent		.02 (.04)	.01 (.04)
Luck		-.04 (.08)	-.03 (.03)
Goal engagement			.04 (.07)
Goal disengagement			.02 (.07)
High reapplication intention			.47 ** (.17)
Control variables			
Female	-.04 (.09)	-.04 (.08)	-.04 (.08)
Age (z-standardized)	.03 (.04)	.05 (.04)	.05 (.04)
Participated in experiment dummy applied	Yes	Yes	Yes
(Pseudo) R^2	.04	.06	.09

Note. Data from the 2nd survey wave. X-col reference category: 0-col. First-time rejected applicants. ** $p < .01$ * $p < .05$. N = 190. Panel weight applied. Source: Medical applicant data, author's calculations.

Table A7.2: Effects of beliefs in meritocratic admission on change in preferred field of study

	Change in Preferred Field of Study (in comparison to no change)	
	margins (std err.)	
	M1	M2
Parental education (ref.: no college-educated parent)		
1 college-educated parent	.03	.03
	(.04)	(.04)
2 college-educated parents	.05	.04
	(.04)	(.04)
Belief that one's own admission depends on ...		
Effort		.02
		(.02)
Talent		-.02
		(.02)
Luck		.00
		(.01)
*Interaction: Beliefs * parental education*		
Effort#1-col		
Effort#2-col		
Talent#1-col		
Talent#2-col		
Luck#1-col		
Luck#2-col		
Control variables		
Female	.02	.00
	(.04)	(.04)
Age (z-standardized)	.00	.00
	(.02)	(.02)
(Pseudo) R^2	.00	.01

Note. Data from the 2nd survey wave. X-col reference category: 0-col. First-time rejected applicants. ** $p < .01$ * $p < .05$. N = 793. Source: Medical applicant data, author's calculations.

Table A7.3: Robustness check including repeat and first-time applicants: Effects of parental education and beliefs in meritocratic admission on persistence in goal pursuit

| | Goal Engagement (1-5) | | | Goal Disengagement (1-5) | | | High Reapplication Intention (0-1) | | | Number of Reapplication Attempts (0-4) | | |
	b (std. err.)			b (std. err.)			margins (std. err.)			b (std. err.)		
	M1	M2	M3	M1	M2	M3	M1	M2	M3	M1	M2	M3
Parental education (ref.: no college-educated parent)												
1 college-educated parent	.01 (.04)	.01 (.04)	-.22 (.21)	-.04 (.05)	-.04 (.00)	.57 * (.24)	-.01 (.01)	-.01 (.01)	.01 (.11)	.37 ** (.14)	.35 ** (.14)	.42 (.54)
2 college-educated parents	.03 (.04)	.02 (.04)	.07 (.17)	-.01 (.05)	-.01 (.05)	.08 (.22)	-.01 (.01)	-.01 (.01)	.04 (.09)	.21 (.14)	.19 (.14)	-.17 (.52)
Belief that one's own admission depends on:												
Effort		.05 ** (.02)	.04 (.03)		-.00 (.02)	.03 (.04)		-.00 (.01)	.01 (.01)		-.08 (.05)	-.04 (.08)
Talent		.00 (.02)	-.01 (.03)		.02 (.02)	.04 (.04)		.02 (.01)	-.01 (.01)		.00 (.05)	.05 (.08)
Luck		.03 (.02)	.03 (.03)		-.02 (.02)	.00 (.03)		-.01 (.01)	.01 (.01)		.02 (.08)	-.07 (.07)
*Interaction: Beliefs * parental education*												
Effort#1-col			.02 (.04)			-.06 (.04)			-.02 (.01)			-.00 (.11)
Effort#2-col			-.03 (.04)			-.03 (.04)			-.01 (.01)			-.12 (.11)
Talent#1-col			.05 (.04)			-.06 (.05)			.02 (.01)			-.17 (.12)
Talent#2-col			.01 (.04)			-.00 (.04)			.02 (.01)			.03 (.12)
Luck#1-col			.02 (.04)			-.07 (.05)			-.01 (.01)			.10 (.11)
Luck#2-col			-.02 (.03)			.00 (.05)			-.02 (.01)			.17 (.10)
Control variables												
Female	-.04 (.04)	-.04 (.04)	-.04 (.04)	.01 (.05)	.01 (.05)	.01 (.05)	.00 (.01)	.00 (.01)	-.00 (.01)	-.10 (.11)	-.10 (.11)	-.10 (.11)
Age (z-standardized)	-.08 ** (.02)	-.07 ** (.03)	-.07 ** (.02)	-.03 (.02)	-.03 (.03)	-.03 ** (.02)	.01 (.01)	.01 (.01)	.01 (.01)	-.06 (.07)	-.09 (.07)	-.09 (.07)
Repeat applicant (ref.: first-time applicant)	.08 * (.04)	.11 * (.04)	.11 ** (.04)	-.14 ** (.05)	-.13 ** (.05)	-.14 ** (.05)	.04 * (.01)	.04 * (.01)	.04 * (.01)	.28 (.15)	.24 (.15)	.25 (.15)
Admitted in semester X dummy applied							Yes	Yes	Yes			
Participated in experiment dummy applied							Yes	Yes	Yes			

| | Goal Engagement (1-5) | | | Goal Disengagement (1-5) | | | High Reapplication Intention (0-1) | | | Number of Reapplication Attempts (0-4) | | |
| | b (std. err.) | | | b (std. err.) | | | margins (std. err.) | | | b (std. err.) | | |
	M1	M2	M3	M1	M2	M3	M1	M2	M3	M1	M2	M3
Constant	4.46 ** (.05)	4.19 ** (.09)	4.24 ** (.14)	1.77 * (.06)	1.77 ** (.12)	1.56 ** (.17)	-	-	-	2.74 ** (.22)	2.89 ** (.34)	3.01 ** (.44)
(Pseudo) R^2	.01	.03	.05	.01	.01	.03	.02	.03	.04	.18	.19	.22
N		1,578			1,578			1,578			603	

Note. X-col reference category: 0-col. ** $p < .01$ * $p < .05$ ° $p < .10$. Source: Medical applicant data, author's calculations.

Figure A4.1: Distributions of societal effort and family background beliefs in NEPS and medical applicant data

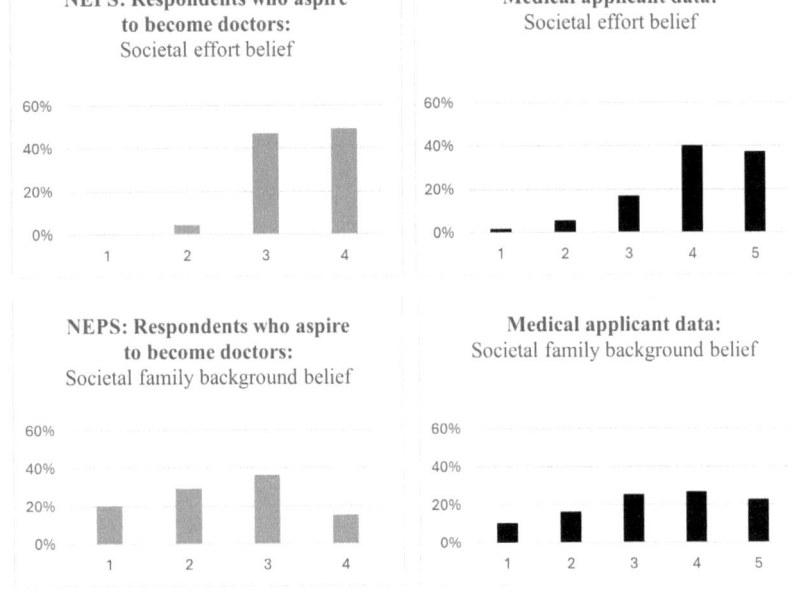

Note. Question wording, reference point, and labels of the scale differ between the NEPS data and the medical applicant data (see Table A4.2 in the appendix).

Figure A5.1: Ordered logistic regression model results: Effects of parental education on domain-specific inequality beliefs

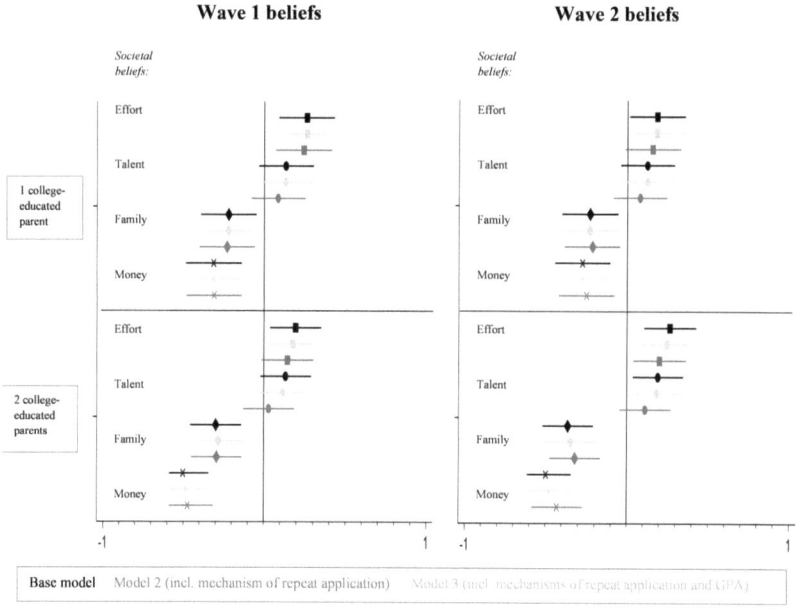

Note. Ordered logistic regression model results. Reference for 1 / 2 college-educated parents: no college-educated parent. N = 4,138. Sampling weight applied Source: Medical applicant data, author's calculations.

Figure A5.2: Ordered logistic regression model results: Effects of parental education on societal inequality beliefs

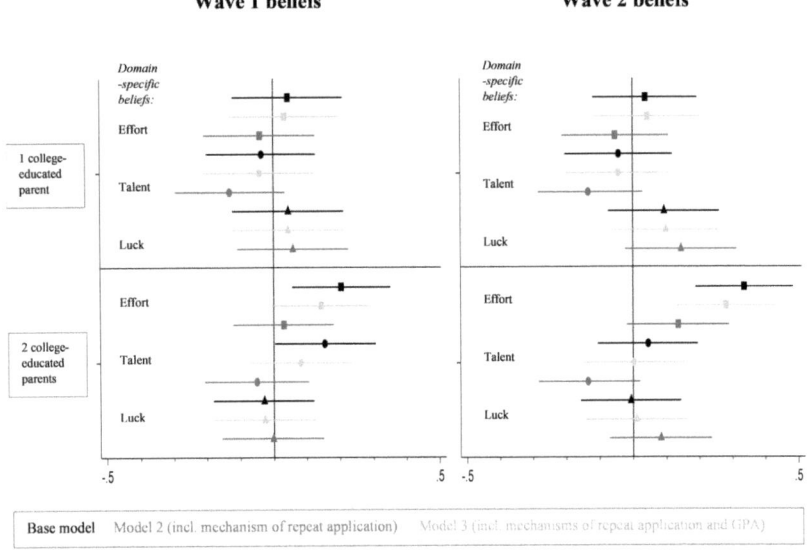

Note. Ordered logistic regression model results. Reference for 1 / 2 college-educated parents: no college-educated parent. N = 4,138. Sampling weight applied. Source: Medical applicant data, author's calculations.

Index

abilities beliefs 43, 73, 77, 130, 136, 138, 140, 150, 182
attributional theory 20, 35–36, 61–63, 68, 97, 122, 129, 150, 169, 182
balanced understanding of success 17
cluster analysis 92, 97, 122
cross-sectional and longitudinal methods 92–93
cultural capital 15, 28–30, 36
cumulative disadvantage 18
discrete-time hazard models 157, 161, 163
distinct types of inequality beliefs 20, 73, 92, 126–130, 132, 136–137, 143, 149–150
diverging paths in inequality beliefs 122, 125, 176, 179, 184–185
domain-specific beliefs 36, 42, 58, 73, 75, 91, 95, 97, 101, 109, 111, 114, 118, 122–123, 128–130, 136, 163, 175, 180
educational attainment 15, 20, 27–29, 32, 62, 170, 172
educational experiences in early adulthood 16, 86
educational gatekeeping 15, 29
educational merit beliefs 73, 183
educational meritocracy 18–19, 35, 49–52, 54–57, 67–69, 77, 126, 128, 133, 136–137, 141–142, 151, 174, 177, 179, 181, 186, 199
elite universities 16, 37, 44

fixed mindset 35, 62, 77, 139–140, 169, 187
formation of inequality beliefs 18–19, 21, 27, 66, 69, 178–179
fuzzy regression discontinuity design (fuzzy RDD) 92, 99, 111–114, 121, 123, 210
German National Educational Panel Study (NEPS) 21, 71, 86–91, 184–185, 203, 220
Germany's stratified educational system 21
growth mindset 35, 77, 139–140, 169, 187
hard work beliefs 73, 75, 150–151, 182
horizontal stratification 15, 30, 69
Individual fixed-effects models 93
inequality-reducing policies 16, 187
intergenerational status transmission 18, 28, 39, 45, 54, 69
interpersonal differences in inequality beliefs 179, 186
legitimation and reproduction of educational inequality 17, 172, 175
linear regression models 98, 103
luck beliefs 73, 150, 183
meritocracy as an inequality-legitimizing ideology 18, 50, 178
meritocratic ideology 15, 21, 27, 32–33, 41, 47, 49, 54, 67, 139

misconception of inequality 16
motivational theory 18, 58, 61, 174
persistence of educational inequality 179, 181, 185, 187
primary and secondary effects 27–28, 30
real-life experience of admission to medical school 17
sampling and panel weights 167
selective university admission 22, 72, 183
self-serving beliefs 40–41, 43, 63, 66, 87, 91, 110, 122, 173, 179
social background beliefs 35, 73, 118, 138, 146, 150–151, 179, 183–184
societal inequality beliefs 19–20, 36, 42–44, 53, 73, 75, 86, 90, 98, 110–111, 114–115, 131, 149, 222
status maintenance 29–30, 174, 180
structural barriers 16–17, 38–39, 44–45, 69, 88, 118, 121, 132, 175, 181–182, 184, 186–187
Structural equation models (SEM) 75, 79, 92–93, 128–129, 135, 149, 177
structural inequality 36, 40, 87, 91, 179, 184, 186–187
success against the odds 15, 44, 67–68, 173
unequal educational opportunities 16
unique medical applicant data 18
winners of the educational game 16, 175